The Literary Sculptors

Margaret Farrand Thorp

THE
LITERARY
SCULPTORS

Duke University Press

Durham, N. C.

1 9 6 5

Several sections of this book have appeared in journals to whose editors I am indebted for permission to reprint them here: the chapter on "The White Marmorean Flock," *New England Quarterly,* June 1959; part of the chapter on Rome, "Literary Sculptors in the Caffè Greco," *American Quarterly,* Summer 1960; a section of the chapter on the *Nudo,* "Rediscovery, A Lost Chapter in the History of 19th-century Taste," *Art in America,* No. 2, 1961.

Printed in the United States of America
by Kingsport Press, Inc., Kingsport, Tenn.

For

Emily Hale

Table of Contents

Plates

The Literary Sculptors

1

The Causes of Literary Sculpture

Early in the nineteenth century our young United States began to feel a need for statues, to honor her great men, to give delight, to uplift the minds of the citizens. Suddenly, as if spontaneously generated by the national will, sculptors appeared to make those statues. Between 1825 and 1876 nearly a hundred workers in clay and marble rose and flourished. To this highly interesting cultural phenomenon far too little attention has been paid. About these so-called literary sculptors only the barest facts have been recorded.

There are several reasons for this. The successors to the literary sculptors did not realize how much they owed to them and so paid them scant attention. The twentieth century has been disdainful because their statues took their being not from plastic ideas but from myths, legends, and historical events as they have been recorded in prose and poetry. The sculptors called their works Orpheus, for example, Hercules, Cleopatra, Eve, Medora, Evangeline. For this reason we label them "literary sculptors" and think them less important than they are.

Actually the literary sculptors performed for American art a century ago services whose benefits we now reap daily. They taught us, for one thing, that statuary, in public parks or private parlors, can be a source of instruction and delight. They raised their voices again and again to persuade us that every proud municipality should boast a gallery where its citizens may enjoy the contemplation of works of art. They convinced us, with difficulty, that nude statues are not obscene, and they did much to explain to the layman the special kind of life and environment an artist needs if he is to do his best work.

Who were these men who decided, out of hand, to be sculptors? What moved them to try? How did they learn the theory and technique of their art? How did they live, in Italy and at home? Why did patrons try to help them? How did critics learn to write about their work? How were Americans induced to buy American statues, to want them in their homes and public squares, to read about them in journals, to admire them in exhibitions, to urge legislators to appropriate funds to erect them? Beginnings have been made toward answering these questions. This book hopes to add more answers.

Patriotism was certainly the strongest motive which inspired the new artists, stronger even than the impulse to create. Profit played its part, too, of course, and so did the desire for personal prestige, but patriotism came first. Americans had in the youth of the nation, as they have today, great faith in the power of education. They were sure that sculpture had an educational mission to perform in the new country, sure that our citizens, if they looked on statues day by day, would be deeply affected by them, would grow in nobility and grace. The rich man who helped a young sculptor toward his training and a start in the profession felt that he was working for the nation.

How powerful the influence of a statue was thought to be one may glimpse in Sylvester Judd's transcendental novel *Margaret*, published in 1851. When Margaret inherits an unexpected fortune she and her husband set to work to convert their mountain farm into a place of beauty and refreshment for the whole neighborhood. They send to Rome a local boy who has shown extraordinary talent for modeling and give him commissions for a score or so of marble statues. About the grounds they place his figures of Truth, Penitence, Fortitude, Temperance, and other virtues. Most significant of all in the influence it is expected to exert is the marble female set up in a hamlet where the people were "notorious for their idleness and dissipation." At a corner where everyone must pass it every day, there rises "a beautiful statue of Diligence."

What his statues must be like if they were to uplift and delight, the American would-be sculptor learned as soon as he turned his eyes toward Europe. He saw at once that they must resemble as closely as possible the statues of the ancient Greeks now adorning the galleries of Rome. They must have beauty, nobility, serenity, repose. They must be made of white marble, and should illustrate, preferably, some classical myth or story. These specifications were not matters of debate; they were accepted by all the contemporary sculptors of Europe.

The fundamental patterns had been set in the middle of the eighteenth century when Herculaneum and Pompeii were being uncovered and Greek sculpture, chiefly of the Hellenistic and Roman periods, was becoming known. The rules were laid down by the German Hellenist, J. J. Winckelmann, and a German painter-scholar, Anton Raphael Mengs. These two proclaimed, in their widely read and learned works, the faults of the baroque and rococo and the absolute beauty of the classical idea. They analyzed its qualities, identified and described the statues which best embodied them.

The neoclassical movement thus had its beginning in theory but it was set soon in solid marble form by the technical brilliance, the charm and skill of an extraordinarily influential Italian artist, Antonio Canova. The son of a stonecutter, with very little education and rather inferior artistic training, Canova settled in Rome in 1781 and accepted the theories of Winckelmann and Mengs. Soon he completely dominated the sculptural art of Europe, and eventually of the United States. His work was ranked so high that when Napoleon carried off to Paris the antique masterpieces of the Greeks, statues by Canova were set upon the empty pedestals of the *Apollo Belvedere* and the Medicean *Venus*. Patrons of all classes bought Canova's work with enthusiasm, from the rich who could afford life-size marble figures to the cultivated impecunious who must be content with small ceramic replicas. Of course the American sculptor thought he should try to emulate *Theseus and the Minotaur* or *Psyche* with a butterfly. Canova's attractive personal qualities, his generosity to younger artists, his readiness to advise and criticize, though he would never take pupils, increased his influence and his power.

Sixteen years later, 1797, when Canova's vogue was beginning to fade a little, when it became permissible to suggest that he was

sometimes too sentimental and too sweet, a Dane, Bertel Thorvaldsen, settled in Rome and began to build a reputation which became
almost as great as Canova's. Thorvaldsen claimed to be even more
classical than Canova, to go back more directly to the true models.
He called himself a Hellenist. Nature, they both insisted, was the
great teacher but it was the Greeks who had best studied, measured,
and understood Nature, so the modern artist could do no better than
to study the Greeks. Thorvaldsen, too, was a generous and effective
teacher who set the neoclassical pattern still more firmly upon the
sculptural world. The painter might move on from academic neoclassicism, to romantic neoclassicism, to realism, to impressionism,
but it was long before the sculptor could think and experiment for
himself enough to be anything but Greek. The American sculptor,
setting to work in the 1830's and 1840's, became of necessity a neoclassicist. He was not, as usually happens in the growth and development of an art, breaking away from some style or form which he
found constricting; the neoclassical was simply the only kind of
sculpture he knew. Because he wanted to make statues he accepted
the current theories wholeheartedly and adapted his work to them as
best he could.

One is tempted sometimes to wonder whether the American literary sculptors would have been better artists had they found themselves in a fashion more congenial to their native temperament.
Suppose they had begun in an age of realism, or at a time like the
present when the artist is fascinated by experiments in the effects he
can produce with different kinds of stone or metal. Certainly to the
nineteenth-century American the neoclassical atmosphere was quite
alien. Only a few of the would-be sculptors had any classical education. Hebe and Ceres and Apollo were for them neither personalities
nor ideas, just names which had to be learned and connected with
certain attributes. The restraint, serenity, and repose preached by
Winckelmann were not virtues in which Americans had had much
practice. Greece did, however, offer them one great hope: the independence of Greece, according to Winckelmann, was a chief cause of
her superiority in art; why might not a young and even more independent nation, a republican nation, too, surpass her? This, at least,
was one more reason for the American sculptors' happy acceptance
of the neoclassical rules as means to their great end. They were not,

to be sure, at all times quite so classical as they thought themselves. Romantic and even sentimental elements intruded and, as the century advanced, there was more and more concern with realism. For the most part, though, the sculptors clung in theory to the classical ideal. It was not until the students of art began to discover in the 1870's the superior quality of French technical training that they turned from Rome to Paris and the power of Winckelmann and Canova was completely broken.

Some of the requirements imposed by the classical pattern were very much to the Americans' advantage; others were for them unfortunate. They are unfortunate for us, too, for they introduce into this early work elements which we find it difficult to accept.

The first essential for the sculptor, the decree ran, was Italy. In Rome and Florence were the Greek statues admired by all Europe. To learn the sculptural art one must know these statues intimately, live with them, analyze and study them day after day. The American sculptor must somehow cross the Atlantic. And he did, by his own efforts or by the generosity of his friends. This was very much to the benefit of the provincial young man from the new country. In Italy he learned many things beside the "secrets" of the Greeks. He discovered, for instance, how good the artist life can be and began to imagine in the United States an intellectual climate which would make the artist life possible. Sometimes he found ways to explain this desirable environment to his countrymen and to promote its development at home. The sojourn in Italy was the happiest of the classical requirements.

Less fortunate was the rule that statues must be made of white marble because this is what the Greeks were supposed to have used. No one during the neoclassical enthusiasm paid much attention to the fact that the statues revered as models were, most of them, Roman copies of Greek works made originally in bronze or of marble painted or gilded. (When the English sculptor John Gibson tried some experiments in coloring marble they were generally frowned upon, despite his high reputation.) Winckelmann emphasized the necessity for marble by his insistence on the importance of white, the color which reflects the greatest number of rays of light and consequently is the most easily perceived. A beautiful figure, Winckelmann said, will be more beautiful the whiter it is. White marble, unfortunately, was a substance with which the American had scant acquaintance. Marble worth working was not accessible in the United States until well along in the century. Americans did not handle it familiarly, as they handled wood and granite. The marble sculptor, too, was obliged to work at an unfortunate distance from his medium. Much of the marble cutting was heavy and time-consuming labor which the artist himself never thought of performing. He kept a contingent of skilled workmen—sometimes a dozen or more—whose work he directed and finished. The process began with a clay model, sometimes of the size of the finished statue, often much smaller, on which the artist worked out his ideas in detail. If a small model was made, a larger one followed. For this the clay had to be built up on an armature of iron, a heavy manual task performed by the workmen; then the artist shaped the clay to his pleasure. This was the most creative part of the process and the clay model was often far more lively and interesting than the finished statue. Hawthorne, who visited many artists' studios, remarks on this more than once in his *Italian Note-Books*. So do other observant writers, but the average man, when he admired a clay model, always longed to see it transfigured in purest marble. The next step was to make a plaster cast of the clay, a task the studio workmen could accomplish; then the marble cutters went to work. The block for each statue was painstakingly selected by the sculptor himself but frequently, for all his care, a hopelessly disfiguring stain or flaw appeared after the cutting had been going on for some time and the whole piece had to be abandoned. Many of the Italian marble workers developed specialized skills in cutting. One, for instance, might always do the hair; another, delicate objects like chains or dress ornaments; another was particularly good at animals; others did the heavy blocking out. They worked from the plaster cast, copying it precisely with careful measurements, but the serious artist insisted always on putting on the finishing touches himself. A remark of Thorvaldsen's was often quoted, that a statue is born in clay, dies in plaster, and is resurrected in marble.

The twentieth century does not share the nineteenth's passion for the beauty of white marble, a beauty of which our forebears seemed never to have enough. The art patron who wanted to be sure that he was getting his money's worth would not set in his drawing-room anything less than Carrara. So far did this predilection go that those who could not afford life-size figures but must be content with minia-ture beauty liked to have their little copies in "Parian," a ceramic ware of unglazed porcelain, very smooth and white. It looked like Parian marble and powdered marble actually was one of its ingredi-ents.

The other possibility was to cast the statue in bronze, a difficult and expensive process, done best at Munich. Americans did not learn to do bronze casting well until after the middle of the century. Bronze was often preferred for colossal monuments which were to stand outdoors but it was also used from time to time for small busts and statues for the hall or library. The woodwork and wallpaper in those rooms were conventionally dark so that they did not require the whiteness of marble ornaments as the light-toned parlors did.

The intricacy and difficulty of the technique of marble sculpture persuaded some of the men who found they could master it that they were artists when actually they were little more than good mechanics. They mistook manual skill for inspiration. From the days of the first settlements Americans displayed an ability to contrive, invent, and make with their hands anything that might be necessary to existence or agreeable to have about. This soon became a national character-istic of which we are aware today in the excellence of our elaborate mechanical products and in the pleasure the average boy takes in tinkering with a car or a radio. The nineteenth-century young man who had the mechanical bent seems, whenever he encountered a new and interesting object, to have responded immediately, "I could make that, too." More than once among the sculptors who compose the literary group we find the tale of a youth who sees for the first time a statue or a portrait bust, exclaims, "I could make that," and goes about it.

Many of the Americans who were internationally admired for their statues were good mechanics and successful inventors. Paul Akers, for instance, while he was working in his father's lumber-mill, constructed a machine for making shingles; Theodatus Garlick performed pioneer experiments in plastic surgery and devised a number of surgical instruments and appliances. Other mechanically gifted sculptors invented devices for use in the making of statues. Joel Hart constructed an elaborate pointing machine with which it was possible to take such accurate measurements of the human head that a portrait bust could be counted on to prove an exact likeness. Hiram Powers devised a tool with which he could finish his statues so that the marble looked like porous flesh, and he constructed a machine for making that tool. Clark Mills and H. K. Brown experimented successfully with casting in bronze. And it is not without significance that the most important of the sculptresses, Harriet Hosmer, was also a good mechanic.

There were neoclassical conventions about the sculptor's themes. He must concern himself primarily with the beauty of the human form, making ideal busts and ideal figures, usually in the nude. (That nudity can be respectable it took the American public a long time to learn.) Each statue was supposed to tell a story and point a moral, too, if it could. This anecdotal element cannot, of course, be blamed on Winckelmann; it was the taste of the age, in painting as in statuary, where it sometimes blocked a normal plastic impulse. There is, for instance, a curious tale of the English sculptor John Gibson who was charmed one day by the lovely contours of a Roman peasant girl looking back over her shoulder at her left ankle. He longed to use the beautiful pose in a statue but did not feel that he could do so until he had invented an incident of a wounded Amazon. He made the Amazon in marble and she was received with enthusiasm.

The sculptor must, then, give his figure a title or at least label it Clytie, Daphne, Hercules. Sometimes he might even desert the classics and permit his statue to illustrate a stanza of Byron or Tennyson or Scott—to whom the Americans added Longfellow. This is an element in the work of our pioneer sculptors which seems to the modern American particularly fortuitous and silly, yet the literary quality of nineteenth-century sculpture was actually of great benefit to the developing art for it was a boon to the layman just learning to look at statues. Here was a point where he was at home, from which he could take off into the new sensations and new emotions generated by a marble figure. Henry James tells us, in *A Small Boy and Others*, that, in his youth, discussion of a work of art hung mainly on the "issue of the producible *name*."[1] He recalls a bust on a pedestal in his parents' parlor which was the subject of constant conversation by visitors. It was called a Bacchante but the general feeling was that it was too gentle for that title; it should be known as a Nymph. And James, in his biography of the literary sculptor Story, confesses to a kind of envy of this simpler critical attitude where the sense to which the work of art appealed "was not, in any strictness, the aesthetic sense in general or the plastic in particular, but the sense of the romantic, the anecdotic, the supposedly historic, the explicitly pathetic." [2]

Permissible also, since the Romans had excelled in them, were the portrait busts. Everyone considered these much lower than the historical and the ideal figures and a few purists, like Harriet Hosmer, would never make them at all, but the majority of American sculptors depended on them as their principal means of support. The public thought them more elegant than painted portraits and, until photography became common and inexpensive, portrait busts were in great demand. Often plaster casts of a small cabinet bust were made and given to one's friends as one now distributes photographs. Busts of great men were also welcome, not only as public monuments but in little replicas for the library. Joel Hart lived in comfort for years on his bust of Henry Clay, of which innumerable copies were sold.

Public monuments were considered, of course, a high form of sculptural art and we Americans, early in the nineteenth century, began to be eager for public monuments. The Revolution had produced a surge of patriotism, of gratitude to our great men and desire to honor them. The first public monument commissioned by a state was a statue of George Washington which North Carolina decided, in 1816, should be set in the State House in Raleigh. They asked advice of Mr. Jefferson, who assured them, quite correctly, that no American sculptor existed capable of executing such a work and urged them to employ "old Canove," which they enthusiastically did. Sixteen years later when the federal government wished to commission a statue of Washington for the national capitol they were able to employ the first Italian-trained American sculptor, Horatio Greenough.*

We ought to know the whole story of each of our literary sculp-

---

* Greenough is usually spoken of as the first American sculptor, but two earlier artists have strong claims to dispute that title with him. William Rush of Philadelphia (1756–1833), a renowned maker of ships' figureheads, carved some charming wooden statues (notably the *Nymph of the Schuylkill* for the Fairmount Water Works) and made some admirable terra cotta busts. John Frazee of New Jersey (1790–1852), a stonecutter, carved in 1825 the first marble bust ever made by an American. A memorial to a distinguished New York lawyer, John Wells, it stands now in St. Paul's Chapel on lower Broadway. Frazee was also the first American to receive a commission from Congress, for a bust of John Jay for the Supreme Court room.

tors. In some cases there is nothing to build on but the name of a patentee of a bust; of three sculptors we have a fairly complete contemporary record: a biography of William Wetmore Story by his friend Henry James; a biography of Harriet Hosmer by an admiring friend; an interesting autobiography by Thomas Ball. Between these extremes the available information varies widely. Sometimes mention of a sculptor is found only in a magazine art note announcing a new statue. Sometimes a man of reputation was written about constantly, by journalists who visited his studio, by travelers who met him at dinner, by critics who reviewed his work in the exhibitions. Sometimes there is a useful account in the books of our earliest art historians, William Dunlap and Henry T. Tuckerman. These enterprising gentlemen persuaded many artists, sculptors as well as painters, to set down for them fairly detailed information about their lives, and they themselves made elaborate records of studio visits and conversations. The twentieth century has produced a few histories of American sculpture and three biographies: of Thomas Crawford by Robert L. Gale, of William Rinehart by William Sener Rusk and of Horatio Greenough by Nathalia Wright. An occasional scholar announces his interest in this or that literary sculptor and publishes some letters or an article. A few local historical societies have been energetic in collecting details about native sons. Incomplete as most of the studies are, they are so illuminating that this book uses many of them to supplement its discussion of general themes.

The period of American literary sculpture drew to its close in the 1870's. It was the Centennial Exhibition in particular which turned the artists' thoughts in a new direction. The statues sent to Philadelphia in 1876 showed that more was going on in France than anywhere else, and already a promising sculptor, Augustus Saint Gaudens, had traveled to Paris instead of Rome for his training. The neoclassical sculptors had been moving since the Civil War more and more toward realism and an increasing interest in American subjects. Some of the younger ones were ready to breathe a new air, though most of the older men who lived on into the twentieth century continued along the road on which they had begun. The Centennial Exhibition, then, marks a convenient end to our history, as Greenough's voyage to Italy marks its beginning.

2

Rome and the Caffè Greco – Thomas Crawford, William Wetmore Story

Horatio Greenough, first of the American literary sculptors, made his way to Italy in 1825. He found Rome so stimulating that he exhausted his energies in long hours of labor, and an attack of malaria laid him prostrate. He was obliged to go home for a year to his native Boston. When he returned to Italy, in 1827, he settled in Florence, as Hiram Powers, the most commercially successful of the literary sculptors, was to do a little later. Florence had always a small and important group of sculptors and painters, but Rome was the real center of artist life. By the middle of the century there were, it was said, four times as many studios in Rome as churches—and there was a church for every day in the year. During the 1830's American artists were only a handful, but each year their tribe increased until by the middle of the century they were an important element in the international artist group. The painters always far outnumbered the sculptors, but the sculptors had a certain prestige. Theirs was thought to be the more difficult and probably the higher art.

The kind of life the sculptors could live in Rome, even when their resources were small, they found so genuinely the good life that most of them were quite unable ever to leave. In their letters, though, and on their visits home they sowed the idea that such an art society might be desirable even in a young, hard-working country. After several decades America began to see the point.

These pioneers did not go to Rome in search of art life—most of them had never heard of such a thing. They went to learn their craft and to practice it. In Rome there were workmen who knew how to put a sculptor's creations into marble. In Rome there were models who would pose in the nude. In Rome one could attend, without fee, anatomical lectures in the medical schools illustrated by the dissection of cadavers. In Rome one could study drawing from life and get criticism, perhaps, on one's work in clay from Thorvaldsen or Gibson. And in Rome were the masterpieces of the Greeks, or at least their Roman copies. The young man who wished to emulate these could contemplate them in the Capitoline and the Vatican.

The hub of art life in Rome, mentioned in every contemporary novel and traveler's journal, was the Caffè Greco on the Via Condotti. Everyone who spent his days with a mallet or with a brush went in the evening after dinner to the Greco to drink coffee, with perhaps some *vino ordinario* or a *mezzo-caldo*, concocted of rum, citron, sugar, and boiling water. The gathering was international and brotherly. Anyone who penetrated the cloud of tobacco smoke and sat down at one of the dirty little marble tables was received as a friend and immediately included in the conversation. It made no difference whether he were one of the great, whom everybody recognized, or a country boy from America who had just, with the usual difficulties, made his way to Rome. The artists thought of themselves as a clan.

This was the first exciting concept to burst upon the young American artist, the idea of a shared and accepted way of life. At home, in Albany or Cincinnati or the country village where he was brought up, he had been lucky to find a well-to-do friend who owned a few engravings from the antique and liked to talk about them or an elderly craftsman who could give him tips on the wielding of his tools. In Rome everyone seemed to be both a critic and a craftsman and never to grow tired of talk. The young sculptor found himself no longer an eccentric, admired occasionally, more often smiled at; he was a member of a respected and accepted profession.

This solidarity was serious as well as gay. Certainly nothing had ever occurred in the United States at all like the meeting of American artists which was called in Rome when Horatio Greenough died in 1852. They not only passed resolutions of regret but agreed that, in manifestation of their regard for the "Pioneer of American Sculpture," they would all wear crape on the left arm for the space of thirty days.

The Caffè Greco (it still flourishes) was purported to have opened in the seventeenth century. Its reputation had been made in the first place by the excellence of its coffee, a Mocha specially imported by the establishment and served always in tall glasses. Location also recommended the Greco to the artists for it was directly across the street from the big cheap restaurant Lepre, where most of them dined. And finally, though this became a matter of less importance under the good Pio Nono (he became Pope in 1846), freer speech was possible at the Greco than anywhere else in the city. The papal spies who, under Gregory XVI, eavesdropped assiduously in most of the *caffè* and restaurants, seem to have thought the artists too irresponsible and unorganized to plot anything dangerous and their wild words, therefore, not worth listening to.

The Greco had no pretensions to charm. Noisy, dirty, smoke-dimmed, crowded—those are the stock adjectives applied to it in the travelers' descriptions. There were just three rooms. The first and largest, its low arched ceiling covered with pretentious allegorical paintings, was occupied chiefly by casual customers—many people came to the Greco just for the coffee—but the artist habitués always stopped as they went through to look in the ancient cigar box which served as a general post office. That box figures in history and fiction: a sculptor comes reluctantly to say goodbye to his friends; his funds are exhausted and he must go back to America on the next boat; he looks into the cigar box from force of habit, and there is an envelope with his name on it—a commission for an ideal figure of Ariadne at a price which will support him through the winter.

After looking hopefully for mail the habitués went on into one of the two back rooms. The younger artists generally packed themselves into the narrow one known as the "omnibus" because of the long benches down each side. Infinitesimal tables were wedged between. In the omnibus the smoke (cigars cost a cent and a half) was even thicker, the noise and singing louder than in the other room, where the more established artists gathered. Here each nationality had its special table, though there was plenty of friendly exchange of talk and jokes between them. Nearest the door were the Germans, the oldest comers (beginning with the Düsseldorf group) who had set most of the customs which the artists from other countries took on. Then came a Russian table, one for the English, and one for English and Americans. The talk around these tables was purported to be both lively and witty but the letter-writers and journalists have furnished us with adjectives rather than examples. We do know that there were endless comparative discussions of all the great artists from the Greeks on down and a lively interest in the work in progress of every contemporary: the bas-relief A had just finished, the ideal bust B had begun, C's difficulties with his client, the commission for a fountain unexpectedly granted to D. Much of this was pure gossip and educational to the American only socially, but there was also plenty of that sharp critical appraisal of one another's work, of what had been intended, what accomplished, which the artist at any stage of maturity finds stimulating.

Their solidarity and their pride in their profession the artists marked not only in their talk but in their dress. Though not so precisely regulated—its note was individuality, not to say eccentricity—the artist costume was quite as distinctive as that of the soldiers or the ecclesiastics who thronged the streets of Rome. The essential was a velvet jacket with sleeves slashed somewhat in the mediaeval manner. The trousers might be velvet or velveteen; they must be very full. The shirt collar was usually Byronic and the cravat a broad gaily colored ribbon tied *alla marinara*. The waistcoat, too, was gay. The hat was high-crowned and conical; the shoes buckled; the stockings of some gaudy color. Most of the garments showed signs of hard wear and were often streaked with paint or gray with marble dust. This costume had the advantage of being cheap to begin with and seldom requiring renewal, for the shabbier it got the more picturesque it became. The total effect, to the eye of the tourist, was dashing and rather wild, especially since every artist felt obliged to wear a beard—great individuality might be exercised in the cut—or at least a pair of fierce mustaches.

Thanks to the artist costume, the Greco, and the Lepre, food, drink, and clothing for the sculptor were comparatively inexpensive. (Roman currency was an easy matter for the American since the coins he most often used corresponded closely enough for all practical purposes with three he used at home. He could think of the *baiocco* as a cent, the *paul* as a dime, and the *scudo* as a dollar.) At the Lepre he could get a hearty dinner, with wine, for three *paul*. This was because, instead of the expensive beef and mutton on which the English visitor insisted, the Lepre offered wild game of every species. "We are regaled," wrote Thackeray's Clive Newcome to Arthur Pendennis, "with woodcocks, snipes, wild swans, ducks, robins, and owls," and he might have added hare, venison, and wild boar, for which the artists had particular gusto.

Yet, though a dollar would buy a good deal more than it could at home, the American legend about the cheapness of life in Italy was not based on very solid fact. Margaret Fuller pointed this out in 1849 in one of her letters to the New York *Tribune* (20 March). The great difference in cost, she said, is for people who are rich. "An Englishman of rank and fortune does not need the same amount of luxury as at home, to be on a footing with the nobles of Italy." The artist can get along with less money than he needs in America if he has an iron constitution and can endure "bad food, eaten in bad air, damp and dirty lodgings." Miss Fuller asked an artist neighbor to make a sculptor's budget for her. "The rent," he reported, "of a suitable studio for modelling in clay and executing statues in marble may be estimated at $200 a year. The best journeyman carver in marble at Rome receives $60 a month. Models are paid $1 a day." [1] The young American, he advised, should have $1,000 placed at his disposal. Many of them were coming with half that amount.

The American worrying about expenses acquired his second new concept of artist life when he compared notes with a French comrade and heard about the Académie de France. Presently his friend would invite him to the Villa Medici, "the most enchanting place in Rome," in the opinion of Henry James. The French government in 1801 transformed it into an academy for students of music, painting, architecture, and sculpture. The twenty-four chosen young men who lived there were nominally superintended by a distinguished elder artist but left, actually, very much to their own devices. "Can there be," asked James, "for a while a happier destiny than that of a young artist, conscious of talent, with no errand but to educate, polish and perfect it, transplanted to these sacred shades?" [2] So it seemed to the young American, and the idea behind the institution was even more startling to his mind than that of an artist society. He had not imagined that any country believed its artists such an asset to the state that national funds were as a matter of course invested in their training. Was this just a French idea, he asked, and learned, with deepening amazement, that other nations shared it. Russia had no Villa Medici but she sent each year to Rome a little group of artists with stipends of $700 each. Germany and the Scandinavian countries granted stipends, too. Even England, or at least the Royal Academy, subsidized, at intervals, an especially promising student.

The co-operative quality of these systems recommended them further to the Americans. The beneficiaries were selected, in theory at any rate, on the basis of their skill and promise. The financing of his own journey to Rome had been largely a matter of luck. It had depended on catching the attention of a wealthy patron who believed that statues were a good thing about the house, or perhaps a group of patrons who wanted to do something handsome for their town and gambled on a local boy with what they took for talent. Some of the aspirants to Rome financed themselves when they could find jobs which allowed them to put a little by each year toward travel.

The $200-a-year studio which embodied the American sculptor's dream often looked to his visitors cold and desolate. The weight of the materials in which he worked made it necessary for him to establish himself on a ground floor so that his windows lacked the views of the eternal city and the glorious sunsets which the painter, on the fourth or fifth *piano*, could command at a lower rent. Even when a sculptor was doing well his studio was likely to have "a good deal the aspect . . . of a stone-mason's workshop," as Hawthorne says of the studio of William Wetmore Story. (Story's *Cleopatra* is the statue described as Kenyon's in *The Marble Faun*.) "Bare floors of brick or plank, and plastered walls; an old chair or two, or perhaps only a block of marble (containing, however, the possibility of ideal grace within it) to sit down upon; some hastily scrawled sketches of nude figures on the whitewash of the wall." [3]

Yet the gardens about a studio, like Crawford's in the Villa Negroni, might be very lovely with cypress avenues, orange walks, and fountains. And Harriet Hosmer put her feminine taste and ingenuity to work to make her studio the prettiest in Rome.

I am going to have a copy of Lady Marian's fountain put up, complete [i.e. with siren, *amorini*, dolphins, and shells], in the entrance room, not only complete, but playing, and I am going to have birds and flowers and every object of beauty, myself included, scattered about among the statues. In fact, I have no doubt people will come to see the appurtenances instead of the fine arts![4]

Miss Hosmer was proud of the economy by which she combined studio, house, and stable—she hunted on the Campagna—at a rent of twenty-eight *scudi* a month, "though it did cost something to furnish, once furnished, house rent comes easy."

Most of the studios, large and small, were in the region behind the Trinità de' Monti where the Via Sistina, the Via Gregoriana, and the Via Capo le Case form an elongated triangle. There the foreign artists had congregated since the days of Poussin and Claude Lorrain and studios had passed from one generation to the next, from Thorvaldsen, for example, to the American Story. The streets were "picturesque" enough to satisfy the most romantic tourist, cobbled, dirty, usually without sidewalks, lighted at night only by dim oil lamps. Since the apartment houses rarely boasted doors, the stairways became extensions of the street, offering the residents close contact with a rich variety of Roman types. James Edward Freeman, in his *Gatherings from an Artist's Portfolio*, describes them:

> Beggars of every degree, from an impoverished count to the most ragged and famished of Rome's multitude of mendicants, mounted the stairs, besetting every door of every story with piteous tales and lamentations. . . . It was not unusual to meet pretty girls in their upland costume mounting to the last floor to sit as models to the painter, or it might be a sunburnt shepherd in his sheepskin jacket, with his wolf-dog in leading. On one occasion I saw an infant donkey being led up the stairs to stand for its picture. Thus animals as well as all grades of humanity could sometimes be encountered on these, so to say, public staircases; the prince, the peer, the fine gentleman, fine lady, tattered mendicant, begging friar with snuff-box, ever ready to proffer the delectable pinch of tobacco-dust, lackeys in livery, bakers' boys, butchers' boys, charcoal men, and hosts of other individuals, jostled each other in mounting and descending these steep thoroughfares.[5]

On each studio door was tacked a little card announcing the hours at which it was open to visitors. The established artist often limited these to one day a week, but the beginner was usually happy to be interrupted on any morning; the visitor, one always hoped, would become a patron. And, as the literary sculptors made America more and more aware of the importance of the fine arts, he did. By mid-century it was the correct thing for even the moderately well-to-do tourist to bring home a portrait bust or a little ideal statue as a memento of his Roman sojourn. A round of the studios became as essential a part of the grand tour as a visit to the Vatican statues by torchlight or seeing the Colosseum under a full moon. Murray's Handbook began in the fifties the practice, which Baedeker later adopted, of publishing a list of addresses of the studios of the more important artists and, ironically enough, the American artist could usually get American commissions more readily in Rome than in New York.

Some of the tourists went through the city at lightning speed but a large number settled down for a whole season of culture, which meant not only walking the galleries but becoming acquainted with contemporary art and meeting some of its practitioners socially. Roman society, as the American observed it, fell into three parts: there were the inner circle of the Italian aristocracy; the English and American colonies; and the artists, some of whom were welcome in both the other groups.

The Romans, when they were in residence during the winter—they spent much of the year at their country villas—entertained elegantly but did not pay much attention to the *forestièri*. The English they thoroughly disliked, for reasons the Americans understood and often shared. The stock caricature of the nineteenth-century British tourist would appear to be erected on very solid fact. He liked the Italian climate, the cheapness of living, and the opportunities for culture, but he had no interest at all in the Italian people, their politics or their problems. The more of England he could carry to Rome the better he was pleased and he succeeded in transplanting so much of it that American travelers constantly expressed disappointment on first setting foot in the Eternal City; it appeared to be an English colony. This was because, coming by the usual route from Civitá Vecchia, the Americans entered Rome by the Porto del Popolo (learning proudly that this referred not to people but to a vanished poplar tree), finding themselves in the Piazza del Popolo and the neighboring Piazza di Spagna, the district which was the center of English life. There were the English church, the English library, restaurants which catered to English tastes and shops offering English goods sold with English manners. Carriages of English make were driven about the street by English coachmen and English was the language heard on every hand. Most of the English lived on streets adjacent to the Piazza di Spagna.

The American soon discovered, however, that this English piazza was only a small section of Rome, that, in fact, he had only to mount the Spanish Steps behind the fountain to find himself surrounded by thoroughly Italian beggars and picturesque artists' models displaying themselves for hire, and that from there he could go on into the great city that belonged to the Romans. He would meet the English again, of course, in the museums and the churches, and, in the churches, would be horrified by their lack of manners. Strongly Protestant as most American travelers were, they were habituated to tolerance and respect for the beliefs of others. That English men and women of apparent breeding could treat the most solemn ceremony at St. Peter's as though it were a circus, walking about at their pleasure, pushing for good seats, commenting freely on the spectacle in high pitched voices, letting champagne corks pop during the elevation of the Host, seemed to the American extraordinarily rude. Distressed or amused as he frequently was by Roman "idolatry," he believed that, until he could put his sentiments into print, he ought to keep them as inconspicuous as possible.

It was these English manners and the English habit of expressing opinions tactlessly which made the average Italian nobleman reluctant to invite an English visitor to his palace, though there were exceptional individuals, of course, whom he welcomed. Toward the American he had no ingrained prejudice; there was simply, in most cases, no point of contact. When the right letters were presented the Americans were hospitably received, especially when they were men of literary or artistic reputation. Sometimes they found the princely entertainments a little too formal or melancholy for their tastes. Julia Ward Howe thought that they held "no great attraction other than that of novelty for persons accustomed to reasonable society elsewhere." But often the Americans were delighted by the brilliance of the scene: the crimson-clad cardinals arriving in coaches

drawn by four black horses, postillions before and footmen behind;
the military men in splendid uniforms; the ladies *en grande toi-
lette;* the great rooms frescoed and hung with tapestry. To perhaps
the most lavish of these Roman entertainments some of the American artists were occasionally bidden. Once or twice a year the great
banker Prince Torlonia offered a reception to his clients, inviting
sometimes two or three thousand. The House of Torlonia was renowned for the elasticity of its interest rate and its readiness to
lend to poor young artists as well as to great entrepreneurs.

Another Roman social affair of a different sort was open to everyone and eagerly participated in by both English and Americans—
the sunset hour on the Pincian Hill. This was a kind of Hyde Park
promenade with an Italian background. The circular drive was far
more effective for its purpose than Rotten Row, for it was so small
that each carriage passed the staring spectator about once in five
minutes. There were equipages French, English, Italian, with handsome horses and footmen behind; there were the pitifully shabby
turnouts of the impoverished Roman aristocracy who still felt impelled to go through the social paces; and there were common Roman
hacks hired by the hour. Most of the pedestrians were well dressed
but there was always an outer rim of beggars. The sculptor, after a
long working day, liked to spend an hour on the Pincio. He could
stroll about the box-bordered paths, listen to the music of the military band, or lounge on a marble bench staring now at the purple
Campagna, now at St. Peter's dome glowing with golden fire, now at
an elegant beauty lying back in her barouche affecting nonchalance
under a little parasol. It was not difficult for the artist's imagination
to assure him that everything at which he gazed in the sunset light
held the potentialities of a future "subject."

Most frequently described of the Roman social gatherings are the
"evenings" in the apartments of the English and American writers,
artists, and "aestheticians" (Freeman's word for those who cultivate
the arts). These affairs glow for us today in the warm light of the
travelers' letters in which they are described, those "intimate" letters
written in the hope that they might one day appear in the *Tribune,*
the *Atlantic,* or even between the covers of a book. The English-
American circle was so small that a single letter of introduction could
easily extend anyone's acquaintance as far as he cared to have it go,

and, in the course of a winter, one could count on meeting, at Miss Charlotte Cushman's or the Crawfords' or the Storys', every peripatetic lion worth encountering. "One sees everybody here at Rome," wrote Harriet Beecher Stowe to her husband in March 1857, "John Bright, Mrs. Hemans' son, Mrs. Gaskell, etc., etc. Over five thousand English travelers are said to be here. Jacob Abbot and his wife are coming. Rome is a world!" [6] Julia Ward Howe is reported to have said that the only lions in Rome who did not mount Mrs. Story's staircase were the carved stone ones on her balustrade.

The American traveler with his thirst for culture found it exciting to be introduced not only to the literary great, whom he might very well meet at home in Boston, but also to American painters and sculptors whose significance to their country was just beginning to be realized. Some of the Americans with established residences had regular evenings with talk and tea and music. Miss Cushman's Saturdays, for instance, were famous. And there were smaller informal gatherings like those Harriet Hosmer described in a letter home (April 1854):

> Every Sunday and Wednesday evening there is a friendly party, as she calls it, at Mrs. Sartoris', consisting of Mrs. Kemble and the Brownings, two young artists [one of them Frederick Leighton] and your humble servant. Mrs. Sartoris sings and Mrs. Kemble sometimes reads, and all in all, it is the perfection of everything that is charming. The Thackerays, too, have been here, and they are such dear girls. Every now and then there is an excursion projected for the Campagna, consisting of these same persons, and we go out for the day picnicking.[7]

Mrs. Nathaniel Hawthorne's diary for January 1859 contains such entries as these:

> Mrs. Story asks us to dine with Mr. de Vere, Lady William Russell, Mr. Alison, Mr. Browning, and other interesting people. . . . In the afternoon I went with E. Hoar to Mr. Story's studio. . . . Mr. Hawthorne and I and Julian went to call on Miss Cushman, and to Mr. Page's studio. . . . I went with my husband to call at Miss Hosmer's studio, and met the Hon. Mr. Cowper, who stopped to talk. Mr. Browning darted upon us across the Piazza, glowing with cordiality. Miss Hosmer could not admit us, because she was modeling Lady Mordaunt's nose.[8]

During all these afternoons and evenings there was continual talk about art. Certain topics seem to have been discussed again and again with unabated ardor: Which is the higher art, painting or sculpture? How do those arts relate to poetry? Which of the marble masterpieces in Rome and Florence stirs in you the deepest emotion? How did you feel when you first confronted the *Apollo Belvedere*, the *Laocoön*, the *Dying Gaul* (they were learning not to say *Gladiator*)? These were not just questions for amateurs; the artists' talk, in the *caffè* and studios, ran in the same channels night after night.

The third form of evening gaiety, the "studio" or "bohemian shine," was an entirely masculine affair. The guests came in their usual Caffè Greco costumes and refreshments were set out, buffet style, on big tables. The standard menu included ham, cold boiled fowl, bologna sausage, bread, cheese, cigars and pipes, and some good inexpensive wine like Marsala. Sometimes a moderately well-to-do artist would dispense Welsh rabbits, carefully superintending in the kitchen their preparation by his Pietro or Giovanni. Talk was the chief entertainment and often it became serious, ranging from art and poetry to politics or even theology. There were cards, too, interspersed with parlor games and stunts. Freeman describes them:

> If we were tired of whist, or other games of cards, our clever host would amuse us with some marvellous trick in jugglery, or droll conundrum; or the latest known puzzle would be produced for the trial of our wits.
> On these occasions [Thomas Buchanan] Read has perhaps recited to us his popular "Sheridan's Ride." Father Burke has sung an Irish song (no one sings them with more feeling and expression than he), Rogers has given us a ludicrous imitation of Forrest as Metamora at the moment when he shakes his false calves to bring down the house.[9]

The gaiety usually went on till dawn.

Parties of this kind were considered so agreeable that at least one was likely to be tendered to any visiting celebrity. There is an account of the elderly Longfellow seated among a lively group around a punchbowl, smoking a long meerschaum, placid and silent, yet thoroughly enjoying the entertainment.

The artists had a few organized gatherings, conducted by their mutual benefit Association of Artists in Rome. The combination of efficiency and *gemütlichkeit* in these affairs indicates their German origin. The initiation of new members, for instance, took place at the *tratoria* Monte Citorio, near the Porta Molle. There was usually an auction of paintings contributed by the more prosperous members for the relief of the poorer, and then a series of tableaux vivants, staged on a table, in which each new member was required to demonstrate his artistic talent by posing as the *Laocoön*, the *Belvedere Apollo*, or one of the other masterpieces. He was then declared worthy to be a Knight of the Baiocco, a penny strung on a ribbon was hung around his neck, and he was presented with a terra cotta quart drinking horn. While all the old members touched beakers with him they sang a German ode composed in his honor. This ceremony had political overtones; it was intended to indicate that the artist should acknowledge no aristocracy except that of genius.

There was also an annual fete, large and picturesque enough to draw many visitors. It took place at Cervara, some ten miles out on the Campagna, to which the artists, most of them in fancy dress, made their way on horseback, assback, or on foot. They dined in the cool volcanic caves, took part in horse and donkey races, performed elaborate mock ceremonies, sang, drank, and enjoyed themselves in a manner which seemed to at least one lady spectator "not the most orderly."

Mingled with all its friendliness and gay camaraderie Roman art life had, of course, a few less agreeable elements. There was jealousy and back-biting and derogation. More than one traveler recorded with amusement that he never heard one sculptor speak well of the work of another, and C. Edwards Lester, American consul in Genoa, quotes in his *Artists of America* a letter written by a painter in 1841: "Strange that so much venom should exist among professors of a liberal art,—but the truth is, that envy and jealousy are our (painters') besetting sins. . . . Except religious sects, I think *we* are the warmest and best haters, and the most malignant devils the sun ever deigned to shine upon." [10]

The supposed "excesses" of artist life seemed to have played a minor part in the Roman society. Drunkenness was not common. Wine, of course, was the chief beverage and not many of the artists could afford too much of that. They adapted themselves, apparently, to the usual Italian limits. As for women, except for occasional tales

of romantic affairs with beautiful peasant girls, accounts of artists'
amours are remarkably few. The affairs of an idol like Thorvaldsen,
which seem to have been perfectly well known, are dismissed with
such statements as that, since he was a bachelor, he probably fell into
the habits too common among foreign artists in Rome. The English-
men and the Americans were not supposed to amuse themselves in
this way. There were, of course, the models, but precise information
on their virtue is a little difficult to come by. The travelers and letter
writers were, after all, making their records for family reading
around the evening lamp and, though there are such sentimental
prose sketches as J. E. Freeman's "My Model, Agata" and W. W.
Story's *Fiammetta*, one is not convinced that that is the whole story.
Some of these tales admit that the profession of modeling was so ill
thought of among the *contadini* that many a young man rejected his
affianced when she undertook it. There is even a pitiful account (also
Freeman's) of the lovely Cesira who was stabbed by her lover because a well-meaning American, tramping through the province with
his sketchbook, had persuaded her to sit for him. The painter's
model, of course, might insist that she posed only in her picturesque
bodice and red skirt, but how could that excuse be urged by the
young woman who stood for the sculptor's Daphne or Eve?

Thomas Ball, writing his autobiography at seventy, sidesteps the
issue.

> Perhaps, as a general rule, female models are just what each
> artist in his heart desires to find them. To me they have been
> invariably patient, obedient, and respectful servants, never in-
> dulging in the slightest familiarity or levity,—coming, patiently
> performing their arduous task, receiving their money, and de-
> parting, precisely as if they had come to mend my coat or scrub
> my floor.[11]

And he goes on to tell of some young women who posed for him in
order to earn money for their *dots*, remarking that a girl could make
in one hour of posing a sum which it would take her from sunrise to
sunset to earn by any other labor. This wage of a dollar an hour was
low from the American sculptor's point of view; it was one of the
reasons which made him prefer Rome to New York, where female
models could be had only at ruinous rates of two or three dollars.

The most derogatory criticism of the model comes from Hiram

Powers. The Reverend H. W. Bellows interviewed the artist while he sat for his bust and published in *Appleton's Journal* "Seven Sittings with Powers, the Sculptor":

> Young women [said Powers] are driven to this employment by the want of bread. I have numerous offers of their services made by parents who are in great distress. I make it a point to discourage all who come to me from entering the business, and am only conquered when I feel sure that, if I decline, they will be driven to other studios. I prefer only professional models, already thoroughly committed to the calling, as I shrink from the responsibility of leading any into so perilous a vocation. They are usually accompanied by their mothers, and I strive to treat them in a way to save their self-respect and delicacy—a very hard task, which too often breaks down in less scrupulous hands.[12]

Life was certainly freer than in the United States, but this did not constitute its greatest attraction for the artist. The thing which delighted him most, after the sense of professional brotherhood, was the tone and tempo of Roman life. This was partly a matter of climate—oleanders and orange trees are not conducive to speed; partly the rich beauty everywhere—a vista down a cypress alley can turn a mind to meditation even at breakfast; but chiefly, perhaps, the impression Italy conveyed that leisure was not necessarily evil, that it might even be a duty. In the bustling young United States anyone who did not labor at his trade from dawn till sunset six days a week usually looked to his neighbors like an idler or a parasite. Americans knew well enough that a field must now and again lie fallow if it is to produce rich grain but it had not occurred to them that a similar condition of repose might be fruitful for the artist. The young sculptor, seeing that none of his friends had such impulses, was constrained to question whether his instinct to complete inactivity now and then was sound. In Rome, when his creative energy flagged, he could discover an array of alibis and comforts. Here were all sorts of devices, beside hard labor, for improving one in his profession. Chief of these, of course, were the galleries and churches. There was an endless file of statues which he might study, which he must study, if he was to understand the possibilities and resources of his art. No day spent in the Capitoline or the Vatican could be considered lost. And at convenient distance from the city itself were individual masterpieces with which one ought to be familiar. Every picnic on the Campagna might, if one liked, have an "object." Moreover, low-pressure workdays need not be spent alone—as he had had to spend them in Vermont. Here the artist was not an eccentric with rather dubious habits but a member of a brotherhood who believed in the virtue of irregular hours. Of course there were temptations to pure idleness and of course there were artists who succumbed to them, but the pressures of poverty kept that number fairly small. Most of them had to turn out at least hack work if they were to continue to eat. The painters made copies of Raphaels and Titians; the sculptors modeled portrait busts.

Sometimes it took a long residence to adjust the American to the Italian rhythm. Greenough, as we have seen, began by working himself into a fever. Crawford in his early years could not bear to stop when the dark made modeling difficult. He fixed a light to a headband like a miner's cap and worked his clay far into the night. Yet both men came to terms with Italy and their own powers. More often the artist felt at once that this was the climate he had always longed for.

> I wouldn't live anywhere else but in Rome, [wrote Harriet Hosmer, 22 April 1853] if you would give me the Gates of Paradise and all the Apostles thrown in. I can learn more and do more here, in one year, than I could in America in ten. America is a grand and glorious country in some respects, but this is a better place for an artist.[13]

And Story, in 1848, was writing to James Russell Lowell: "As the time draws near I hate the more to leave Rome, so utterly exhaustless is it, and so strongly have I become attached to it. How shall I ever again endure the restraint and bondage of Boston?"[14]

Yet for all their devotion to Italy the sculptors, like most of the American visitors, were singularly unconcerned with her struggle for unity and independence. The revolution of 1848, Garibaldi's great march, the valiant defense of Rome Americans watched as though they were dramatic spectacles arranged for their benefit. The proclamation of Italian independence in 1860 left them comparatively unmoved and many of them were actually sorry in 1870 when Victor Emmanuel entered Rome and it became the capital of the new nation. Pio Nono seemed to them such a good old man that they did not like to see him shorn of his temporal power, confining himself to the Vatican, and reducing to a minimum the processions and illuminations which they had found so picturesque and enjoyable.

To the average Protestant American the Catholic Church as an institution was anathema but he took great pleasure in its elaborate and handsome ritual, so different from the cold Presbyterian or Methodist ceremonies to which he was accustomed. He was quite ready to admit that the ecclesiastical government of Rome was inefficient and oppressive but these faults weighed little on his daily life and he felt no responsibility for their reform. "I am not a Catholic, I am much the contrary," said Harriet Hosmer telling of her experiences in Rome in 1870, but she went on to relate how she joined the black-robed throng in St. Peter's when a mass was celebrated to protect the Pope against his enemies, the Italians, and how she sobbed with the rest at the sight of Pio Nono in tears among his weeping cardinals. Rome, she thought, was spoilt for the artist by the presence of the Italian soldiers. She had stayed on in the city when the troops entered because she was "not likely to have another chance of seeing a bombardment." [15] The Pope's French guard, overwhelmingly outnumbered by the Italians, were expected to make only a token resistance but actually the cannonading went on for five hours, during the course of which the adventure-loving sculptress had her cheek grazed by a rifle bullet and found herself standing next to a man whose hand dripped blood. She took him home, bound him up, and wrote that she "wouldn't have missed it for the world." [16]

William Rinehart, on 4 November 1871, wrote in the same vein. "Rome will never be old Rome again." [17] He did not object to the cleaned houses nor to the opening of new streets, but he hated the bustle and confusion caused by the influx of politicians for the sessions of Parliament and the restrictions on visiting papal collections of art. "We are to have no Easter ceremonies, no illuminations," he wrote a few months later (18 March 1872), "the old cuss is real mad and won't do anything. One can only enter the Vatican now with a permit and then only two hours at a time—what nonsense." [18]

Even the Storys, whose intimate friendship with Margaret Fuller Ossoli brought them close to the anxieties and dangers of the siege of Rome, assisted, Henry James tells us in his biography of Story, "as in an opera-box" at the battle of the French troops against the

popular government of Rome. "The flight of the Pontiff, the tocsin
and the cannon, the invading army, the wounded and dying, the wild
rumours, the flaring nights, the battered walls, were all so much grist
to the mill of an artistic, a poetic nature, curious of character,
history, aspects." [19] Margaret Fuller brought them news on 25 April
of the French landing at Cività Vecchia and a few days later they
went to watch the building of barricades at the Porta San Giovanni,
where the sculptor seated himself on a pile of timber "destined to be
used in the defense" [20] and sketched the movements of the workmen
who seemed to him agreeably lazy and graceful. On 30 April, when
they heard the first cannon, the Storys moved the children to the
Casa Dies, where Americans were gathering for protection under
their flag and from which they had a fine view of the whole battle.
They went with Margaret Fuller to her hospital and gave her money
for the wounded she was tending, then to the Vatican Gardens to see
Ossoli engaged in the defense. "Pleasant days and evenings," wrote
Mrs. Story in her journal, "the weather cloudless; our balcony,
which overlooks the city, a rich source of interest." [21]

There were exceptions, of course. Crawford in 1848 was invited by
his Italian friends to become an officer in the Civic Guard. Greenough left Florence for the United States because he could not bear
to see his beloved city under Austrian domination. But the majority
of Americans managed to remain detached from the whole process of
the Risorgimento.

Two of the highest Roman reputations, European as well as
American, were those of Thomas Crawford and William Wetmore
Story, men of totally different backgrounds and temperaments but
admirers of each other's work and excellent friends.

Crawford (1813–1857) is actually the first Roman American
among the sculptors, for Greenough, though he set foot first in
Rome, was identified through his whole artistic life with Florence.
The admiration with which Crawford's contemporaries regarded
him seems excessive by modern standards, but one must not forget
that to the average American just to carve a figure, any kind of
figure, in marble seemed miraculous. The man who could do it must
be a genius. And when a marble statue expressed an idea or told a
story how could one not be deeply moved? America knew that she had

raised up statesmen as able as any that England had to show, or Rome, or Greece. Why might she not, fresh, young, strong, republican, produce a sculptor as fine as Phidias? Many of his contemporaries thought that Crawford was that man. His personality and his virtues were shaped in the finest American pattern.

Crawford, to begin with, was a poor boy who made his way to fame and wealth not only by his sculptural skill but by the exercise of good American qualities: persistence, courage, and hard work. In his success he was modest, in his manner of life hospitable but simple. He was, too, in the right American way, always optimistic about the future and "his moral nature was as pure as his genius was high. The temptations to which the sensitive organization of artists exposes them had no power over him." [22] This is the testimony of a lifelong friend, George Hillard.

Crawford was born on 22 March 1813 in New York City. His father and mother had recently emigrated from North Ireland and lived in circumstances neither very comfortable nor very poor. The father is reported to have had a university education and to have belonged to a family of landed gentry who disapproved of his marriage. The member of the family who mattered most to Thomas was his sister Jenny, a few years older, who was his counselor and confidante through life.

Except for Jenny, who seems to have been a person of taste and fond of reading, there was little in his environment to nourish or even suggest an artistic career, but the boy had an innate desire to draw everything he saw and a good deal of facility in handling a pencil. This is common enough in the young, but Thomas was so totally uninterested in lessons of any other kind that the family finally placed him in a drawing school, where he was perfectly happy. Just what the curriculum of this establishment was Crawford's biographers do not say but he had evidently less than the usual elementary education when, at fourteen, he was expected to begin contributing to the family income. He flatly refused the conventional opportunities that presented themselves in stores and offices and apprenticed himself to a wood-carver. He wanted to earn money by making beautiful things and he showed a real aptitude for the work he had chosen. He began, too, to think about being an architect and tried to teach himself something about the art from what books he could command. He read also many biographies of artists and gathered from them that the way to eminence is often long and hard. He was not discouraged by the prospect. An artist, he was sure, was what he was meant to be; he was strong; and he liked to work—at labor of his choice. Of statues New York had at that time almost none but there were shops full of prints and engravings which introduced him to the neoclassical tradition. He hoarded his earnings and bought what he could, spending his time at home in copying or coloring his purchases while sister Jenny read poetry aloud. It was possible, too, he found, to purchase inexpensive casts of some of the great works of antiquity and of the present and he built gradually a rather impressive little collection. The one he cared for most was Thorvaldsen's bas-relief *Triumph of Alexander*. This was the kind of thing a nineteenth-century man could make, the sort of thing he himself dreamed of making some day.

We know little about Crawford's other amusements at this time or about his companions. He was always in later life so engrossed in his work that he was very happy in solitude and he was never gregarious though he made warm and enduring friends who thought him both admirable and charming. In appearance he was picturesque, tall and graceful with thick waving chestnut hair and eyes of a remarkable bright blue. In manner he was sometimes distrait—his mind, his friends supposed, off on artistic dreams—so that he seemed, till one knew him, cold and reserved. With success and marital happiness he grew mellower.

By the time he was nineteen Crawford felt that he had exhausted the possibilities of wood and must begin to work in a more important medium. He found himself a place in the stoneyard of James Frazee and Robert Launitz. This was a piece of good fortune, for both men were not only stonecutters but artists. Frazee was, as I have said, the first American to carve a bust in marble and to receive a sculptural commission from Congress; Launitz was a Pole who had worked for four years in Rome with an uncle who was a pupil of Thorvaldsen. While he worked in the stoneyard Crawford began to attend the anatomy classes—taught from books and charts—at the National Academy of Design. He knew now that the art he wanted to practice was sculpture. Both Frazee and Launitz were impressed by Crawford's skill in carving, by his ability to work long and hard, and by

his genuine interest in art. Finally they encouraged him to go to
Rome and supplied part of the funds which made the journey possible. Even more valuable to the aspiring sculptor was Launitz's
letter of introduction to Thorvaldsen. The famous sculptor
welcomed the young American warmly and offered him a place in his
studio until he could make his own arrangements. From the beginning and all through a long friendship he was generous with criticism and advice.

Rome was even more exciting than Crawford had anticipated.

You can imagine [he wrote Launitz] my surprise upon seeing the
wonderful halls of the Vatican—after leaving Barclay Street
[Academy of Fine Arts] and the National [Academy of Design].
Only think of it—a green one like me, who had seen but half-a-
dozen statues during the whole course of his life—to step thus
suddenly into the midst of the greatest collection in the world.[23]

Crawford plunged eagerly into work as soon as he arrived in
Rome. He visited the galleries constantly, writing elaborate analyses
and criticisms of what he saw, most of them in letters to his sister. He
drew daily in the life class at the French Academy—the first opportunity he had ever had to work from a nude model. He modeled in
Thorvaldsen's studio, copying the antique and setting up little statues of his own which he labored over for a time and then, unsatisfied,
destroyed. He worked always rapidly and impatiently and this was
the explanation his admirers later gave for any faults in his execution. It was an amused saying among his fellow artists that whenever
Crawford had an idea he threw some clay together with a trowel,
struck it first with his right hand, then with his left, turned it round
three times on the pedestal—and there was a finished statue.

Rome set Crawford's mind whirling with new impressions and new
impulses. He could not begin to get into clay, or even down in
sketches, half the ideas which came to him. The days were far too
short; he worked late into the night. His friends began to worry
about his health.

This eagerness and fecundity never slackened. "I regret," he
wrote when he was thirty, "that I have not a hundred hands, to keep
pace with the workings of my mind." [24] And years later, when he had
an established reputation and was executing commissions for the
Federal Government, he found it necessary to stop again and again

in the long course of constructing a monument to jot down in clay some insistent idea which he could not bear to lose. There was a little room over his studio filled with these clay sketches on which he hoped to work some day. His ideas at first were classical— *Orpheus, Genius of Mirth, Vesta, Sappho,* and so on; then he tried Biblical stories—*David and Goliath, Daughter of Herodias, Christ Disputing with the Doctors;* and finally historical themes.

It is this fecundity of Crawford's as well as his instinctive impulse toward sculpture which makes one feel that he may actually have been, as so many of his contemporaries thought, the truest artist of them all. With his manual skill and his imagination he might have accomplished great things—if only he had had a little education, if he had learned how to read about his art and how to think about it as his contemporary Greenough did. Sure as he was of his vocation, Crawford had only elementary ideas of what its practice required. He recognized the necessity for knowing anatomy and learned what he could. He had a quick and penetrating eye and gathered much by looking at statues as well as at people. He believed Beauty to be all important and tried hard to find out what Beauty is by struggling with Burke on the Sublime and Alison on Taste, but they were too much for him. His knowledge of Rome and Greece came from translations of Ovid and Homer. He read Pope's translation first, then Cowper's, which seemed to him much closer to the simplicity of the original so he worked from that. In English he liked best the poets, Byron and Shelley particularly, who gave him ideas for statues and bas-reliefs. The training he got from Frazee and Launitz was valuable, but technical only. The National Academy of Design taught him that the source of all excellence was to be found in the work of the Greeks, but they did not tell him why. Crawford, when he went to Rome, thought of sculpture as a wonderfully exciting way to tell a story or present a character. He was perhaps the most completely literary of all the literary sculptors. His thronging ideas for statuary sprang always from myth or poetry or portraiture, real and ideal. One is struck also by the fact that, quite late in life, he spoke with profound gratitude of an early piece of advice from Thorvaldsen: that in making a statue one must think first about mass and volume and action, not about detail. That fairly obvious observation came to him, apparently, as a revelation. "These few words of instruction from this great artist gave me more insight into my art and were of more service to me than all else put together that I have ever seen and heard." [25] Thorvaldsen did not mean, of course, that details were unimportant, quite the contrary, only that they should be attended to in their place. And Crawford was very skilful in details; he loved to invent accessories and to carve them carefully, as he had once carved wreaths on mantelpieces.

Crawford enjoyed the *caffè* and studio life in Rome, the talk with artists from England, Germany, France, Russia. The only other American artist there at the time was the painter Frederic Philip, with whom he formed a warm friendship. He also became greatly attached to the American consul, George Washington Greene, a painter and a literary man as well as a government official, who has left us a useful biographical sketch of the sculptor. Perhaps because there were so few Americans in Italy when he arrived Crawford identified himself more closely with the Italians than many of his countrymen later did. He picked up the language with ease—his ear was as quick as his eye—and it is characteristic that though he came to speak it so well that his Italian friends liked to say that he had the true *bocca Romana*, he never acquired any grammatical accuracy. When, at the time of the siege of Rome, he was asked to become a member of the Civic Guard, some American friends questioned the propriety of his putting on a foreign uniform. Crawford replied that he had property in the city which he wanted to protect and that in any case to be a defender of liberty would not alienate him from his own country.

Happy and exciting as the first years of Crawford's artist life were, they were also hard. He had practically no funds beyond his passage money and it took many months for word to spread among the wealthy travelers that there was an American sculptor in Rome; but it did spread. The American patron, usually looking for a bargain and always in a hurry, was glad to hear about a countryman who worked swiftly and would undertake a commission at any price he could get. In one period of ten weeks Crawford modeled seventeen portrait busts and though the payment he received barely covered his expenses he felt justified in taking a studio of his own. He found a good situation on the Via Negroni but fortune was against him. That summer Rome experienced an epidemic of cholera and the depression of 1837 in the United States reduced markedly the number of travelers to Italy. While he waited for orders Crawford set up ideal figures and finally made one which he wanted to put into marble. This was the *Orpheus* (*Pl. 3*), which was to be the start of his reputation.

> I am writing [runs a letter to the faithful sister] in the midst of a terrible thunderstorm, and can scarcely proceed for the incessant flashes of lightning, which dart every moment into the windows of my studio. . . . I have been thinking of the story about Phidias and his wonderful statue of Jove. You know, that upon finishing it, he requested some sign from the god, to know if he were pleased with the representation. It seems the nod was given, for at that moment the statue was circled by lightning, which came and passed off with such a noise as could only be produced by heaven's artillery. Were we living in that age, or were ours the religion of the ancient Greeks, I, too, might interpret the sign in my favor.[26]

Jove's sign to Crawford was the advent of Charles Sumner. The future Senator was a close friend of Crawford's Roman colleague W. W. Story, who introduced them. A strong friendship grew out of Sumner's admiration for the *Orpheus* and Crawford's other work. He became a vigorous proclaimer of Crawford's excellence and a promoter of commissions.

Sumner, like most of Crawford's contemporaries, was impressed by the fact that he chose for his statue a scene from the Orpheus legend which none of the ancient sculptors had ever depicted: the moment when Orpheus, having, with his lyre, lulled Cerberus to sleep, steps forward into the darkness of Hell. Crawford seems to have conceived his statue not only as an illustration of the myth but as an allegory of the artist seeking the ideal which always eludes him. The slender figure of Orpheus leans forward, peering into the darkness, shading his eyes with his right hand; in the left he holds a lyre; a short cloak floats from his shoulders. Beside him is Cerberus, introduced, Crawford wrote, so that the spectator might recognize at a glance that this figure with wreath and lyre is not Apollo. The great dog's three heads are properly drowsy—this is essential to the story—but his anatomy is very confusing. The heads seem to have been stuck on almost anyhow, one on top of another. It is probably Cerberus which made William Rimmer declare this group "one of the worst examples of modern art." Rimmer knew more about anatomy than almost any other artist in the nineteenth century and he was especially interested in the anatomy of animals. But Rimmer was almost alone in his opinion. That the Boston Museum of Fine Arts, which inherited it from the Athenaeum, no longer keeps the *Orpheus* on prominent display would seem incredible to Crawford's contemporaries. John Kenyon, the English poet, for instance, wrote:

> Some of the best judges, even in the mould, compare [it] to the Apollo. Gibson, chary and cold in praise, spoke of it to me as a most extraordinary promise of eminence in the art. I know that Thorwaldsen (himself the greatest of modern names, not even excepting Canova) has expressed the same opinion, and esteems Crawford as his successor in the severe classic style of sculpture.[27]

Sumner, in an article for the *United States Magazine and Democratic Review* (May 1843) says of *Orpheus:*

> Too much cannot be said in praise of the manner in which the artist has arranged his little group. The attitude of the principal figure, the position of the arms, and the apt employment of drapery, strike the most careless eye. But it is in the selection of the scene, and the poetical conception of it, that Crawford challenges our warmest admiration. It is not known that any other sculptor—we believe no other artist of any kind—has illustrated this scene. From the pictured urn of the past, our young countryman first drew it forth and invested it with the light of his genius.

The excitement and labor of creation, imposed upon the long previous stretch of overwork, brought on a fever which might have had serious consequences had it not been for the friendly and official efficiency of Greene, who saw to it that Crawford had the best of medical care and, when he could be moved, took him into his own home for convalescence.

As soon as he was on his feet again Crawford went vigorously to work, but his funds were running dangerously low when a letter came from Charles Sumner announcing that he had obtained subscriptions to the amount of $25,000 for the purchase of the *Orpheus* for the Boston Athenaeum. This was the beginning of success. As soon as *Orpheus* arrived in Boston orders for statues began to come in and soon Crawford was very profitably busy.

At the same time that his professional reputation began to flourish Crawford's personal life burst into flower with a fine romantic courtship and marriage to the beautiful New York heiress Louisa Ward. It pleased the couple, in later life, to recall that they saw each other first in 1832 when Crawford's employers, Frazee and Launitz, sent him to carve an elaborate marble mantel, with caryatids, for the dining room in Samuel Ward's new mansion on Bond Street. The young workman took small heed of the little daughter of the household, who was only nine years old, but when the two met again in Rome she was a lovely creature of twenty-one, spending the winter with her sister Mrs. Samuel Gridley Howe. Louisa and the sculptor fell rapidly in love. Some of her relatives were skeptical about the lasting quality of this attachment, but the real obstacle was the guardian uncle in New York who had small use for artists and was quite sure that the young man was only after Louisa's fortune. Crawford, refusing to be put down, followed her to America and after a few weeks presented himself with such an impressive number of commissions in his hand that the uncle gave way. The marriage took place on 2 November 1844 and, after spending some months more in the United States and acquiring more commissions, Crawford, with his bride, went back to Rome. There they took a ninety-nine-year lease on the second floor of the huge old Villa Negroni, with permission to build as many studios as Crawford needed over the reservoir of the Baths of Diocletian in the garden. Here they settled happily, brought up four brilliant children, one of them the novelist F. Marion Crawford, and hospitably entertained their friends.

Crawford's expanding popularity was not merely the unsophisticated enthusiasm of Americans hoping for a national genius. Europeans admired him, too, Gibson and Thorvaldsen, as we have seen, and the artists of other countries. He was made an honorary member of the Royal Academies of Munich and St. Petersburg and of the Academy of St. Mark at Florence. From the Germans came also a spectacular recognition when his *Beethoven* was cast in Munich.

Charles C. Perkins, the Boston art historian, had commissioned from Crawford a bronze statue of Beethoven for the Boston Music Hall. So impressed were the Munich foundry workers and all others who saw it with Crawford's great brooding figure that it was decided its completion in bronze must be celebrated with an art-music festival. No tribute like this had ever before been offered to an American. The date set was 25 March 1855, the anniversary of Beethoven's death. The statue, banked high with flowers and lit by a hundred gas lamps, was placed in the Concert Hall against a background of green velvet and golden pillars. Three hundred musicians performed some of the composer's finest works. King Maximilian and his Queen attended in state and expressed their regret that "this masterpiece of art" could not remain in Munich. When the statue arrived in Boston that New England city almost rivaled Munich in a ceremony which included music and a poem by Crawford's fellow sculptor Story.

A few years before this, while the Beethoven statue was still in progress, Crawford was making a visit to America with his family when the state of Virginia announced a competition for a monument to Washington to be erected in Richmond. This was a kind of work of which Crawford had long dreamed; he wanted to make statues not just for drawing rooms but for public places where they might influence many people every day. He had, at different times, made little models of Washington statues and it did not take him long to complete a design which he submitted to the Virginia commissioners. That he found himself in competition with seventy others is some indication of the number of aspiring sculptors the United States was nurturing. The commissioners took a long time to come to a decision, reducing the number of possibilities by little and little, but finally they accepted Crawford's design.

> The sun shines at last, dear Lou! [he wrote to his wife on 2 February 1850]. I have beat them all, and the monument is mine! Here is truly glorious news to send you, darling. . . . I have at last been permitted to realize all my artistic dreams and have received a work that any artist might be proud to have the honor of executing. My position in art is now defined, and I speak of it as calmly as I can under the first excitement produced in my mind by the action of the commissioners. . . . I long wished to offer you something that would command the respect of our country, and I have at last found it.[28]

This monument displays strikingly both Crawford's strengths and his weaknesses. The idea is entirely literary, an equestrian figure of Washington on a very high pedestal surrounded by standing statues of six distinguished Virginia statesmen; beyond these, on six outlying plinths, six eagles. (Randolph Rogers, who finished the monument after Crawford's death, replaced these by six allegorical female figures.) General Washington is well modeled—his casting caused another demonstration in Munich—but his horse stands on a narrow rectangle from which one step forward would precipitate him to the earth. The two figures—Jefferson and Patrick Henry—which Crawford himself completed are admirable in pose, gesture, and expression—the Henry, in particular, is an excellent portrait statue—but neither they nor the four other figures are placed in any significant relationship to Washington. They do not look at him or seem to be aware of him in any way. The monument sculpturally is a collection of parts.

Crawford succeeded no better in the composition of the first large-scale work he executed for the Federal Government. This commission came while the Richmond monument was in progress. Captain Meigs, the engineer in charge of the additions to the Capitol, invited Crawford and Hiram Powers to submit designs for the north pediment. Powers thought it beneath his dignity to accept anything less than an entirely free commission but Crawford was perfectly ready to submit models and take suggestions. Meigs found him so agreeable to work with that other commissions followed, for the bronze doors to the Senate and House wings, and, most spectacular of all, for the figure of *Armed Freedom* (*Pl. 5*) to crown the Capitol dome. The hoisting into place of this gigantic goddess took place six years after Crawford's death, in 1863 when Washington was full of soldiers. When the huge head, which had to be lifted separately, was set in place a salute of cannon thundered the triumphant moment to the nation.

The Capitol pediment was planned to present a careful literary idea, the disappearance of the Indian race and the emergence of the new American types which were taking its place. Crawford had seen and admired the Elgin marbles but, like most of his contemporaries, he had not deduced from them anything about the relationship between sculpture and architecture. The position of one figure in relation to another he thought of as a matter of narrative, not of mass or line. But these points were not matters of concern to the majority of his contemporaries. They rejoiced to watch an American do something no American had ever done before and they were proud to see their new Capitol embellished with American works of art. Crawford's reputation was at its height when in 1856 he took his family to the United States while he straightened out some details too complex for letters in the erection of the Richmond and the Washington statues. It was arranged that Mrs. Crawford should spend the winter with her family so that the children might have some American schooling, while sister Jenny accompanied her brother back to Rome. Not long before he sailed Crawford began to be troubled by a swelling in his left eye which blurred his vision and produced severe headaches. He made light of it, sure that it was only a temporary affliction, but when he was back in Rome it grew steadily worse, the doctors could give him little help, and soon he was quite unable to carry on any work except the supervision of what was going on in his twelve studios. Finally, in Paris, the swelling was diagnosed as a tumor pressing on the brain; an operation was impossible and his days were numbered. His wife was sent for; they went to London where a surgeon was able to give him some relief from pain by the removal of the eye. Both Crawford and his wife met the long months of suffering with a courage and patience which made a deep impression on his friends; it all fitted into the romantic pattern of his life. Crawford was not only an artist but a hero.

"He rests from his labors," wrote George Hillard, "death alone could make him rest. His works follow him; his example follows him, too." [29]

William Wetmore Story (1819–1895) was a man of many talents. He might have made a success in several very different professions and it took him a long while to decide to which one he really wanted to devote his life. It was fortunate for the new American art that he finally determined to be a sculptor, for though, by modern standards, he never became an artist of high distinction, he brought to the new art some of the things which it most needed and which only a few Americans were then equipped to lend it.

Story might have been a writer, and he did publish a good deal both in prose and verse. He cared greatly for music—he had a fine baritone voice; he was enthusiastic about the theater and was an excellent amateur actor; but the great rival to sculpture was the law, to which he was born. His father was the distinguished Judge Joseph

Story who sat on the bench of the United States Supreme Court and was the first professor in Harvard's Law School.

William Story was born in Salem in 1819 but brought up in Cambridge, to which the family moved when the Judge became connected with the Law School. A Harvard A.B. degree was of course taken for granted for him and he followed that with an LL.B. in 1840. As a student he enjoyed his books and made good friends, some of whom, in their different fields, became as distinguished as he. The ones to whom his most interesting letters are addressed were James Russell Lowell and Charles Eliot Norton.

Story began his practice of the law in the office of Charles Sumner and George Hillard, former pupils and close friends of his father. Both of them shared William Story's interest in the arts and their legal discussions sometimes wandered into greener fields. In 1843 Story married Miss Emelyn Eldridge of Boston, about whom the chroniclers like to use the adjectives "beautiful" and "queenly." She was to become famous as a Roman hostess. During the six years when he practiced law Story published his first book of verse and also two important legal volumes, a *Treatise on the Law of Contracts* and a *Treatise on Sales of Personal Property*. Both of them went into six editions and were adopted as textbooks in the Harvard Law School. A little later he published a three-volume *Reports* of law cases, which was also received with respect. Everything pointed toward a distinguished legal career when, by what seems to us a curiously inverted process, he turned into a sculptor. Actually the manner of his transformation was not uncommon in the new country looking for artists. Story learned to model because he was asked to make a statue.

When Judge Story died in 1845 some of his friends wished to place a memorial to him in the Chapel of Mount Auburn Cemetery. They knew that his son William had often modeled little clay figures for his own amusement; so they commissioned him to make a life-size statue of his father and suggested that he visit Europe to learn how such work was done. Story accepted happily and in 1847 took his wife and two children to Rome.

The Storys stayed in Europe until 1850, spending a winter in Germany and six months in London, Paris, Venice, and Florence but coming back always to Rome, which they began to think of as their home and for which their attachment grew. Story found that he had an aptitude for the carving of marble and the work gave him much pleasure, but that is unfortunately all we know about his initiation into the art. Who taught him technique beyond the amateur modeling he had done at home, whether he made any study of anatomy, what sort of work he tried his hand at first, and who, if anyone, criticized it, we do not know. We have a highly interesting biography of Story written by his much younger friend Henry James, but it omits many details which one would like to have. James remarks on the curious circumstance of Story's being asked to make a statue before he had learned how but he does not tell us how he did learn. James is chiefly concerned to re-create the social and artistic milieu of Rome and London and Cambridge in which Story moved and to present personalities and relationships—he calls the book *William Wetmore Story and His Friends from Letters, Diaries and Recollections.* This gives us a setting for Story far more vivid and interesting than the background we can conjure for any of the other literary sculptors, but it leaves many questions unanswered.

Story was fascinated at once by the tone and temper of art life in Rome. He had expected to enjoy the beauty of the country and the pleasure of being in constant presence of fine pictures and statues, but he had not realized how different the life of an artist in Italy was from the life of a lawyer in Boston. The freedom from convention, the pleasant spontaneous ways of passing one's time, the absence of hurry and pressure seemed to him infinitely preferable to the tenor of the life he had been living at home. He went back to Boston and took up his practice of law, but he could not forget the experience of what seemed to him the truly good life. Finally, in 1851, to the consternation of his mother—she said he was a fool—and of many of his friends, he decided that it was as an artist that he wished to live. He severed his connection with the law, and took his family to Rome.

At the beginning all went well. He found quarters and a studio and went happily to work on the statue of his father. In 1853 it was ready for shipment to Mount Auburn and Story wrote to Lowell (10 August) : "I do believe you will like it despite its faults, and I really think that it is not stupid." [30] Story the artist was partly satisfied, as he was with the work of different tone which he undertook next, a bas-relief, *The Flight of Youth,* and a large statue of a piping *Arcadian Shepherd Boy,* eventually purchased for the Boston Public Library. To model in clay gave him real pleasure, but he was daily becoming more and more aware of his artistic insufficiency. He had the temperament but not the training. It seemed improbable that he could ever be the great artist he had dreamed of becoming. Something more was needed in the making of a sculptor than the study and appreciation of the work of the Greeks. The air of Italy could not unaided, as he and the commissioners of his father's statue had more or less assumed, produce an artist. Story had begun too late. He had had no elaborate training in anatomy, no months of drawing and of modeling copies of the antique, no long practice with chisel and modeling stick, no years of making portrait busts, not even the discipline, with which many of his colleagues began, of carving mantels and tombstones. He was ten years behind. Had he been less sensitive and less well educated he might not have been aware of his deficiencies. Other sculptors no better prepared for their work than he—Clark Mills is the conspicuous example—went blithely ahead unaware of their limitations, but Story's only solution seemed to be to give the whole thing up and return to the law. His mother's serious illness was an additional reason for a return to America in 1855.

There was family business to attend to at first—he was met at the dock with news of his mother's death; then Story went back to his legal writing.

What do you think I have been about these three months? [he asks in a letter to Lowell] Why, writing law—in Little and Brown's back room. I have actually written about 400 pages in that time to add to a new edition of my "Contracts," and I feel like a wet rag after it. Now it is nearly over, and I am thinking of making a basso rilievo of the Pied Piper with the children flocking after him. But what encouragement to do it? Nobody will buy it, nobody cares for it. There would be real interest if I had imported a cargo of saltpetre.[31]

He expatiates further on his dislike of Boston and its attitude toward the arts.

We love nothing, we criticize everything. Even the very atmosphere is critical. Every twig is intensely defined against the sky. The sky itself is hard and distant. Earth takes never the hue of its heaven. The heart grows into stone. The devil-side of enthu-siasm (irritability) possesses us. There is no hearty love of any-thing, for we are afraid of making a mistake. We love unhap-piness.[32]

This is, unfortunately, as far as we are able to get into Story's state of mind. He does not say as much as we would like to know about himself but he would seem to be one of the few American sculptors who was conscious of his own limitations. He decided, nevertheless, in spite of them, that a career of second rank in Rome would be a better life than Boston and the law. The possibility of a merely dilettante existence abroad—he could have afforded it—he seems to have been too thoroughly American to consider. "If I did not work I should die," he is reported to have said later in life and now he determined to work as a sculptor, to be a respectable artist if not a supreme one. He sailed in 1856 and took up permanent resi-dence in Rome.

There was another occasion, years later, when Story considered the possibility of giving up the attempt to be an artist. He speaks of it this time in a letter to Charles Eliot Norton (15 August 1861). He has been describing his *Libyan Sibyl*, which he thinks the best thing he has ever done. "This I am now putting into marble, and if I can afford it shall send to the new Exhibition in London. . . . If it is returned on my hands I shall abandon sculpture, or at all events shut up my studio." [33]

But the *Sibyl* and the *Cleopatra* (*Pl. 7*) who accompanied her were received with enthusiasm at the London Exhibition of 1862, were praised by the critics, purchased, and ordered in replica. Story went happily on to fame, though one supposes him always to have been aware that his reputation was above his deserts. This may be read between the lines of the James biography and is definitely, though conjecturally, stated in Hawthorne's *Italian Note-Books* (4 October 1858).

> Mr. Story is the most variously accomplished and brilliant per-son, the fullest of social life and fire, whom I have ever met; and without seeming to make an effort, he kept us amused and enter-tained the whole day long. . . . Still, though he bubbled and brimmed over with fun, he left the impression on me that . . . there is a pain and care, bred, it may be, out of the very richness of his gifts and abundance of his outward prosperity.[34]

Story's decision to devote himself to the art advanced the cause of American sculpture in several ways. He lent prestige to the profession when, in 1857, he settled his family in the Palazzo Barberini, where they were to live hospitably and happily for forty years. They rented the *piano nobile* of the right wing; the left wing contained the Barberini Library and the famous portrait of Beatrice Cenci. Their quarters were commodious, with fine views, a beautiful garden, and spacious salons for entertaining, at which they were adept. One of the rooms Story fitted up as an elegant little theater where he produced many warmly applauded amateur performances. He liked to do scenes from Shakespeare, for whom his admiration was profound, and he tried out plays by his friends and his own verse dramas before putting them into print. Every interesting American or English visitor to Rome was certain to ascend the Storys' winding stairway, and their Italian friends were many. During the years of tension between Church and Monarchy they were proud of the fact that Whites and Blacks, who would not mingle otherwise, met at their receptions in perfect harmony. Many of these ecclesiastical connections—the Storys were, of course, stout Protestants—were made through their neighbor Cardinal Pecci, who occupied the *piano* below them and thought highly of the Story family. It was probably he who brought Story's work to the attention of the Pope who played an important role in the sculptor's career. It was Pio Nono who bore the expense of shipping the *Cleopatra* and the *Libyan Sibyl* to the London Exhibition, proud to have them exhibited in the Roman pavilion.

That Americans could entertain as agreeably and as well as the pair in the Palazzo Barberini made an excellent impression on the various foreign colonies in Rome, and many American guests, inclined to be skeptical about artist life, found themselves with a new interest in sculptors and sculpture. Story's studio was not far from the Palazzo, on the Via San Niccolò de Torentino. In the seventies he built himself more commodious quarters, on the model of Crawford's, on the Via San Martino a Macao.

The Storys' happy family life had been saddened during the early years in Rome by the death of their eldest son, Joseph, but the other three children flourished. Edith, the eldest, married the Marchese

Simone Peruzzi di Medici; Julian became a painter; Waldo, a sculptor.

More important than the prestige he added to the burgeoning American art was Story's other contribution, the romantic-dramatic quality of his statues. He never consciously opposed the neoclassical theories; indeed, he thought of himself as a true follower of the Greeks, but the whole cast of his mind and imagination was of a different type. His statues were much easier for Americans to like and understand than the ideal nudes which most of the sculptors presented for their admiration. Not all the critics, on the other hand, approved. James Jackson Jarves, usually an acute critic, was inclined to think that Story's choice of subjects was influenced by something morbid in his nature. " 'Cleopatra poisoning Herself,' 'Judith having slain Holofernes' [actually she is depicted before the slaying], 'Media [*sic*] intending the Murder of her Children,' 'Delilah after betraying Samson,' 'Saul Mad,' and 'Sappho meditating Suicide' are hazardous topics even for genius." [35] Despite the fine Freudian possibilities here it seems more probable that Story's choice was inspired by his enthusiasm for the dramatic, and this the layman shared. The features and gestures of Story's figures expressed passions and emotions it was interesting to watch and analyze. Great actors did this sort of thing on the stage. Many painters showed scenes like this in their pictures. The layman liked this kind of drama in his statues.

Another thing the layman enjoyed in Story's work was the costuming of the statues and their elaborate accessories. *Cleopatra*, for instance, wears on her head the *uroeus* or twining basilisk of sovereignty; about the neck of the *Libyan Sibyl* hangs the Tetragammaton, and the *Cumean Sibyl* carries on her forehead the winged dragon of Eternity. Story delighted in this kind of archaeological research. All of his ideal figures are draped, though some of the drapery is quite slight, and this makes them easier for the inexperienced spectator than the usual ideal nudes. Occasionally, too, one could tell what Story's statues meant by reading his verse, for he sometimes composed a poem on the theme he was depicting in sculpture.

Another quality in Story's female figures which pleased his public, though they may not have been directly aware of it, was their American character. He observed his countrywomen, so James tells us, with pleasure in their suppleness and grace and it is their outlines he gave to Judith and Sappho and the rest rather than the conventional proportions of the Venus. It was the London Exhibition of 1862 which brought these various qualities to public attention as a "new note" in sculpture, and after that Story could count on selling whatever he chose to model and having a pleasant number of orders for replicas.

Some public commissions came in, too, most of them for monuments resembling the statue he had made of his father. There was, of course, no chance here for drama but Story tried to make his portrait statues "expressional," not simply monuments but real renderings of a personality. Most of his subjects were men he had known and admired: *President Josiah Quincy* of Harvard, *Edward Everett* for the Boston Public Garden, *George Peabody* for the City of London, *Chief Justice Marshall* for the National Capitol. This was Story's only federal commission.

Of portrait busts on which so many of his colleagues supported themselves Story made only some thirty and these were all of family and close friends, like Lowell and the Brownings, or of great men he admired, Keats, Shakespeare, Beethoven. Contrary to the practice of his contemporaries, he liked to do the major part of his marble cutting himself, particularly with his ideal statues.

> I work my models with great care [he told a curious inquirer in 1877], and finish them perfectly. I suppose I might let the stone be cut by other hands if I could find other hands to suit me; not but what they would copy my model accurately, but I do not feel bound to copy my model. Don't you see how much freer I am than they could be? If I want a line different—a blow, and there it is.[36]

Story's career as a writer ran parallel with his career as a sculptor and he often said that it gave him equal pleasure. In 1851 he published an excellent biography of his father; during the Civil War he turned his legal knowledge to effective articles for the Northern cause in the London *Daily News;* but most of his writing was poetic or "literary." These poems and tales and essays seem today even more dated than the statues, but his contemporaries read them with enthusiasm, especially *Roba de Roma* (1862) and *Conversations in a Studio* (1890). The first of these was reprinted in condensed form and became a popular guidebook. *Roba*, Story explained, is "everything—from rubbish and riffraff to the most exquisite product of nature and art," and the book was an agreeable combination of personal impressions and experiences joined to curious bits of history, fact, and legend which he had unearthed in his wide reading.

Story's general plan of life was to spend eight months of the year in Rome working steadily at his sculpture. He breakfasted at eight and put in usually an eight-hour day. During the summer months, when the city was supposed to be intolerable, the family traveled or went into *villeggiatura*, sometimes near Rome, sometimes at the Baths of Lucca, often near Sorrento, arranging whenever they could to be neighbors of the Brownings. An acquaintance made during the first experimental years in Italy had ripened and deepened into a close friendship. Browning's letters when he returned to England after the death of his wife speak of their shared Italian days with a touching affection and Story wrote to Charles Eliot Norton, 15 August 1861:

> You cannot imagine how I shall miss him. For three years now we have been always together; . . . all the long summer evenings of these last summers at Sienna he was with us, and we sat on our terrace night after night till midnight talking together, or we played and sang together above stairs. All the last winters he worked with me daily for three hours in my studio, and we met either at my house or at his or at that of some friend nearly every evening. There is no one to supply his place.[37]

During the sixties the Storys spent most of their summers in England, usually as guests of the many English friends made in Rome and through Story's work. It was during the summer months that he did the major part of his writing, though even when he was hard at work in his studio he was constantly moved to put his thoughts and emotions into verse in which one sees, naturally, a good deal of influence from Browning. He wrote constantly but did not try to publish more than a small portion of what he set down.

In 1877 Story made a visit to the United States which had the pleasant effect of convincing him that his countrymen really did hold him in high regard. He had been hurt that recognition had to come first from the English. Now he found himself welcomed as a distinguished sculptor and poet. He was entertained lavishly, urged to lecture, consulted by the Government on what should be done with the still unfinished Washington monument. The decision to be a sculptor had proved a good one both for the artist and for the United States. The remaining years—he died in 1895—were rich in accomplishment and in a full and happy Roman life.

3

Florence and the Caffè Doney —
Horatio Greenough,
Hiram Powers

Art life in Florence moved in a pattern very like that of art life in Rome, only it moved more slowly and more quietly. Which city you preferred was a good deal a matter of temperament. Florence's most distinguished American sculptors, Horatio Greenough and Hiram Powers, thought Rome dizzying. Greenough had gone there on his first Italian excursion in 1825 and was so overstimulated by the crowding impressions of past and present that within a year he had worked himself into a fever and had to go back to Boston to recuperate. When he returned to Italy in 1829 he settled in Florence and lived there, at a more reasonable speed, for twenty-two years.

Powers began with Florence (1837) and during the thirty-six years of his residence made only two visits to Rome. These he described to a sitter who kept a record of the sculptor's conversation while his bust was being "taken."

His first visit to Rome, Powers said, was made in the company of William Preston of South Carolina, one of the patrons who had made it possible for him to come to Italy. Mr. Preston was already well acquainted with all the lions of Rome and was eager to rejoin his family as soon as possible. Sightseeing was done, in consequence, at a rate which left poor Powers breathless and thoroughly confused. The second expedition had the same effect. "I have felt, on both my visits, as if I were riding in an express train through a cane-brake, and was called upon to number the reeds." Rome, Powers felt, was saying to him, "What is the use of adding to this superfluity, or to the materials of this sure destruction?" [1] The riches of Florence were oppressive enough, but in Rome he thought it would be impossible to preserve one's artistic independence.

The majority of the American sculptors, on the other hand, felt that just because of its abundance Rome was the more compulsory residence of the two. The essential monuments in Florence could be assimilated on visits. One must, of course, be acquainted with *the* Venus, the Niobe, and the statues ringing the Tribune in the Pitti Palace, but these were almost the only works which required long study. The statues of Michelangelo, Donatello, Cellini, and the other Renaissance masters were to be looked at, of course, wondered at, perhaps admired, but, under no circumstances, imitated. The men of the Renaissance were powerful but they were barbaric, not in the great Greek tradition.

The opportunities for study which Florence offered the sculptor were good, and cheap. The medical schools made no charge for their classes, to which artists were gladly admitted. Anatomy was taught by dissection, with, always, a live man, naked, standing beside the cadaver so that the student might see the action of any muscles under discussion. There were also groups which gathered weekly to draw from live models and though the sculptors in Florence were fewer in number than they were in Rome, they educated one another in the same way. They visited each other's studios and they gathered nightly at the Caffè Greco's equivalent, the smoking room of the Caffè Doney on the Via Tornabuoni. (The main *caffè* was a fashionable place for the consumption of pastry and ices.) The Doney was less crowded than the Greco, less dirty and smoke-stained, and the conversations were carried on in somewhat lower voices but there was the same warm comradeship and the talk was eager and stimulating. The group was perhaps less cosmopolitan than in Rome for, as Elihu Vedder tells us, the Doney was frequented chiefly by the English and American artists. The Italians gathered most often at the Caffè Michelangelo.

We know that some of the American literary sculptors who came to Florence were attracted there not only by the tempo of the life but by the presence of Greenough and Powers and the distinguished Italian Bartolini. The Florentine American sculptors numbered per-

haps a dozen during the forty years with which we are chiefly concerned. The painters were, of course, more numerous and so were the
men of letters. Lay visitors to Italy, in search of culture or a salubri-
ous climate, often chose Florence because it was cheaper than Rome.
In climate Rome had something of an advantage. It was said of
Florence that no one could die there in the winter and no one could
live there in the summertime. There were ardent Protestants, like
Theodore Parker, who came to Florence because they could not live
at ease under a papal government. And there were other Americans
who chose Rome because Florence was too much like Boston.

This amusing, if not remarkably accurate, comparison was established in American minds partly on the authority of Margaret
Fuller, who wrote (22 August 1847) that Florence is "more in its
spirit like Boston than like an Italian city"; its citizens are "busy and
intellectual." [2] William Wetmore Story capped this by announcing
from his Roman studio that "Florence is nothing but a Continental
Boston in its spirit." [3] The practical development of the theory was
made by Charles W. Eliot in 1865, a few years before he assumed the
presidency of Harvard. In a letter (29 May 1865) to his sister-
in-law, Miss Anna Peabody, he says that

> As a place wherein to wait for death on a small income, Florence
> struck me very pleasantly. It is clean and sweet, the people are
> not in the extreme of misery, one may study painting and sculp-
> ture to great advantage there, a man-servant in a tail-coat and
> white tie costs $8 per month and a chambermaid $4, there is a
> considerable society of English who live there for economy, there
> is a capital reading-room where all periodical literature can be
> had, and the protestant cemetery is a very neat and pretty spot.
> When you add that the climate is tolerably healthy, that spacious
> apartments of the dirtiest description may be had for $100. a year,
> that cabs cost 80 centimes the course, and that the environs pre-
> sent the finest views of a city set down in an amphitheater of
> fertile and villa-ed hills, you have combined a very unusual num-
> ber of advantages for persons whose object is to secure food and
> drink, and aesthetic enjoyments at moderate rates. When ill-
> health, unsympathetic relatives, or ungratified art-longings drive
> Bostonians into exile, let them try Florence for a season.[4]

Bostonian spirit aside, there was an important social difference
between Florence and Rome which affected the *forestièri* of all

classes almost as much as the native citizens: the government of Florence was not ecclesiastical but ducal. Life, in consequence, had less pageantry but it was freer and gayer.

Il Gran Duco Leopoldo II, who succeeded his father in 1824, was actually an Austrian despot, but a kind, well-meaning despot, if not a very bright one. His subjects often referred to him as *Il Gran Ciuco* (the Great Ass) but they said it with more affection than contempt. He was not at all a bad ruler over his million and a half Tuscans; he had been well educated and approved of artists and literary men; and his little court was pleasant and hospitable to strangers. It was hospitable really of necessity, for without the visiting foreigners ducal entertainments would have been scarcely large enough to be worth attending.

Leopold gave a ball at the Pitti Palace every Tuesday evening and any foreigner who had been presented to him had a standing invitation. The delicate problem of who should be presented most of the ministers—Austrian, French, Prussian, Russian (the other countries were represented by *chargés d'affaires*)—solved by presenting any of their countrymen who had been received at court at home. Lord Holland, however, British minister for many years, set the custom of introducing almost anyone who asked for the privilege, and whoever happened to be in charge of the citizens of the democratic United States—sometimes an Italian, sometimes an American —was quite ready to present all of them. The Grand Duke, who was a gauche and awkward person, very shy with strangers, made the briefest possible appearance at his own entertainments, but everyone else stayed for the whole evening, half way through which a sumptuous supper was served. T. A. Trollope, in his *What I Remember*, gives a circumstantial account of the way the Duke's subjects pillaged the supper tables:

> I have seen large portions of fish, sauce and all, packed up in a newspaper, and deposited in a pocket. I have seen fowls and ham share the same fate without any newspaper at all. I have seen jelly carefully wrapped in an Italian countess's laced *mouchoir!*[5]

The English confined their depredations to bonbons, both men and women emptying whole plates into their pockets. The Americans did

Plate 1

Horatio Greenough, *Washington*. The first statue commissioned by Congress from an American sculptor, 1832. It was intended for the rotunda of the Capitol but the lighting proved impossible. (*Courtesy of the Smithsonian Institution*)

Plate 2

Horatio Greenough, *The Rescue*. Designed for the east steps of the
Capitol and intended to show the superiority of the white
man to the savage. (*From the collection
of the Library of Congress*)

Plate 3

Thomas Crawford, *Orpheus and Cerberus*. Charles Sumner
collected the subscription which presented the work
to the Boston Athenaeum. (*Courtesy of the
Museum of Fine Arts, Boston*)

Plate 4

Thomas Crawford, *The Chief Contemplating the Progress of Civiliza-tion*. From the east pediment of the Capitol. (*Courtesy of the New-York Historical Society, New York City*)

Plate 5

Thomas Crawford, *Armed Freedom*. A bronze cast of this
figure surmounts the dome of the Capitol. (*From
the collection of the Library of Congress*)

Plate 6

Anne Whitney, *Roma. (Courtesy of the Wellesley College Library)*

Plate 7

William Wetmore Story, *Cleopatra*. (*The Metropolitan Museum of Art, gift of John Taylor Johnston, 1888*)

Plate 8

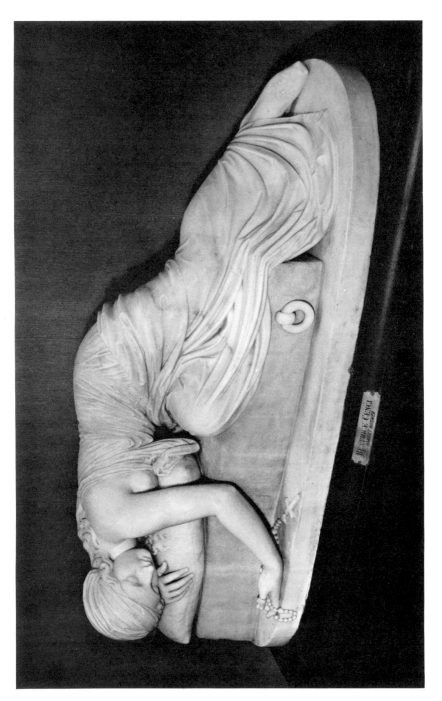

Harriet Hosmer, *Beatrice Cenci*. (*Courtesy of the Mercantile Library, St. Louis*)

Plate 9

William Henry Rinehart, Latona and her Children, Apollo and Diana. (The
Metropolitan Museum of Art, Rogers Fund, 1905)

Plate 10

Hiram Powers, *The Greek Slave*. (*In the collection
of the Corcoran Gallery of Art*)

Plate 11

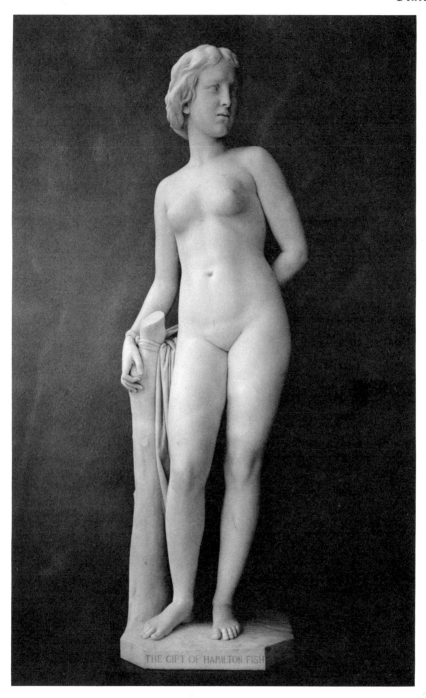

Erastus Dow Palmer, *White Captive.* (*The Metropolitan Museum of Art, gift of Hamilton Fish, 1894*)

Plate 12

Clark Mills, *Andrew Jackson.* Lafayette Square, Washington.
(From the collection of the Library of Congress)

Plate 13

H. K. Brown, *Washington.* Union Square, New York, *ca.* 1860. (*The J. Clarence Davies Collection, Museum of the City of New York*)

Plate 14

John Rogers, *Wounded to the Rear or One More Shot, The Slave Auction, Weighing the Baby.* (*Courtesy of the New-York Historical Society, New York City*)

Plate 15

William Rimmer, *Despair.* (*Courtesy of the Museum of Fine Arts, Boston*)

Plate 16

William Rimmer, *Centaur.* (*The Metropolitan Museum of Art, gift of Edward Holbrook, 1906*)

no pillaging at all, though the ladies happily accepted bonbons from their English admirers.

In addition to the ducal balls there was a weekly ball at the Casino dei Nobili; many of the foreign ministers gave large balls and receptions, and so did many of the resident English. The Italians themselves did not trouble to do any very large scale entertaining but most of them were at home in the *prima sera* (seven to nine) in a way the American visitors found very pleasant. The guest might come and go as he pleased, play cards, drink tea, listen to music, chat with his hostess, even, if he liked, settle into a comfortable chair with a book. Many members of the American colony had regular "afternoons" or "evenings," as they did in Rome. Margaret Fuller writes in 1849 that her countrymen meet twice a week at the house of Joseph Mozier (who had made a comfortable fortune in business before he became a sculptor): "I am often present, on account of the friendly interest of those resident here." [6] Mrs. Hiram Powers' "Wednesdays" (tea and home-made cookies) were well attended and one could count on meeting there any visiting celebrity, political, literary, or artistic.

Another popular evening gathering place was the opera at the Pergola. The repertory for the season consisted of two, or perhaps three, operas performed over and over again, but everybody went four or five times a week because the Pergola was so pleasant a place in which to meet your friends. The audience talked and circulated during the whole performance, pausing to listen to the music only during the more important arias. This, since the applause was vigorous, seems to have satisfied the singers, whose amiability was more distinguished than their skill. The nobility and the well-to-do rented boxes by the season in which to receive their friends. Admission to the pit included the privilege of visiting the boxes and, since the cost was two and a half *crazie* (i.e., one cent), even the most impecunious artist could attend whenever he felt inclined.

There was also a daily occasion of general meeting at sunset on the Cascine, the equivalent of Rome's Pincian Hill, which had its counterpart in every Italian city. The Cascine offered three miles of beautifully wooded drives near the banks of the Arno and a little square, in front of the Duke's dairy (*cascina*), where the carriages drew up to exchange visits and receive them from gentlemen on horseback or on foot. The Duke and his family—the sons on horseback—usually joined the carriage promenade, bowing and smiling graciously. Another family group, mentioned by all the travel chroniclers, was that of the Irish novelist Charles Lever. Like all his heroes he was a dashing figure in the saddle and rode accompanied by a picturesque troop of sons and daughters with flying hair, all mounted on piebald horses. The rest of the Florentine world was at the Cascine, too, but the observant tourist noticed a curious division in nationalities. If he arrived just after sunset—the fashionable English moment—he found all the Italian carriages drawn up outside the gate, exchanging their visits, while the English and Americans were still in front of the dairy among the bosky trees. Evening air, filtered through the thick foliage, was considered by the Florentines almost as dangerous to the health as Rome's miasmas, but the Anglo-Saxons refused to be intimidated.

Most Americans enjoyed greatly what they saw of Florentine society, though N. P. Willis, writing in 1833 to the New York *Mirror*, warned them that it was dissolute in a way that it is "scarce possible for an American to conceive." [7] This was chiefly because the *cavaliere servente* still flourished and was always invited to any gathering with his lady, who would seldom talk to anyone else. By the forties, however, cicisbeism had declined; Adolphus Trollope, writing in 1843, makes no mention of it.

When Florence in the summer became intolerably hot the residents and visitors who did not possess the means or energy for a real migration, went into *villeggiatura* up in the hills at the Baths of Lucca. "The Saratoga of Italy," as Willis called it, was a charming and amusing little resort which offered its patrons not only mineral springs but really beautiful scenery—Mrs. Browning thought it the most beautiful in Italy—and, according to choice, restful solitude or an entertaining small society. The Baths ran up the mountainside in three stages and the more you wanted to be alone, the higher up you went. Living was even less expensive than in Florence so the artists sometimes made excursions there. On 18 August 1837, for instance, Horatio Greenough wrote to his brother Henry: "I have been lately for ten days to the Baths of Lucca, where I had the finest air and scenery in Italy. The heat in Florence was overpowering." [8] Story even thought it worth while to go to Lucca from Rome. "We are all at the Baths of Lucca now," he wrote to Lowell (10 August 1853), "high up on the hills, amid the thick chestnut-trees, . . . leading the most *dolce far niente* of lives." [9]

The two most important "Florentine" sculptors, Horatio Greenough (1805–1852) and Hiram Powers (1805–1873), are good examples of the different kinds of temperament, education, and environment which produced sculptors in the young United States. Born in the same year, 1805, they had little in common except the thorough enjoyment of their vocation. "Forty-seven years of joy I have lived," [10] was Greenough's answer when Emerson asked him his age, and the admiring visitor to Powers' studio often took note of his contentment with himself and his way of life.

The artistic inclination of Powers, the more typically American of the two, derived from his native skill as a mechanic. Greenough's impulse toward art—also a common one in the United States—was the sight of a marble statue. But our first American sculptor did not, like most of his brother artists, see his statue suddenly and briefly; he grew up with it. It stood in his father's Boston garden.

The statue of Phocion was a copy in marble of an ancient work, brought from Italy, probably, because the elder Greenough had read his Plutarch and admired the Athenian general whose level-headed integrity would have been an asset to the Massachusetts legislature. Young Horatio, too, knew the story of Phocion's unjust accusation and Socratic death but what stirred him chiefly was the look of the marble figure on its little mound, outlined against the garden's green. The classical proportions and balance, the play of mass and line and shadow roused lively sensations in the boy's mind. His response was not at all the mechanical response of Powers and so many other Americans: How did he make that? I could do it too. Greenough's chief feeling was a desire to create beauty which would move other men as this statue, every day, moved him. He tried to reproduce its effect with such materials as he could command—clay, chalk, plaster of Paris. Then he began to make heads and figures of his own, copying them from line engravings in the books and magazines in his father's library. By the time he was twelve he could exhibit, set on little pine shelves, an impressive row of small busts of ancient heroes.

The young Horatio was very serious about what he was doing and this earnestness, his skill, and his personal charm—he had both good manners and good looks—won him several excellent teachers. Samuel Willard of Boston, impressed by the boy's attempt to learn clay modeling from an article in the *Edinburgh Encyclopaedia*, showed him how it should be done. Alpheus Cary, a Boston stone-cutter, taught him to carve marble. Binon, a French sculptor, then living in Boston, let him come to his studio and model there. A friend of his father introduced him to William Smith Shaw, librarian of the Boston Athenaeum, who gave him permission to copy freely in its gallery of casts.

Horatio's father, David Greenough, was a Boston businessman who did well in building and real estate. At one time he owned the greater part of Brattle Street but he over-extended his investments and became bankrupt. He re-established himself later. He might have been expected to discourage a would-be artist son. On the contrary, he set no obstacle in the boy's way except the sensible requirement that before embarking on the artistic life he take a degree at Harvard. And he encouraged the sculptor, though often he could not give him financial aid, as he encouraged the three others among his eleven children who embraced artistic careers. The eldest of the family, John, was a landscape painter who exhibited at the Royal Academy as well as in New York. Henry Greenough was a good architect who did some painting and carving for his pleasure and also wrote a novel of artist life, *Ernest Carroll* (1859). Richard Saltonstall became, under his brother Horatio's tutelage, a competent and respected sculptor.

Horatio Greenough, during his four years at Harvard, was a hardworking, serious student who did not let the pleasure he took in outdoor exercise or the company of his contemporaries interfere with his fundamental business. Six feet tall and "perfectly symmetrical," as a classmate described him, he was so handsome that the *Achilles* he modeled in the 1830's was reputed to be a self-portrait. He was a good horseman, a good swimmer, a good walker; young ladies delighted in his company and eventually he married a Boston heiress. As a student he did well in Latin, Greek, modern languages, and English, not so well in mathematics. Anatomy, in which as a sculptor he was intensely interested, he studied informally in the office of Dr. George C. Parkman. A classmate of Greenough's, who roomed in the same house with him, was a medical student in whom **Dr. Parkman** was interested so he generously lent the two young men his medical books and bones and preparations from his collection.

But the most important educational influence during his undergraduate days was, Greenough thought, his friendship with Washington Allston. He was introduced to the distinguished painter by Edmund Dana, in whose house he was fortunate enough to occupy a room during his years in Cambridge. Edmund Dana, brother of Richard Henry Dana, the elder, was a wise and learned man whom his student roomers called "the Master." He and Allston were old friends, and the painter, then living in Cambridgeport, was accustomed to visit him every Saturday evening. Dana's young lodgers liked nothing better than to listen to, and sometimes share, their elders' talk, on aesthetics, poetry, philosophy, the theory and practice of painting and sculpture. Allston was delighted by the young sculptor's artistic enthusiasm, so like his own, and their acquaintance became a real friendship. Greenough spoke of Allston as his spiritual father who had taught him "how to discriminate—how to think—how to feel." [11]

It was during Greenough's senior year at Harvard that the city of Boston announced its intention to erect a monument to commemorate the Battle of Bunker Hill and invited artists to submit competitive designs for a memorial column. Young Greenough sent in a design, not for a column, an architectural element which, he said, should never stand alone, but for an obelisk. An obelisk, he wrote years later ("Aesthetics at Washington"), "says but one word, but it speaks loud. If I understand its voice, it says, Here!" [12] The committee unanimously adopted this idea, though the obelisk finally erected was not Greenough's design—he was no longer in this country.

With his father's permission Greenough had decided that as soon as he took his Harvard A.B. he would go to Europe. Vessels making the voyage were in those days not many so when he found that one was sailing for Gibraltar in May, shortly before the Harvard commencement, he asked permission of the authorities to take passage on her. His academic standing was so good that they readily agreed to let him go and to send his diploma after him.

Horatio Greenough, sailing for Italy in 1825, was a real pioneer, the first of the long line of American sculptors who were to feel that journey an essential stage in their professional development. Like many of the young artists who crossed the Atlantic, he was obliged to borrow the funds for the voyage, but intellectually he was far better prepared for the experience than most of those who followed him: he could read Latin, he had made a beginning in Italian, he knew some anatomy, and he had a good deal of elementary instruction and practice in his craft; but he was quite unprepared for the emotional shock of the Italian experience. How that shock came and how he responded to it we know in some detail from his own record.

When passing through Genoa on the way to Rome, so Greenough related years later to the art historian Henry Tuckerman,[13] he plunged at once into excited exploration of the old city. In the cathedral he was struck by the beauty of a statue which seemed to him finer than anything he had ever seen. As he gazed at it in delighted wonder he noticed with surprise that no one else—and there were many people in the church—seemed even to notice it. Is this country, he thought, so full of marvelous things that this statue, the finest I have ever imagined, does not command even a passing glance? How can I hope ever to make statues at which people will stop to look? The would-be sculptor found a dark corner and wept some bitter tears.

The mood of discouragement was brief. Greenough was sure that a sculptor was what he was meant to be and Rome filled him with excitement. How he responded and how he lived there William Dunlap tells us in some detail in his *History of the Rise and Progress of the Arts of Design in the United States*.[14] In preparation for his book Dunlap wrote to various artists asking for accounts of their lives. Greenough responded very modestly but at some length and his brother Henry furnished many additional details.

Though Horatio Greenough was the first American sculptor to reach Rome, some American painters were there before him and among them he found his friend Robert Weir, who had just come from Florence. The two young men took rooms together on the Pincian Hill, opposite the house which had been occupied by Claude Lorrain and near those once lived in by Salvator Rosa and the great Poussin. This they felt, in Weir's words, was "holy ground."

Greenough flung himself with eager enthusiasm into a study of "all the galleries of Rome." He was excited to discover that the plaster casts he had so admired in the Boston Athenaeum were only shadows of the real marbles and that there were many more beautiful creations of which he had never even heard. New ideas seethed in his mind, generated not only by the works of art and architecture but by "the genial forms of Italy," the people and the landscape which fascinated him. He plunged headlong into work and study on a plan he had laid out with the advice of Allston.

He rose early, went to the French Academy and there, or in one of the galleries, drew during the morning from the antique; in the afternoon he worked in his studio, modeling some subject of his own composition, thus exercising his invention and his imagination. At six he rejoined Weir for dinner at the Bocca di Lione, followed by a session of talk with fellow artists at the Caffè Greco. The two then went to the English life school, where they drew until nine. Later, if the night was fine, they made up a party to explore the ruins of ancient Rome. From his fellow students, Italian, French, English, Russian, German, Greenough learned much about the techniques of his profession. For expert guidance he turned to Thorvaldsen, to whom he had letters, and Thorvaldsen, as he did with so many young artists, gave him generous encouragement and criticism.

Everything interested Horatio Greenough; the days were never long enough. He pushed himself far beyond his strength and, in his high-strung weariness, became an easy mark for the Roman fever. The attack of malaria made him not only desperately ill physically, it plunged him into a deep melancholy. (There is considerable evidence that he was a manic-depressive.) Weir, who had moved to cheaper lodgings, came back to Greenough's rooms and nursed him devotedly during the fever. Then, on the doctor's advice, he took his friend to Naples, but the change of scene had no effect. Greenough was quite unable to direct his life himself and it was decided that he must return to the care of his family. With a generous disregard of his own work and plans Weir made the arrangements for the journey and accompanied Greenough on the steamer. The long voyage, the rest, the sea air, and some violent seasickness worked a complete cure; Greenough landed in Boston his usual lively self. He decided, however, to spend some time with his family and at first he lived at home, working steadily at drawing and modeling. Then he went to Washington to make a bust of President

Adams. He modeled also a bust of Chief Justice Marshall and one or two others for the Gilmors in Baltimore. In May 1828 he returned to Italy.

The first three months he spent at Carrara studying the details of putting a clay statue into marble. He always did much more than most of his contemporaries of the marble cutting of his statues. Then he settled in Florence. There the tempo, as we have seen, was slower than in Rome and the stimulus more gentle. It suited him exactly. He became warmly attached to the city and deeply involved in Italian life and Italian hopes. He soon spoke the language with fluency. He had a natural gift for tongues and it was with a grammar and an exercise book that he regularly read himself to sleep.

Florence had fewer distinguished artists than Rome, but Greenough put himself under the tuition of Bartolini, whom he thought the best of portrait sculptors, and went happily to work. He had his artistic balance now and knew what he wanted to do, though he never quite succeeded in doing it. Taught by his studies in the galleries he tried to draw his inspiration, as he believed the Greeks had done, directly from Nature. "I had before adored her, but as the Persian does the sun, with my face to the earth." [15] But he was never able to disentangle himself completely from the neoclassical and the literary traditions. Nor had he any great gift for the chisel. Even those who admired his designs and his theories admitted, now and then, that he was deficient in manual dexterity. Jarves thought him a true artist, though in execution unequal to his conception. His "tongue was far cunninger in talk than his chisel to carve," [16] Emerson wrote to Carlyle in 1853. Professional recognition came slowly. This was owing, of course, not only to his own limitations but to those of the American public, for whom sculpture was a totally new thing. They did not at all know how to look at it; they thought it strange, puzzling, and often indecent. It was James Fenimore Cooper who finally set Greenough's professional life in motion. He "saved me from despair," wrote Greenough in his biography for Dunlap. "He employed me as I wished to be employed": with a commission for original work.[17]

Even earlier than this Cooper, who was pleased with Greenough's bust of him, had helped the young man when he wanted to make a bust of Lafayette. He found the great Frenchman was at first unwilling to pose. He had just sat for a bust to David d'Angers and they had agreed together that this was the likeness which should go down to posterity. Cooper, however, succeeded in persuading the General that posterity ought to know him not only from the French but also from the American point of view. David's bust was the French Lafayette, the idealized neoclassical hero; Greenough's bust would give the American naturalistic impression. Lafayette accepted the idea and Greenough's American bust was considered highly successful.

Cooper's commission for an original work came in 1829 when he was with his family in Florence. The *Chanting Cherubs* was suggested by Raphael's *Madonna del Baldacchino* (Cooper refers to it as the *Madonna del Trono*) in the Pitti Palace. Cooper's daughters had been greatly interested by the picture. One of them had made a careful drawing of the two little winged boys who sing before the Virgin's throne and they thought the pair full of sculptural possibilities. Greenough seems to have used Raphael's painting merely as a suggestion for a composition of his own but the relationship weighted the frequent charge that he had no originality. Cooper's reasons for choosing the subject were two, as he said in a letter to William Dunlap:

> The first was a due regard to my purse, which would scarcely bear the drain of a heavier work, and the second was a notion I had imbibed that the bias of Greenough's mind just then, was adverse to his success in his art. I found him bent altogether on the Michaelangelo or the heroic school; certainly a noble and commendable disposition in a sculptor, but one that was not so well suited to the popular taste, as that which is connected with the more graceful forms of children and females. It was my wish, that he should do something to win favor from those who are accustomed to admire Venuses and Cupids, more than the Laocoön and the Dying Gladiator.[18]

The *Cherubs*, Cooper supposed, would accomplish the mission for which he had designed them; actually it was not Cooper but Allston who helped Greenough to a government commission. In 1832, Congress decided to order a statue of Washington for the Capitol and Leonard Jarvis, chairman of the Committee on Public Buildings, accepted Allston's recommendation and named Greenough as the sculptor.

The *Washington* required eight years of work before it was ready to be shipped to the United States, but the announcement of the granting of the commission had an immediate effect upon Greenough's reputation. American visitors to Florence began to think that a bust or a statue by this American sculptor might make as impressive a souvenir of one's journey as a work by any Italian artist. Orders came in agreeable numbers, and Greenough undertook them with pleasure as relaxation from his monumental figure. In addition to portrait busts he made a few ideal figures, most admired of which, though its nudity was even more shocking than the *Cherubs'*, was the Corsair's bride *Medora* lying on her bier.

In 1837 Greenough married Louisa Gore of Boston, of whom we know chiefly that she had money and that she made him happy. They had three children. Henry Tuckerman, meeting Greenough after an absence of years, wrote with pleasure of what marriage had done for him. "As he had once talked of art he now talked of life. His affections had led him to reflect upon human destiny; and I found him as eloquent and as ingenious in the discussion of the religious sentiment and educational theories as he was wont to be when intent upon the vocation of the artist." [19]

As a householder doing well in his profession and with his wife's money behind him, Greenough now built himself a studio which Tuckerman thought a model of its kind, unsurpassed in Europe. Greenough's architectural ideas were full of originality and common sense. Emerson once remarked that if he were going to build himself a house Greenough was the first man he would consult. Tuckerman's enthusiastic description of the studio is not very specific but he gives us some interesting details. The building, surrounded by a beautiful garden, stood on the Piazza Maria Antonia, a new square recently laid out on the Fiesole side of the Arno. The entire structure was only one story, built with great strength and with some fine ornamental stone work. There was a spacious and admirably lighted exhibition room, a private studio for the sculptor, a large apartment for the workmen, a gallery of plaster casts, and a vestibule hung with pictures.

Cooper had warned Greenough that Americans are all *ex nato* connoisseurs and that he must expect his own "matured and classical thoughts" about his *Washington* to be estimated "by the same rules, as they estimate pork, and rum and cotton. Luckily you get a pretty good sum, and the statue that has cost *them* $20,000 may stand some chance." [20] There were other complications which Cooper had not foreseen. Some were caused by the figure's semi-nudity; others by matters of lighting and position. Congress had purchased only a few statues and no one knew what kind of advice and help to give the artist. Greenough designed his great seated figure as a sort of deified Washington, the pose suggested by Phidias' Zeus in the temple in Olympia; one arm is raised in beneficent admonition, the other presents a reversed sword. The spectator in the rotunda of the Capitol was to look up at the Father of his Country glorified by light descending from the dome. Greenough was appalled to find that the light, instead of being diffused as he had expected, came down from above in heavy vertical rays which threw the whole lower part of the face into deep shadow and destroyed all the effects he had worked for with the folds of the drapery. He tried various experiments with artificial lighting but they did not work and he was finally constrained to petition Congress to remove the statue to the lawn in front of the Capitol. This was done, but the erection of a building to protect *Washington* from the weather was never provided for and for years the great figure sat out in rain and frost, his classical drapery looking sadly inappropriate to the climate, the deep furrows in the marble, designed to catch overhead light, acting as troughs for running water. Eventually he was protected from the public by a railing, which only made things worse for it was now impossible to get a proper view of the whole work, and a trimming of flower-beds and lamp-posts did not improve the effect. The statue looked not so much impressive as incongruous and cruel jokes began to be made about it.

> Had I been ordered [wrote Greenough in a letter published by Tuckerman] to make a statue for any square or similar situation at the metropolis, I should have represented Washington on horseback, and in his actual dress. I would have made my work purely an historical one. I have treated the subject poetically, and confess I should feel pain at seeing it placed in direct and flagrant contrast with every-day life.[21]

At long last, in 1908, the *Washington* (*Pl. 1*) was removed to the Smithsonian Institution where modern lighting technique eventually illuminated the statue as Greenough imagined it and gave us an impressive noble figure. It is now in the Museum of History and Technology.

That Congress was not entirely displeased with the *Washington* was made evident when, in 1839, it gave Greenough a second commission, for a group for one side of the east entrance to the Capitol. On the other side Luigi Persico, an Italian sculptor, had created a *Landing of Columbus*, which had artistically very little to recommend it. Greenough was to complement this symbol of Discovery with a symbol of Settlement. His *Rescue* (*Pl. 2*) shows a frontiersman saving his wife, her baby in her arms, from an Indian who has his tomahawk raised to strike.

The placing of *The Rescue* when it arrived after Greenough's death was delegated to Clark Mills, the contriver of the Jackson monument on the amazingly rearing horse. Mills set the group up quite incorrectly. The wife and baby, who should be in front of the murderous Indian, he placed to one side and a little to the rear, balanced, more or less, by the other figure, an indifferent dog. Friends of Greenough who had heard him talk about the group knew that Mills' arrangement was wrong, but since Greenough had left no written directions their objections were disregarded and the imbalance remained.

Greenough had not shipped instructions with his statuary because he had expected to assemble it himself. He took his family with him on this visit to America in 1851 because he was pretty certain that his stay would be more than a matter of months. Florence under Austrian rule was becoming intolerable to him as a place of residence. The American consul at Leghorn had given him a nominal diplomatic office which prevented the Austrians from quartering troops in his house but he witnessed every day acts of persecution and injustice to his Italian friends which he was powerless to prevent. He believed, too, that America was becoming daily a better place of residence for artists. He had not thought so in 1843 when he wrote to Richard Dana, at the time of Allston's death, that "America has always acted toward her artists like a hen who has hatched ducklings. She cannot understand why they run to the water instead of thriving upon the dunghill—which only asks to be scratched in order to feed them all!" [22]

By 1852 Greenough thought she was learning and in any case he was ready to express gratitude to his native country: "I would not pass away and not leave a sign that I, for one, born by the grace of God in this land, found life a cheerful thing, and not that sad and dreadful task with whose prophecy they scared my youth." [23]

Since Greenough did not succeed at once in finding the place in which he wanted to set up his home and studio, he established his family at Newport and himself moved about, to Washington, New York, Boston, as his various projects demanded. The arrival of *The Rescue* was annoyingly delayed by various governmental and transportation inefficiencies but he was happily occupied in making plans for a monument to Cooper, which he proposed to erect in Newport, and an equestrian Washington for New York City. He chose the site in Union Square but the statue was made after his death by H. K. Brown.

Looking at American architecture with eyes trained by daily walks in Florence, Greenough was moved to lively criticism. It was in writing, perhaps, rather than sculpture, that his real gift lay and it is in his essays far more clearly than in his statues that we glimpse today the mind which so stimulated and delighted Emerson. In 1843 (July and August) he had published in the *United States Magazine* articles on "American Architecture" and "Remarks on American Art." Now he got out a small pamphlet, "Aesthetics at Washington," and began to think of gathering some of his thoughts into book form.

Most important of Greenough's artistic ideas was the essential connection between form and function. This theory was current then in Europe but no one in the United States was much aware of it. Greenough astonished his countrymen by saying that the clipper ship was the most beautiful work of art America had yet produced, "something I should not be ashamed to show Phidias." He admired, too, the functionalism of the New England farmhouse and the trotting sulky. His "Stonecutter's Creed" announced:

> Three proofs do I find in man that he was made only a little lower than the angels—Beauty—Action—Character.
> By beauty I mean the promise of function.
> By action I mean the presence of function.
> By character I mean the record of function.[24]

We can trace an almost genealogical descent for this theory from Greenough to Frank Lloyd Wright. Emerson took up and disseminated with enthusiasm the concept that form follows function. Frank Furness, son of Emerson's friend W. H. Furness, was a progressive architect in Philadelphia who tried to put the theory into action, and it was in his office that Louis Sullivan started his career.

When he began to think of publishing his various papers in a book, Greenough sent the pages, printed but not bound, to Emerson with a request for frank criticism. He called the volume *Travels of a Yankee Stonecutter* and signed it Horace Bender (Bender was his mother's maiden name). Emerson was excited by the originality of the essays and by their seminal ideas; they must certainly, he thought, be printed.

> I have read your little book twice through, to say the least [he wrote on 6 September 1852]. I have gone back, and up and down, and criss-cross, and now am in a course of reading passages to my neighbors: and I assure you, it is a very dangerous book, full of all manner of reality and mischievous application, fatal pertinence, and hip-and-thigh-smiting personality, and instructing us against our will. . . . it contains more useful truth than any thing in America I can readily remember; and I should think the entire population well employed if they would suspend other work for one day and read it.[25]

Emerson was distressed, at the same time, by the casual way in which the book was put together—"you have been unpardonably careless in your proofreading"—and horrified by some of Greenough's thoughts on subjects other than art. He took particular exception to the essay on Abolition with its strong dislike of the Negro and its insistence that he is quite incapable of directing his own existence and is far happier and better off in slavery than he ever was in Africa. There were other essays he thought might be omitted, some trivial, some simply unilluminating, but Greenough, who did not think writing worth the hard labor he put into his sculpture, decided to let the book go as it was, in a small edition. Most of this was later destroyed. Only two copies survive, but a facsimile edition was printed in 1958. The *Memorial*, which Tuckerman published after Greenough's death, contained, in addition to eulogies and a biographical sketch, the essays from the *Yankee Stonecutter* of which Emerson particularly approved.

Greenough's dangerous, instructive ideas were not combined in any coherent system but gleamed out in flashes as they must have done in his conversation.

> The susceptibility, the tastes, and the genius which enable a people to enjoy the Fine Arts, and to excel in them, have been denied to the Anglo-Americans, not only by European talkers, but by European thinkers. . . . Seeing us intently occupied during several generations in felling forests, in building towns, and constructing roads, she [Europe] thence formed a theory that we are good for nothing except these pioneer efforts. She taunted us, because there were no statues or frescoes in our log-cabins; she pronounced us unmusical, because we did not sit down in the swamp with an Indian on one side, and a rattlesnake on the other, to play the violin.[26]

> There is at present no country where the development and growth of an artist is more free, healthful, and happy than it is in these United States. It is not until the tyro becomes a proficient —nay, an adept—that his fortitude and his temper are put to tests more severe than elsewhere.[27]

American architecture, Greenough thought, had developed no distinct national style because, though the country was young, the people were old and "as Americans we have no childhood, no half-fabulous, legendary wealth, no misty, cloud-enveloped background."[28]

Attempts to copy European styles seemed to him totally ineffectual.

> The commonwealth, with that desire of public magnificence which has ever been a leading feature of democracy, has called from the vasty deep of the past the spirits of the Greek, the Roman, and the Gothic styles; but they would not come when she did call to them![29]

> Captivated by the classic symmetry of the Athenian models, we have sought to bring the Parthenon into our streets, to make the temple of Theseus work in our towns.[30]

Yet the ancients have much to teach us: "As a Christian preacher may give weight to truth, and add persuasion to proof, by studying the models of pagan writers, so the American builder, by a truly philosophic investigation of ancient art, will learn of the Greeks to be American."[31]

Yet while Greenough admired the potentialities of his countrymen he made a sharp attack upon some of their tendencies which he thought needed subduing:

> It [the Washington Monument] is another example of the arithmetical sublime—an attempt to realize in art the physical truth that many little things united form one great one; which *in art is not true.*[32]

> We tire of sameness and ask change, true, and therefore did a beneficent God put the stars out of our reach—we change what we can, and what we cannot we adore![33]

In November 1852 Greenough delivered two lectures in Boston on "Art in Relation to Life," using some of the material from his book. It was during these that his memory began to fail him and his mind to give way. A few days later he was dead. The contemporary diagnosis was brain fever. Tuckerman believed that the hustling pace of American life had driven Greenough to exertions which wore him out. Today it seems that the trouble may have been a brain tumor but, whatever the cause, the country had lost too soon—he was only forty-seven—a vivid, original mind which might have served in many other ways the art in which he was the American pioneer. Greenough left, Tuckerman tells us, sketches for work which would have occupied him for the next twenty years. "I account that man," wrote Emerson in his *Journal* (July 1853), "one product of American soil (born in Boston), as one of the best proofs of the capability of this country—"[34]

Some of Hiram Powers' contemporaries thought that the United States had lost by his devotion to sculpture; he might have been a distinguished inventor. This, perhaps, is true, though as a sculptor he did much toward the artistic education of his countrymen.

For whatever role he was to play Powers' early life followed a sound American pattern. He was born in Woodstock, Vermont, the son—the eighth of nine children—of an impecunious farmer who tried to improve his lot by moving his family to New York State and then to Ohio. They had scarcely settled in a small town near Cincinnati when Stephen Powers contracted malaria and died. Hiram, faced with the necessity of self-support, worked at a variety of odd jobs, as a library attendant, tavern boy, bill collector; finally, when he was seventeen, as a mechanic in Watson's Cincinnati clock factory, where his accurate eye, skilful hand, and Yankee ingenuity made him very useful. Six years later he moved to a better paid and more interesting situation in Dorfeuille's Western Museum, which combined "scientific" exhibits of stuffed birds and geological specimens with wax figures in the style of Mme Tussaud's. Mrs. Frances Trollope, then in Cincinnati, had suggested to Dorfeuille that he set up a Dante's Inferno. He had just purchased some second-hand dilapidated wax figures and he engaged Powers to repair and mechanize them. Mrs. Trollope, so her son Adolphus has reported,[35] was interested, as many literary people were later to be, by Powers' personality; he had many Yankee traits: energy, shrewdness, a good conceit of himself, and a love of talk. She described to the young man the Dante scenes and incidents she thought he might use and was pleased when he seized her suggestions with alacrity and skill. The Infernal Regions, or "The Regions" as it came to be known locally, was a huge success. The gaping crowds were so large and pressed so close to the groaning, gesticulating waxworks that Powers was obliged to protect his creations by a wire fence, which he charged so that it administered sharp electric shocks, to the amazement and admiration of the over-eager spectators.

In 1832 Powers married Elizabeth Gibson of Cincinnati, of whom we know little except that she was mechanical-minded enough— perhaps she, too, had worked in the clock factory—to help him with his mechanisms. It was not long after his marriage that Powers discovered his real vocation. Visiting one day the studio of a German sculptor, John Eckstein, he saw for the first time a marble bust. He was fascinated and curious, demanded details of the method of making it, borrowed a lump of clay, and began to experiment. His mechanic's hands manipulated the new tools and material easily and his accurate eye enabled him to capture the likeness so highly valued in that day when the portrait bust performed the functions of the modern cabinet photograph. He learned a little anatomy and was soon taking orders.

Eckstein had two other young pupils, H. K. Brown and Shobal Clevenger, and for a time the little group shared artistic ideas and enthusiasms in a way that American sculptors rarely enjoyed. All three eventually became successful professional modelers.

After Powers had been making busts for two or three years, Nicholas Longworth, a distinguished fellow-townsman, suggested to him that he try his artistic skill in the national capital. Longworth believed ardently that the United States needed artists, especially sculptors. He gave Powers not only the financial means of making the journey to Washington but letters of introduction to some important public figures. Powers modeled Chief Justice Marshall, Webster, Calhoun, and even President Jackson, who kindly agreed to pose when he was assured that the young sculptor could take his likeness without covering his face with plaster. This stern portrait (now in the Metropolitan Museum) ranks high among Powers' achievements.

After he had done three years of successful work in Washington, Powers set out for Italy, aided by loans from Longworth and the Prestons of South Carolina. Senator William Preston had interested his rich brother, John Smith Preston, in the young sculptor. These loans Powers, after he began to prosper, conscientiously repaid and he further expressed his gratitude by naming his two sons, born in Florence, Longworth and Preston. The Powers already had two children, a four-year old daughter and a baby in arms, when they embarked on the long sailing voyage to Europe. The children prospered on the journey but Mrs. Powers contracted smallpox from a case which developed in the next stateroom and the family had to make a long stopover in Paris for her convalescence. Powers used the time profitably in visiting the Louvre and other museums. They reached Italy in the fall of 1837 and took up their residence in Florence. Greenough, almost the only other American artist there, was kindly solicitous for the welfare of his countryman.

Powers had brought with him a number of busts to put into marble and was at first distressed to find no competent workmen to help him. Four busts—the Jackson among them—he chiseled himself at great cost of time and labor. At last he discovered an unsuccessful Italian sculptor who understood his style of modeling and was glad to serve him as a marble worker. Powers had enough commissions to keep him going but his margin of profit was not large. Mrs. Trollope, settling in Florence for the winter of 1843, was distressed, when she redis- covered her Cincinnati protégé, to find that he could not afford to put into marble the ideal figures he was modeling when his portrait work allowed. It was not until the mid-forties that Powers achieved real success. His wide fame—and he was the best known of all the American literary sculptors—was established by his *Greek Slave* (*Pl. 10*), exhibited first in London in 1845 and in the United States two years later.

The *Greek Slave* not only demonstrated to Americans the possibility of combining nudity and chastity, it showed many of them for the first time what, beside a portrait bust or a public monument, a work of sculpture might be. This glimpse of ideal beauty was to many citizens of the new country most exciting. It is a little difficult today to imagine an American city in which no statue of any kind exists, where there is nothing which tries, at least, to give delight by plastic qualities and proportions. For even where the local works of art are quite without distinction most houses are flooded with photographs, in books, in newspapers, in magazines, of one form or another of sculptural beauty. But to hundreds of people in the mid-nineteenth century the appearance of the *Greek Slave* was a revelation. They paid gladly for the privilege of looking at her and, once inside the exhibition hall, spent hours in enjoying their new sensations. No wonder they thought her better than she is; they had never seen anything remotely like her.

Even in European countries more accustomed to the sight of works of art the *Greek Slave* created a sensation. In England, in 1845, she attracted so much attention that Summerly's Art Manufacturies got out a diminutive statuette in Parian ware which sold well at two guineas. The *Slave* made an even greater impact when she appeared at the Crystal Palace in 1851. Some Americans in London, distressed by the poverty of the United States' contribution to the Great Exhibition and the lack of imagination with which it had been composed, managed to borrow a replica of the *Slave*. It became at once one of the most eagerly visited attractions in the Crystal Palace.

After this Powers was able to make and sell without difficulty, on either side of the Atlantic, his other ideal figures. The busts of *Faith, Hope, Charity, Proserpine, Hesper,* and so on are, to the modern eye, pretty much alike, despite their carefully chiseled attributes. There were two *Eves*, one before, the other after the Fall. There was a *Penseroso*, one of Powers' few draped statues, carefully costumed according to Milton's description. There was *California,* purchased by John Jacob Astor for his New York mansion. There was an *America,* in tunic and helmet, which Powers intended for the Capitol, but small government recognition ever came to him. He declined to enter competitions or even to submit designs for approval because he thought that for an artist of his importance directions and restrictions were unnecessary. President Pierce, he believed, had been instructed by Congress to purchase his *America* but was prevented by various trickeries and chicaneries. Powers was so far out of touch with his own country, Hawthorne records, that he believed its political state to be far worse than it was. Finally, partly to appease him, partly because his reputation was so great that it was considered essential to have some work of his among the Capitol's adornments, Congress purchased life-size statues of Franklin and Jefferson to stand at the foot of the stairways to the Senate and the House. This was something but not enough, for Powers, in his own opinion, was far superior to all his contemporaries. Even Canova he criticized for making all his portrait busts in his own likeness and he had no praise for Thorvaldsen who had warmly admired him. It is not surprising that, with the exception of his close friend Thomas Ball, he was on bad terms with most of his brother artists. "No wonder!" said Hawthorne. "He has said enough in my hearing to put him at swords' points with sculptors of every epoch and every degree between the two inclusive extremes of Phidias and Clark Mills." [36]

Laymen, on the other hand, especially literary men, seem to have admired Powers as a picturesque personality and to have enjoyed his company. That wide-ranging genius George Perkins Marsh, who played with Powers as a boy in Woodstock, Vermont, remained his friend through life. Lowell liked him though he thought him "not a poet." The Brownings enjoyed his company. Mrs. Browning has left us a vivid description of his eyes, which seemed to his contemporaries to shine with genius. They were, she said, "like a wild Indian's, so black and full of light. You would scarcely wonder if they clave the marble without the help of his hands." [37] Several people thought it worth the trouble to record at length Powers' "millstream of talk."

C. Edwards Lester, American consul at Genoa, took pages of it down in shorthand. When he brought it for correction, Powers was amazed at the accuracy of the transcription and agreed to its publication as part of Lester's book *The Artist, the Merchant, and the Statesman* (1845).

One of Powers' sitters, the Reverend Henry W. Bellows, made careful notes after each session. His portrait bust required seven sittings and the topics Powers covered, partly spontaneously, partly directed by his sitter's skilful questioning, ranged wide. In the summer of 1869 Bellows published in *Appleton's Journal* "Seven Sittings with Powers the Sculptor."

More unexpected is the interest of Nathaniel Hawthorne, but he analyzed the quality of the millstream as the other men were not acute enough to do.

> I have hardly ever before felt an impulse to write down a man's conversation as I do that of Mr. Powers. The chief reason is, probably, that it is so possible to do it, his ideas being square, solid, and tangible, and therefore readily grasped and retained. He is a very instructive man, and sweeps one's empty and dead notions out of the way with exceeding vigor; but when you have his ultimate thought and perception, you feel inclined to think and see a little further for yourself. He sees too clearly what is within his range to be aware of any region of mystery beyond. [27 June 1858] [38]

Powers' "instructive" talk was concerned, some of it, with empirical remedies he had invented for such ills as burns or congestion of the lungs. He took pride in his medical successes. But his favorite subjects were mechanics and engineering. He thought much about flying machines and was certain that they would some day become a means of transportation. When, in 1858, an unsuccessful attempt was made to lay an Atlantic cable between England and the United States he was sure that it could be accomplished by a method he had worked out. He was always ready to discuss the devices he had invented and constructed for the better practice of his art: a file, for instance, for giving a special, much admired surface to his marble, a machine for making these files and for punching holes in iron, and other instruments to assist him in his modeling, for he did not work, like most sculptors, in clay (except for portrait busts) but in plaster. There was a special room connected with his studio where he tinkered happily with these mechanical inventions. He occasionally showed them to special friends.

There were other topics, beside the mechanical ones, on which Powers liked to dwell. One of these was the distinguished men who had sat to him, about whom he had a fund of characteristic and amusing stories, made even more entertaining by the fact that he was an excellent mimic. Another topic was spiritualism, to which he and his wife gave a good deal of attention until he decided that to dwell on that subject was morbid. He preferred to talk of Swedenborgianism, a faith he finally embraced. He was baptized by the Reverend Thomas Worcester who, traveling in Italy with his bride, sat to Powers for a bust which Lowell thought equal to anything done by the Greeks.

In 1867 Powers built himself a villa with a fine garden. There he entertained freely and well. His studio was now one of the sights no tourist could miss and those travelers fortunate enough to be invited to Mrs. Powers' Wednesday evenings could count on meeting all the visiting celebrities. The young woman from Cincinnati seems to have played capably the role of distinguished hostess without losing any of her homespun American qualities.

His financial and artistic success sharpened, apparently, some of Powers' more unattractive traits. He was Yankee enough to drive a sharp bargain and to take very good care that no one got the better of him financially. He and Miner Kellogg, his American agent for the exhibition of the *Greek Slave*, had a protracted, disagreeably public dispute over the receipts and expenditures of that, to Powers, very profitable transaction. With dilatory clients, also, Powers had small patience. He invented a scheme for their reform which amused some of his friends and distressed others: to a shelf in his studio he tacked a card reading, in large letters, "Delinquent," and on that shelf he set the portrait busts whose owners, for one reason or another, were delaying payment.

Thirty-six years Hiram Powers spent in Florence. During all that time he returned just once to America, but he remained throughout his life a complete Yankee with speech, manners, and ideas flavored by the Ohio and the Connecticut; not the Arno. He learned of necessity to talk Italian but he spoke it always with a Vermont twang. And his Italian-bred children were just as American as he. In his tastes he was always genuinely democratic. He was annoyed by any attempt on the part of his countrymen to ape aristocratic manners. He had "no compassion," he wrote to Nicholas Longworth during the panic of 1857, for the suddenly impoverished "Mr. Mc's and G's, who after making fortunes at home, by boiling soap and dipping candles, come out here and sport carriages with coats of arms blazoned upon them, and trick out servants with liveries." And he went on to describe "another specimen of this sort, who prides himself on a better turn out than the *Grand Duke's*. He has been seen indeed, dashing through the streets with *eight* pair of horses to his carriage, but this was a little too much to be bourn [*sic*], and the police interfered." [39]

Powers did not make many Italian friends and in Italian politics he took no interest at all. When, in 1851, Greenough returned to the United States because he could not bear the daily sight of Austrian soldiers in the Florentine streets, Powers remained in his studio working competently and contentedly on.

Except for the proximity of good marble and the cheapness of models and sculptor's workmen, Powers might just as well have been modeling in Cincinnati. He made, during his Florentine residence, only two trips to Rome, which, as we have seen, he found merely bewildering. He visited few other cities, and those for change of air rather than the study of works of art. When he first arrived in Florence he had been, like most young Americans, filled with despair by the artistic richness of the city—why should one add to this superfluity?—but this mood did not last long. He was soon busily finding fault with Phidias and Michelangelo, convinced, as he had been at home, that his own way of working was the right one. He made minute study of the statues of the elder artists but chiefly, it would seem, to remark on their anatomical deficiencies. Character-istic is his discussion with Hawthorne of the *Venus de Medici*. Her figure he thought admirable but the face was "that of an idiot"; the eye, "less like a human eye than a half-worn buttonhole"; the ear set too low; both mouth and forehead, "altogether wrong." [40] Haw-thorne was convinced for the moment but when he saw the statue again decided that Powers was mistaken; the Greek sculptor had carefully calculated his proportions for the total effect.

It was perhaps his complete Americanism which made Powers so popular with his countrymen. He looked at statues much as they did during the first half of the century, as works of craftsmanship rather than of art. His far wider experience of the great productions of the past seems to have increased his technical but not his critical abilities. He went perhaps as far as a mechanic turned sculptor can go and did more for his countrymen in encouraging them to look at statues than he would have done by pre-imagining one of Edison's inventions.

The presence of Greenough and Powers attracted a number of American sculptors to Florence. Richard Greenough shared his brother's studio for a time. Paul Akers and William Barbee were pupils of Powers. Many asked for their advice and criticism. Other American sculptors took studios in the Tuscan city simply because it was reported to be cheap and pleasant. Some of these, like Thomas Ball, became devoted permanent residents; others, after a year or two, moved on to the livelier artist life of Rome. From their choice one can deduce something about their temperaments. There were, as one might expect, always more Roman than Florentine Americans but the Florentines had an amused affection for their little city which is pleasant to contemplate. Horatio Greenough, writing on a visit to Paris, summed it up neatly and nostalgically. A letter to his brother Henry, dated 3 September 1834, concludes: "Dear, compact, bird's eye, cheap, quiet, mind-your-own-business, beautiful Florence, how does my heart yearn for you!" [41]

4

"The White, Marmorean Flock"

> I should mention, too, Miss Hosmer . . . the young American sculptress, who is a great pet of mine and of Robert's, and who emancipates the eccentric life of a perfectly 'emancipated female' from all shadow of blame by the purity of hers. She lives here all alone (at twenty-two); dines and breakfasts at the *cafés* precisely as a young man would; works from six o'clock in the morning till night, as a great artist must, and this with an absence of pretension and simplicity of manners which accord rather with the childish dimples in her rosy cheeks than with her broad forehead and high aims.[1]

Thus, writing from Rome in May 1854, Elizabeth Barrett Browning described the first American sculptress. Mrs. Browning was emancipated enough herself to admire female presumption when it managed to keep itself "pure," but not all critics of Harriet Hosmer (1830–1908) were so charitable. She was the leader, and the bravest, of that little band to which Henry James (in his life of Story) attached the epithet "white, marmorean flock," [2] making it impossible thereafter to refer to them by any other term.

To be an American "sculptress" in the nineteenth century was far more difficult than to be an American sculptor, and that, as we have seen, was hard enough. The nineteenth-century woman who adopted any profession beyond homemaking was immediately suspect. Was she discontented? unladylike? strong-minded? And, if she must practice one of the arts, why could she not confine herself to painting? Sketching, if not done to excess, was a proper pastime for a young woman, but the working of clay and marble was indecorous and required hard physical effort. This disapproval was intensified by the general ignorance of the way a sculptor works. Most Americans imagined that, with chisel and mallet, he hacked his statue out of a block of marble, a labor far too arduous, surely, for any woman. And suppose she did attempt it, would she not have to wear some costume as undesirable as trousers? There was a still more serious problem. Even if the sculptress presented her marble figures thoroughly draped, she must model them with some knowledge of the bones and muscles under the cloaks and scarves. She must know anatomy, and how was anatomy to be learned? By dissecting corpses and studying nude models!

Against these obstacles, real and imaginary, Harriet Hosmer went stoutly to work. Masculine energy and strength she had already. Because her mother, two brothers, and an elder sister had died of tuberculosis, her doctor father determined to give her, in her childhood, stamina to withstand the malady. He saw to it that she lived a vigorous outdoor life. He taught her to row, to swim, to skate—they lived in Watertown, Massachusetts, on the Charles River—to ride horseback, to shoot, with pistols and with bow and arrow. She responded with joy, added to her exercise tree climbing and other unfeminine activities, and became a notorious tomboy. She developed also a fine self-confidence, a pleasant impudence, and a gay propensity to mischief which often went far enough to provoke gossip and to be a real nuisance to the neighbors. More than one school dismissed her in despair and, by the time she was sixteen, Dr. Hosmer felt quite incapable of managing her. He took advice and packed her off to Mrs. Charles Sedgwick's school at Lenox in the Berkshires.

The atmosphere in Lenox proved to be exactly right. Harriet made warm friends among her schoolmates and attracted the interest of several distinguished older women, notably Mrs. Sedgwick's novelist sister-in-law Catherine Sedgwick and the actress Fanny Kemble. These ladies thought it quite proper for a female to show a little independence and to devote herself seriously to a profession. They tamed Harriet sufficiently for company and taught her how she might employ her energies to advantage. She had often modeled clever little figures in the clay pit in the garden in Watertown and she decided to become a sculptor.

The impulse which directed her choice was the same one which turned so many of her masculine contemporaries to the art: the American mechanical genius. Harriet Hosmer liked to work with her hands; she liked to invent things, contrive things, "fix" things; she was constantly constructing ingenious little household devices and setting up small machines. All through her life she carried on mechanical experiments, as Joel Hart did and Hiram Powers. She invented a method of modeling in plaster of Paris instead of clay, then coating the plaster with an inch of white wax on which it was possible to do minute and careful carving while the figure retained its shape without the constant care that clay demands. She patented an— unsuccessful—process for transforming limestone into marble, and in the latter part of her life spent much time and money on a machine to solve, by means of magnets, the problem of perpetual motion.

When this young artist-mechanic came home from school to Watertown, her father built a little studio for her in his garden where she shaped her clay and worked out some of her contrivances. She took lessons in drawing and modeling from the Boston sculptor Paul Stephenson, but instruction in anatomy was harder to come by; the New England medical schools flatly refused her applications for admission. In the winter of 1850, however, she went out to St. Louis to visit a favorite schoolmate, Cornelia Crow, whose father, Wayman Crow, was impressed by the seriousness of her artistic ambition. He induced his friend Dr. J. N. McDowell to admit Harriet to the class in anatomy at his medical school, which was then a branch of the state university at Columbia. "With intuitive delicacy," says Cornelia Crow in her biography of her friend, Dr. McDowell "offered to give her, each morning, in his library, an abstract of the lecture prepared for his students, with the opportunity of examining each specimen used in exemplifying the lesson of the day." [3] At the end of the term Harriet passed the examination and was duly certified.

She surmounted successfully also the social hazards of the long daily walk to the school which stood on the outskirts of the city. Local gossip had it that no medical student ever offered any impertinence to the eccentric young woman for the very good reason that she carried a pistol in her belt and was known to be a crack shot.

Before she went back to New England Harriet determined to see something more of the West and, to the wide-eyed admiration of her friends, made, quite alone, a steamboat journey on the Mississippi. She went down to New Orleans, which delighted her, and then up to

St. Paul. On the way she explored a copper mine and smoked a pipe of peace with the chief in a Dakotah village. She also won a wager that she could climb the highest bluff in the Mississippi valley (near what is now Lansing, Iowa) faster than any of the young men among the steamer's passengers. It is still called, in her honor, Mount Hosmer.

Back in Watertown, Harriet executed her first "ideal" work, a head of *Hesper*, the Evening Star—and began to dream of Rome. Her father had income enough to finance her modestly and, in the autumn of 1852, they sailed for Europe. With them went an older friend, Charlotte Cushman, the actress, in whose care Harriet was to be left. Her dear hope was to be admitted as a pupil to the studio of the English sculptor John Gibson, who, she wrote, "has been resident in Rome for thirty-four years, and leads the van." [4]

Harriet's eagerness to begin her career was such that the party stayed only a week in England and another in Paris before pressing on to Rome. There a friendly young English sculptor offered to make the overtures for her to Gibson, though he was not optimistic; Gibson was often heard to lament the hours he had wasted on English ladies who supposed that they had artistic talent. The kindly young man, nevertheless, took the daguerreotypes, front and profile views of *Hesper*, which Harriet had carefully brought with her, and laid them on the little marble table in the Caffè Greco where Gibson was drinking his morning coffee. At first the great old man was reluctant even to look at them but when he did, he became immediately interested. After a close inspection he asked to have the young lady brought to his studio. "Whatever I can teach her, she shall learn." Harriet went at once to the Via Fontanella and insisted on starting her lessons the next day.

Gibson was captivated by the girl's talent, by her seriousness about her work, and by the gaiety which always endeared her to older companions. Mutual respect ripened rapidly into a warmly affectionate friendship and the distinguished sculptor, who could never make a sensible purchase or get to a train on time, became gratefully dependent on his young pupil's practical good sense. Harriet referred to him always as "the Master," and his little notes to her were signed "Your slave, John Gibson."

Gibson assigned for Harriet's use a little room in the garden which had once been occupied by Canova and set her to work drawing and copying from the antique. As soon as he was satisfied with the precision of her eye he encouraged her to undertake an "ideal creation." She made a bust of *Daphne* as a gift for Mr. Crow and a *Medusa* head which was purchased, with a copy of the *Daphne*, by Mrs. Samuel Appleton of Boston. Copies of the *Medusa* went also to two titled ladies in England. Then Wayman Crow sent her a commission for a full length statue, whenever she was ready to make it. In 1856 she sent him an *Oenone*, mourning her desertion by Paris.

Harriet's father, still careful for her health, had made her promise to take daily exercise and to leave Rome during the hot summer supposed to be so dangerous to northern constitutions. Accordingly she purchased a saddle horse which she rode daily on the Campagna, quite alone when it suited her convenience, until the police objected; the sight of an unescorted female equestrian caused commotion in the Roman streets. The summer of 1853 Harriet spent in cool Sorrento and for 1854 she planned a trip to England. Just as she was setting out, however, a letter arrived announcing that Dr. Hosmer had had serious financial reverses, could no longer support his daughter in Rome, and wanted her to come home at once.

This was the most serious obstacle Harriet Hosmer had encountered in her pursuit of art but she met it with pluck and energy. To leave Rome was unthinkable; she must arrange to support herself. She called into consultation her young sculptor friend (her discreet biographer never reveals his name), experienced in economies, and together they evolved a plan. The visit to England was canceled. Harriet decided to stay in Rome during the summer when the general exodus reduced the cost of rent and food to an almost negligible sum. She sold her horse—a real sacrifice—and took to energetic walking for exercise. The summer weeks, it was decided, must be devoted to making a statue which would surely sell. With genuine good sense she capitalized that capacity for "fun" which so continuously delighted her friends, and modeled a very amusing little *Puck*. The naked, bat-winged baby sits on a toadstool, grasping in his upraised right hand a beetle which he seems about to throw at the spectator; his left hand holds down a lizard and his plump crossed legs caused the Crown Princess of Germany to exclaim, "Oh, Miss Hosmer, you have such talent for toes!" *Puck* charmed at once and orders for replicas began to come in. When the Prince of Wales bought one for his rooms at Oxford, the imp's prestige rose so high that fifty copies, at $1,000 apiece, were eventually sold.

Mrs. Ellet, in her *Women Artists*, remarks, apropos of the helpful anonymous young sculptor, that platonic friendships between the sexes are thought to be impossible but probably they can exist when the woman has an absorbing interest in her profession.[5] Certainly love affairs played small part in Harriet Hosmer's life, and this seems to have been by her own choice. When she was twenty-four she wrote to Wayman Crow:

> Even if so inclined, an artist has no business to marry. For a man, it may be well enough, but for a woman, on whom matrimonial duties and cares weigh more heavily, it is a moral wrong, I think, for she must either neglect her profession or her family, becoming neither a good wife and mother nor a good artist. My ambition is to become the latter, so I wage eternal feud with the consolidating knot.[6]

When Harriet's life-long friend Frederic Leighton first met her in Rome at about this time, he wrote to his mother that the "little American sculptress" was "the queerest, best-natured little chap possible," [7] and this is the way her many warm friends seem to have felt about her. They combined admiration for her work and her serious pursuit of art with amusement at her eccentricity and delight in her gaiety. Their letters are couched often in extravagantly affectionate terms. For instance:

From Robert Browning, Florence, 19 October 1857:

> Dearest Hattie: You know whether or not we are glad to hear from you, and more glad to expect your very self to come, and most glad of all to hope to be along with you at Rome this winter. . . . Ah! Won't we have a time of it! It's too good to prove true, that's the word: but you're a darling.[8]

(It was in 1855 that Harriet Hosmer made a cast of the clasped hands of the Brownings. Several bronze replicas are now in the United States.)

From Lydia Maria Child, Wayland, 21 August 1858:

> I was delighted to receive your little love-note, which exhilarated my old heart, as wine does the nerves, but unlike wine, it left no headache or depression.[9]

From Fanny Kemble, London, 9 December 1854:

> My very dear little Capellina [a play on Hat-ty and the sculptor's beret]: How often I wish I could see your funny and pleasant and beloved little physiognomy for five minutes![10]

And Mrs. Browning tells us how Lady Marian Alford, the Marquis of Northampton's daughter, "knelt down before Hatty the other day and gave her—placed on her finger—the most splendid ring you can imagine, a large ruby in the form of a heart, surrounded and crowned with diamonds. Hatty is frankly delighted, and says so with all sorts of fantastical exaggerations."[11]

A good many people set down, in letters or journals, their impressions of Harriet Hosmer. Most perceptive is Hawthorne's in the *Italian Note-Books,* April 1858:

> We found Miss ——— in a little upper room. She has a small, brisk, wide-awake figure, not ungraceful; frank, simple, straightforward, and downright. She had on a robe, I think, but I did not look so low, my attention being chiefly drawn to a sort of man's sack of purple or plum-colored broadcloth, into the side-pockets of which her hands were thrust as she came forward to greet us. She withdrew one hand, however, and presented it cordially to my wife (whom she already knew) and to myself, without waiting for an introduction. She had on a shirt-front, collar, and cravat like a man's, with a brooch of Etruscan gold, and on her curly head was a picturesque little cap of black velvet, and her face was as bright and merry, and as small of feature, as a child's. It looked in one aspect youthful, and yet there was something worn in it too. There never was anything so jaunty as her movement and action; she was very peculiar, but she seemed to be her actual self, and nothing affected or made up; so that, for my part, I gave her full leave to wear what may suit her best, and to behave as her inner woman prompts.[12]

Hawthorne was quite right; Miss Hosmer was wearing a "robe" below her mannish jacket, though its skirt was probably a short one. Outside her studio she dressed conventionally and with some care. She did, however, cut her curly hair short so that she might have less trouble with marble dust and worked in the beret Hawthorne speaks of. She even, when occupied with a colossal statue, put on a pair of full trousers not unlike Mrs. Bloomer's. To Cornelia Carr, 4 March 1858: "I am busy now upon Zenobia, of a size with which I might be compared as a mouse to a camel. . . . To-morrow I mount a Zouave costume, not intending to break my neck upon the scaffolding, by remaining in petticoats." [13]

After *Puck*, Harriet Hosmer's star rose rapidly, aided, as Hawthorne shrewdly observed, by the fact that visitors to Gibson's studio always saw her work. A *Beatrice Cenci* (*Pl. 8*), commissioned as a gift to the St. Louis Mercantile Library, was exhibited in London on its way and much admired. *Zenobia* occupied a preferred position in the London Exhibition of 1862. A *Sleeping Faun*, shown at the Dublin Exhibition of 1865, was purchased for the city by Sir Benjamin Guinness. Soon Miss Hosmer was fashionable and making a very comfortable income, although she steadily declined to do the remunerative portrait bust, believing, with Gibson and the majority of her contemporaries, that the ideal statue was the higher form of art. It was not long before she had more ideal commissions than she could fill. She designed gates and tombs and fountains for English estates; she met the demand for companion pieces to some of her statues: a *Waking Faun* and a *Will-o'-the-Wisp;* she turned out replicas of *Puck, Zenobia*, and the *Sleeping Faun*. A photograph taken in 1867 shows Harriet Hosmer in diminutive command of the score of burly, bearded stonecutters whom she kept in constant employ. In 1865 she set up her own house and studio, kept a fine horse again, and even two, and was one of the founders and promoters of the hunt which met twice weekly on the Campagna. Her daring jumps became a legend. She entertained hospitably and well and traveled freely, to the United States, to England, Germany, Switzerland, accompanied, for propriety as much as convenience, by a faithful German maid.

Harriet Hosmer's patrons included not only the English aristocracy but European royalty: three successive Kings of Bavaria, the Empress of Russia, the Empress of Austria, and the Queen of Naples, whose beauty and charm so moved the American sculptress that she took no exception to her politics. Sometimes Roman friends became patrons, sometimes patrons developed into friends, so that her English summers became a round of castles and country houses whose historic names her biographer takes a democratic pleasure in recording. She quotes, for instance, a letter written by Harriet from Ashridge in October 1867:

Well, I had a delightful visit at Raby, and then I came here to Lady Marian Alford, who is more darling than ever. On Monday I go to the Duchess of Buckingham for a few days, then Lady Ashburton claims me for a few more.[14]

This sort of success on the part of a female seemed to a good many of the struggling artist brotherhood quite preposterous. It deprived them, too, of the weapon of ridicule which they had often used against the student Harriet Hosmer. Detraction took a malicious turn. It began to be said at the Caffè Greco that Miss Hosmer did not produce her own statues; those exhibited under her name were actually the work of Gibson. In 1862 when her *Zenobia* was set in the best location in the London Exhibition, this assertion was made in print, in communications to the *Art Journal* and *The Queen*. Miss Hosmer promptly brought suit for libel, withdrawing only when the editors agreed to publish a retraction not only in their own pages but also in the London *Times* and the Roman *Galignani's Messenger*.

A variant slander—credible because the public knew so little about the processes of sculpture—credited the good points of Miss Hosmer's statues entirely to the skill of her Italian workmen. In answer to this she wrote for the *Atlantic Monthly* (December 1864) a perspicuous article on "The Processes of Sculpture," explaining just what part the sculptor (male or female) performed in the creation of a statue and how much of the heavy physical labor was always done by skilled but not creative workmen. She gave precise details about the working practices of Thorvaldsen and Canova and it was quite evident that she was stating facts.

In Harriet Hosmer's own country her reputation grew rapidly and the calumnies took no root. *Zenobia*, exhibited in Boston in 1863, was visited in a few weeks by fifteen thousand admirers and, in the course of its American tour, accumulated eulogistic criticism, poetic garlands, and $5,000 for its creator. It was purchased by Almond Griswold of New York; a replica was ordered by Mrs. Potter Palmer of Chicago and another by Robert W. Emmons of Boston, who presented it to the St. Louis Museum of Fine Arts. "In looking at it," wrote John Greenleaf Whittier, "I felt that the artist had been as truly serving her country, while working out her magnificent design abroad, as our soldiers in the field and our public officers in their departments." [15] The comment of that acute art critic James Jackson Jarves seemed to most Americans far too cold.

> Harriet Hosmer is an example of a self-made sculptor, by force of indomitable industry and will. She alone of the women of America who have essayed sculpture has achieved a reputation. Puck displays nice humor, and is a spirited conception; but Zenobia is open to the charge of mere materialistic treatment. The accessories of queenly costume overpower the real woman. Indeed, Miss Hosmer's strength and taste lie chiefly in that direction. She has not creative power, but has acquired no small degree of executive skill and force.[16]

Miss Hosmer's executive skill and force were both called into play when she received the accolade of a public commission. The State of Missouri, wishing to erect in St. Louis a monument to their great Senator Thomas Hart Benton, intrusted the design to Harriet Hosmer and, in 1868, unveiled proudly her somewhat ungainly colossal figure. Huge crowds attended the ceremony and approved both the art and the likeness. They were not too much disturbed by the sculptress's device for turning their Senator into a Roman statesman. Miss Hosmer wrapped him in a long cloak such as he actually wore, draping it like a toga, and shod his feet in sandals. The city of San Francisco was equally pleased with the *Queen Isabella* which Harriet Hosmer made for its celebration of 1892.

Harriet Hosmer was a pioneer but she was not the only one. Other women among her contemporaries began to see the same vision: an America made beautiful by marble forms. The records we have of most of this brave little band are meager but the stories are always interesting and often exciting. Few of these sculptresses had Harriet Hosmer's energy and endurance but each of them had some real force of character or she would not have committed herself to so unorthodox an occupation; sculpture was a new profession even for a man. To the imaginative feminine mind the art shone with romantic nobility; it was a way of improving the world. That anything more than dedication and industry were needed for its practice most of the sculptresses did not realize. They were content with the anatomy they could learn from charts and lectures and their technical training was, in many cases, meager. They produced, nevertheless, work which, in its day, roused genuine admiration and emotion. They taught the United States a great deal about art.

We have record of two amateur sculptresses—and there must have been others—whose work preceded Harriet Hosmer's. Mrs. Wilson—we know only her last name and that she was active about 1850—discovered her talent, like some of her masculine contemporaries, by a visit to a sculptor's studio. It may have been that of Hiram Powers since she was living in Cincinnati. She began at once to model a bust of her husband at which, so Mrs. Hannah Lee tells us in her *Familiar Sketches of Sculpture and Sculptors,*

> . . . she worked with so much energy that sometimes she would faint away, and on one of these occasions he [her doctor husband] said, "If you are not more moderate, I will throw that thing out of the window!" But it was finished, proved a perfect likeness and she chiseled it in stone. It is in her parlor, at Cincinnati, a most beautiful bust and an admirable likeness.[17]

> She has a family of children [Mrs. Lee concludes] and is a devoted mother. We think *stone* will have but little chance with these beings of flesh and blood, whose minds and hearts she is carefully *modelling.*" [18]

The artistic history of Mary Ann Delafield Dubois [19] (Mrs. Cornelius Dubois, 1813–1888) of New York has the same happy ending. She discovered her talent when she was asked to criticize a bust being modeled of her father. She pointed out to the artist several errors he had made in the details of the likeness and then, exclaiming, "I could do that!" took a bit of clay and modeled a very creditable portrait of her husband, who was also present. She decided to take lessons but her health was so frail that her teacher never advanced beyond the dictum to keep her clay always moist. Mrs. Dubois succeeded, however, in modeling a *Cupid and Psyche* and likenesses of her children. Then she attempted the head of a Madonna in marble but the heavy labor so affected her health that "her physician interdicted her devotion to the arts." After that she confined herself to cutting cameos, occasionally instructing a class of artistic young ladies, and, so far as her means would allow, extending a helping hand to aspiring artists. One of these was Edward Brackett.

The most considerable female accomplishment next to Harriet Hosmer's was Anne Whitney's (1821–1915). She, too, oddly enough, was born in Watertown, Massachusetts. She was Harriet's senior by nine years but her junior in clay for her artistic impulse found its outlet first in verse. She had achieved a pleasant Boston reputation as a poetess before a comparatively trivial circumstance turned her attention seriously to sculpture. A wateringpot, accidentally upset in a greenhouse, produced a damp clay which could be effectively manipulated. Miss Whitney, who had modeled little figures from time to time, found that working this properly malleable material gave her a profound pleasure; she decided that sculpture was her true vocation. She began to study and model seriously and with success.

After the war she went to Rome, spending nearly half the next decade there. In Boston she and her close friend Adeline Manning, the painter, made their studio a center of hospitality, talk about the arts, and the promotion of good causes. For Anne Whitney, in her concern for art, was not distracted from the concern for reform in which she had been brought up. She was an abolitionist, a suffragist, and even interested herself in socialism. Many of her statues were touched with propaganda. She made an *Africa* and a *Toussaint l'Ouverture*. She made busts of many of the reformers: *William Lloyd Garrison, Frances Willard, Lucy Stone, Harriet Martineau,* and a statue of *Charles Sumner*, now in Cambridge.

Boston admired and patronized Anne Whitney. Her *Leif Ericson* stands on Commonwealth Avenue and Massachusetts commissioned a *Samuel Adams* for Statuary Hall in Washington with a bronze replica for Boston's Dock Square. She lived a long, busy, and interested life, dying in 1915 at the age of ninety-three.

A New Englander also, born in Salem, was Louisa Lander (1826–1923) whose call to the vocation of sculptress was, like Anne Whitney's, a gentle one. As a small girl she gave evidence of her talent by modeling, in wax, heads for broken dolls. Her admiring mother thought them so remarkable that she would not let Louisa use them as playthings. The family seems from this time to have taken for granted her artistic vocation and in 1855, when she was thirty, sent her to Rome to study with Thomas Crawford. There, in addition to an *Undine*, a *Sylph*, and a *Ceres Mourning for Persephone*, she made two more original figures, an *Evangeline* and a *Virginia Dare*. Busts she modeled, of course, including one of Governor Gore for the Harvard College Library and one of Hawthorne who sat at her request when he was in Rome. He went several times to her studio, "large, high, and dreary from the want of a carpet, furniture, or anything but clay and plaster." He was amazed by Miss Lander's independent way of life, as the Brownings were by Harriet Hosmer's, and used it as a pattern for Hilda's and Miriam's in *The Marble Faun*.

> During the sitting I talked a good deal with Miss Lander, being a little inclined to take a similar freedom with her moral likeness to that which she was taking with my physical one. There are very available points about her and her position: a young woman, living in almost perfect independence, thousands of miles from her New England home, going fearlessly about these mysterious streets, by night as well as by day; with no household ties, nor rule or law but that within her; yet acting with quietness and simplicity, and keeping, after all, within a homely line of right.[20]

Emma Stebbins (1815–1882) of New York came also to her vocation by a somewhat arbitrary decision. She had painted contentedly for years when, at forty-two, influenced probably by the success of Harriet Hosmer, she decided to become a sculptress. She went to Rome, where she studied under Paul Akers and formed a warm friendship with Charlotte Cushman, in whose shadow she thereafter contentedly lived. Miss Stebbins commemorated her actress friend in a rather dull biography and an interesting bust. She worked quietly and steadily at her modeling and her work was well thought of by her contemporaries. Both Boston and New York gave her commissions, though Boston was not thoroughly pleased with her *Horace Mann*, if we may accept the testimony of Mrs. W. W. Story, prejudiced a little, perhaps, because her husband would have liked to do the statue: "Miss Stebbins' statue of Horace Mann," she wrote to her daughter, "has been received by the populace very unfavorably and is everywhere denounced. In fact it is the very worst thing I ever saw." [21]

The history of Margaret Foley (1815 [1825?]–1877) is touched with pathos. Her father was probably a hired man, laboring on Vermont farms. She attended school for a time in Vergennes, working for her board and room in the house of Samuel Wilson. Like other children in the neighborhood, she used to bring stones she picked up to "Grampa" Tucker (Philip C. Tucker) for his geological collection, but Margaret Foley's stones had faces cut on them and she often offered "Grampa" little figures whittled from chalk or wood. Mr. Tucker, with the strong American impulse to discover and foster talent, invited Margaret to use his library and to read and study with his daughters. She always regarded him with gratitude as her first patron.

When she had finished her own education Margaret Foley taught school for a time—she gave her pupils little figurines as rewards of merit—and worked briefly in the Merrimack Mills in Lowell, attracted by her "idealization of the life there, as it had been reported." So says Lucy Larcom in her *New England Girlhood*. Miss Larcom gives us, too, in *Idyl of Work*, a little portrait of Margaret which seems, by more prosaic accounts, to be accurate:

> That broad-browed delicate girl will carve in Rome
> Faces in marble, classic as her own.

The twelve-hour day at the loom did not leave, Margaret found, much energy for the pursuit of culture but she made such clever carvings on the bobbins that her foreman urged her to make art her career.

In 1848 she went to Boston, where she learned and practiced assiduously the art of cameo cutting. "My success," she wrote to Mr. Tucker, "was sudden and unexpected, for my second cameo, a likeness after Rev. John Pierpont, established my reputation as an artist." [22] After seven years of cameo cutting, some school teaching in Westford, and teaching of drawing and painting at the New England School of Design, Miss Foley managed, with the help of admiring friends, to fulfil her dream of Rome. Once there she came home only on one brief visit. She could support herself frugally; she loved the Roman life; and she made warm friends in the English colony, chief among them the daughter of William and Mary Mitford.

Margaret Foley's reputation as a cutter of cameos rose high but she was not content to confine herself to that comparatively minor art. She began to make medallions in clay and marble. One of these, of William Cullen Bryant, was hung in the English classroom at Amherst College. Others included the Howitts, Longfellow, Julia Ward Howe. She went on to busts of Theodore Parker and Sara Josepha Hale, and then, stretching her abilities perhaps too far, attempted ideal figures—*Excelsior, Little Orpheus*, the *Flower Girl*.

Finally she determined to try her hand on a large composition. She spent years of thought and labor on an elaborate fountain, the water held in a basin of overlapping leaves, beneath which sported three happy children. This, with her heads of *Joshua* and *Cleopatra*, she planned to send to the Centennial Exhibition in Philadelphia. Overwork and anxiety brought to a serious state her "malady" and the kind Mitfords took her off to spend the summer with them in the Tyrol. She came back to Rome with renewed vigor but soon exhausted it, and her slender savings as well, in the elaborate business of putting her fountain into marble and shipping it to Philadelphia. When she heard that it had been given an admirable position in the Exhibition's Horticultural Hall she was full of eager hope, but, since the fountain was set up among the flowers, not in the hall with other statuary, none of the critics noticed it in their report and no one purchased it. Bitter disappointment increased the effects of Margaret Foley's illness and, taken again by the Mitfords to Medina, she died there in the summer of 1877. Not long after her death the fountain was purchased by George Whitney and presented to a Philadelphia park.

Another literary sculptress made her way up against odds, odds even greater than Margaret Foley's or Harriet Hosmer's. The Negro-Indian Edmonia Lewis (1845– ?) was born near Albany, New York. When she was barely three both her parents—her father was a Negro, her mother a Chippewa Indian—died. Some of her mother's people took pity on her and she lived for years among the Chippewas. Somehow she made her way to Oberlin and an education. In 1865, when her course was finished, her teachers sent her to find work in Boston, equipping her with letters to William Lloyd Garrison and other abolitionists. The story goes that, entering the strange city alone, she wandered about and finally sat down on the steps of the City Hall to munch the crackers which were all her slender resources allowed her for lunch. As she gazed about her, bewildered but by no means in despair, her eye was caught by Richard Greenough's statue of *Benjamin Franklin*. A statue the size of life was something she had never seen or heard of. That a great man of the past could be made to appear before her eyes seemed very wonderful. Could she perhaps learn to perform such an act of creation? She had often modeled little figures in clay; how was it to be done in stone?

She took her letter of introduction to Garrison and asked him the question. Garrison, impressed by her eagerness, sent her to the sculptor Edward Brackett, who gave her a lump of clay and a plaster cast of a foot. "Go home and make that," he said; "if there is anything in you, it will come out." The girl toiled over her clay until she produced a fair imitation of the cast. When she took it to Brackett he broke it up and told her to try again. She did try, over and over, and began to learn. Finally she succeeded in making a medallion head of John Brown and then, working from photographs, a bust of Colonel Robert Shaw, who had been killed at the head of his Negro regiment. A Soldiers' Relief Fair was then being held in Boston to raise money for the Sanitary Commission and plaster casts of Edmonia Lewis' bust were put on sale. One hundred of them were purchased, and with the proceeds she sailed for Rome. Her Boston friends, now many, gave her letters to Harriet Hosmer, who persuaded Akers and Gibson to give her instruction, and to Charlotte Cushman, who invited her to become a member of her feminine artistic household.

The first ideal figure Edmonia Lewis made in Rome was *Hagar* in her despair in the wilderness. "I have a strong sympathy," she said, "for all women who have struggled and suffered." *Hagar* was promptly sold to a gentleman from Chicago; her next work, a *Madonna*, was purchased by young Lord Bute, and Edmonia Lewis was launched. Her statues sold and her studio became one of the fashionable places for the tourists to visit. They thought her a picturesque figure with her Negro features and straight black Indian hair and they were fascinated by the contrast of her black hands working the white marble.

Edmonia Lewis continued to draw her subjects from the Bible but added to them scenes from her Chippewa experience, giving them, however, the requisite literary touch. *Hiawatha's Wooing* and *The Marriage of Hiawatha* were much admired. The *Wooing*, according to a contemporary description, "represents Minnehaha seated, making a pair of moccasins, and Hiawatha by her side, with a world of love-longing in his eyes." Features, costumes, and all the accessory objects were impressively accurate. Miss Lewis continued, too, to make portrait busts, though not from life, of her heroes: Longfellow, Charles Sumner, Lincoln. To the classics she turned only once—for a *Death of Cleopatra* which she sent to the Centennial Exhibition in

Philadelphia. This curious work was quite original, totally different from the *Cleopatras* of Story, Gould, and other literary sculptors; it was designed to show the effect of death upon beauty and was so startlingly realistic that contemporary critics found it "absolutely repellent," even while they admired its power.

There must, one fancies, be other details worth knowing in the curious story of Edmonia Lewis, but they have not been recorded.

Unsatisfactory as these brief histories are—and there are probably some even shorter careers of which we have no record at all—they do give us a fairly clear idea of what it was like to be an American sculptress in the middle of the nineteenth century. Certainly it was a field much easier for a woman to enter than medicine or lecturing or even journalism. Neither parents nor husbands looked askance at any of these women when they announced their artistic intentions, and in Rome, though they faced a little ridicule and a good deal of grumbling by artists who resented any intrusion on their masculine Bohemian society, there was no persecution. Most of the barriers Harriet Hosmer had already broken, though obstacles appeared now and then in unexpected places, as Anne Whitney discovered when she entered Boston's competition for a colossal statue of Charles Sumner, a memorial planned immediately after his death in 1870. From the twenty-eight designs anonymously submitted, hers was unanimously selected by the committee in charge, but when they read the sculptor's name they declined to award her the commission; no woman, they thought, could possibly understand and delineate the features of a man. She never entered another competition but at the age of eighty she made from her original model a seated statue of Sumner for Harvard Square. Most Americans were ready to accept the sculptresses' work on its merits, more often than not to overpraise it just because it was woman's work.

There were several reasons for this. In the first place, the sculptresses were not active reformers, like the women writers and lecturers. Those women made their way into masculine territory because there were causes they wanted to advance: abolition, temperance, women's education, women's suffrage, and it was these causes rather than their bold defiance of St. Paul which enraged their contemporaries. The sculptress, on the other hand, even when she made a statue with a propaganda theme, could be treated as an artist rather than a reformer, her propaganda was just a subject. Of course any woman who devoted herself to a profession was more or less suspect but the artist's was considered a good deal less dangerous than other callings. In the arts the line between amateur and professional was a little blurred; landscape sketching, china painting, and cameo cutting might be perfectly proper pastimes for a young woman.

And the female sculptor was not merely tolerated; she was encouraged. Her fellow citizens urged her on in her dangerous course because America wanted statues and there were not nearly enough masculine sculptors to go around. Sex was a minor matter.

The women, moreover, came into the field only a little later than the men; except in Rome and Florence, there was no tradition of masculine prerogative, as there was in oratory, for instance, or homiletics. So women's statues were bought gladly and women even received commissions for public monuments.

When, in 1862, Harriet Hosmer was entrusted with the modeling of Missouri's Benton monument, Gibson congratulated her on having attained a female eminence unknown as yet in England. There no woman had ever designed a public statue. Actually, America enlightenment was even greater than Gibson supposed. Harriet Hosmer's was not the first female public commission. As early as 1858 Louisa Lander had made a bust of Governor Gore for the Harvard Library. In 1860 Emma Stebbins designed her *Angel of the Waters* for New York's Central Park and, a few years later, a *Columbus* for New York and a *Horace Mann* for Boston. Anne Whitney, as we have seen, made statues for the Commonwealth of Massachusetts.

Once at least a woman received a commission just because she was a woman. The first federal commission granted to a sculptress went, in 1867, to pretty twenty-year old Vinnie Ream (1847–1914), who had some real ability in modeling but almost no training or experience. This choice of an artist, made it was said by "susceptible senators," met wide disapproval, some of it outraged, some amused, yet the life-size statue of Lincoln Miss Ream made for the Capitol rotunda is a quite respectable piece of work. It is a pity that we have only the outline of her life history, for it is a real American success story.

Vinnie Ream was born in a log cabin in Wisconsin Territory, of which her father was then Treasurer, and it was on the Missouri frontier that she grew up. During the war the family went to Washington, where Mr. Ream found work in the Treasury Department and his daughter obtained a clerkship in the Post Office. Vinnie was very pretty, small, slender, bright-eyed, with soft brown curls. She had not only great charm but a strong will, a capacity for hard work, and complete self-confidence. Her artistic vocation was discovered through a jest when she was visiting with a friend the studio of Clark Mills. Miss Ream picked up a bit of clay and playfully tried to work it, saying that she would model a portrait of her host. The result was so surprisingly good that everyone present thought they had discovered a genius. Mills offered to give her instruction and she began to spend most of her free hours in the pursuit of art. Some members of Congress who admired her persuaded President Lincoln that he would be helping a poor and ambitious young girl if he would permit Miss Ream to model him and he gave her permission to come for half an hour every morning before she went to the Post Office, sit in a corner of his office and study his face and figure while he went about his daily business. She saw Lincoln on the morning of his assassination and it was not difficult to persuade the Congress that she was precisely the person to make the $10,000 statue they immediately voted. The change in Vinnie Ream's fortunes was so sudden that at first she could not believe it and refused to give up the security of her job in the Post Office, but finally, when the clay model of her statue was completed, she set off for Rome to put it into marble. She took her parents with her, for she was now supporting the family in great comfort. In Rome she rapidly became a personage with many orders for portrait busts and a crowded social life. Her independence and unconventionality were accepted as fascinating characteristics of the American frontier and her charm was as effective upon distinguished Europeans as it had been on the less sophisticated congressmen. Gustave Doré and Père Hyacinthe, among others, permitted her to model their heads and so, to the general amazement, did the forbidding Cardinal Antonelli, papal secretary of state. She accomplished this, by her own account, simply by putting on her prettiest white dress and asking for an audience with His Eminence, who immediately granted her request.

That Vinnie Ream's frontier charm was "pure" in the best American manner we have testimony from the Danish scholar Georg Brandes, who, as a young man, met her in Rome just before her return to America. After she sailed for home he wrote in his diary a little account of Vinnie Ream, concluding thus: "This recollection of her is retained by One who knew her for seventeen days and will never forget her." She was his first American girl and in the beginning, he says, he did not understand her. "I had a few unpleasant conjectures ready. I had to have many conversations with her before I understood her ingenuousness, her ignorance, her thorough goodness, in short, all her simple heartiness of soul." [23]

In Washington Vinnie Ream's social and professional life flourished as it had in Rome. Congress gave her another commission, a statue of the Admiral for the center of Farragut Square, and she had plenty of private orders for busts and even for ideal figures, *Sappho, Miriam, The Spirit of Carnival.* In 1878 she married Lieutenant Richard L. Hoxie, an engineer, and abandoned sculpture to become a highly popular Washington hostess, but in later life she turned again to her art. Her most admired work was *America or the Four Sisters*, North, South, East, and West.

Two other sculptresses are represented in the Capitol: Anne Whitney, as we have seen, with her *Samuel Adams* in Statuary Hall, and Sarah Fisher Ames (1817-1900). Her bust of *Lincoln*, which she patented in 1866, was purchased by the committee charged with buying works of art for the Library of Congress and the Capitol.

Sarah Ames, wife of Joseph Ames the painter, was born in Lewes, Delaware, in 1817, studied modeling in Boston and in Rome, and then lived in Washington, where she moved in artistic, literary, and abolitionist circles. During the Civil War she was a Sanitary Commission nurse, serving in field hospitals and at one time in charge of a hospital in Washington. Her other works of which we have record are also busts, including one of General Grant which won an award at the Paris Exhibition of 1900.

In one respect the sculptresses were actually in advance of the sculptors; they did not hold so closely to classical themes but experimented with genuinely American subjects far more than most of the men were doing. This was probably in part because of the almost complete absence of the classics from female education but it was certainly a result too of feminine "strong-mindedness." These women thought for themselves; conventions did not seem to them immutable; and, like all the feminine pioneers, they were concerned not so much for their own self-expression as for the improvement of the world; they labored to uplift America by making statues which would teach, each one of them, a lesson, in patriotism or reverence or reform. Anne Whitney, for instance, who wanted passionately to see the abolition of slavery, made, during the war, a statue which she called *Africa*. The colossal ideal figure is just rising from sleep. She supports herself upon her left hand and, with her right, shades her eyes against the breaking light. "Doubt, fear, wonder, hope, pain, are all marvellously blended in the half-awakened face," wrote Mary A. Livermore in her biographical sketch of Miss Whitney in *Our Famous Women*. Later, in Italy, Miss Whitney made a *Roma (Pl. 6)*, showing her as an ancient beggarwoman seated on a broken Corinthian capital. Her gown, bordered with medallions of antique sculpture, is rent and tattered. This conception of the decay of Rome under the papal power roused so much excitement in the eternal city that *Roma* had to be transferred to Florence, where she was kept in the house of the American Minister until she could be shipped to the United States.

It was pure patriotism which Louisa Lander wanted to inspire with her group of the *Captive Pioneer* and with an "ideal female" whom she called *Today*, crowned with morning-glories and draped in a flag, fastened at her breast and shoulder with clusters of stars. *Today* was not very different from the troops of *Hespers*, *Faiths*, and *Minervas* who preceded her but Miss Lander treated later a quite original American subject, *Virginia Dare*, the first white child born in the New World. A member of Raleigh's lost colony of Roanoke, Virginia Dare, according to the legend, was said to have been brought up among the Indians and the statue shows her as an Indian princess, her face exhibiting, says a contemporary description, "the thoughtfulness and spirituality that would naturally be derived from the dreamy recollections of her early life. The figure is semi-nude; the drapery, a light fishing-net, is charmingly conceived and executed, being worn like an Indian blanket." [24] It was the same pleasure in America's developing legends which moved Anne Whitney to make her *Leif Ericson*. And both Miss Lander and Miss Lewis were moved to illustrate the poems of that American weaver of legends, Longfellow. Vinnie Ream made an *America* and a *Young West* and even the quiet Emma Stebbins was among the first to introduce into American art such figures as *Industry* (a coalminer) and *Commerce*.

This movement toward native themes is only one of the debts which the twentieth century owes to the literary sculptresses. The white marmorean flock, gentle as their activities were, exerted a real influence on the awakening artistic consciousness of the United States.

5

The Exception: William Rimmer

In the middle of the nineteenth century one sculptor, never well known to his contemporaries, made a small number of statues so different from any of those we have been considering that it is difficult to believe they belong to the same period. To the modern observer they are far more interesting than most of the work of the literary sculptors. This is in part because their maker seems to have had, in addition to an extraordinary knowledge of human and animal anatomy, an instinctive feeling for real sculptural qualities, but, beyond this, these statues are charged with a kind of passion none of the neoclassicists seems ever to have felt. Looking at them today we are inclined to agree with Daniel Chester French that their maker "just missed being great." Most of these figures present struggle or death: *St. Stephen* suffering martyrdom, *The Falling Gladiator*, *The Fighting Lions*, *The Dying Centaur (Pl. 16)*.

They were made by William Rimmer (1816-1879) of Boston, a painter of pictures as passionate as his statues, a doctor, a lecturer on art anatomy, an eccentric, fascinating, and infuriating person. He had great gifts of which he never made more than partial use. Some of his contemporary admirers thought that his small success during his lifetime was the fault of nineteenth-century America, not yet prepared to recognize and cherish a true artist. This is certainly not so, as it is not true—E. P. Richardson has convincingly demonstrated it—that Washington Allston shriveled in an unfriendly New England atmosphere. Opportunities were offered to William Rimmer again and again. He spoiled them or threw them away. What prevented him from making use of his powers was his temperament and that was the product of singular circumstances: he had been brought up to believe that his father was the lost Dauphin, heir to the throne of France.

Thomas Rimmer, William's father, was told, as soon as he was old enough to understand, that he was the son of Louis XVI, that as a baby he had been spirited away to England and given in charge to a yeoman's family in South Lancashire. (Their name was Rimer from which Rimmer derived the name he assumed when he emigrated to America.) The Rimers brought up Thomas as a Catholic, treated him with far more deference than the other children in the household, and supervised an elaborate education, paid for, so he was told, by the privy purses of Great Britain and Russia. He was taught Latin and most of the modern tongues, including Russian, mathematics, chemistry, history, drawing, music, fencing, all of which he absorbed with what seems to have been an excellent mind. He had also great skill with his hands, was as clever with them as any mechanically minded American. Thomas Rimmer believed implicitly in his future and believed that military glory would be important to it. He joined the British Army, where he was advancing well when, in 1815, the Bourbons were restored to the throne in the person of Louis XVIII. Thomas Rimmer felt that he had been betrayed. He threw up his commission, married an Irish servant girl, and emigrated to America. Fearful, apparently, of pursuit or even perhaps of persecution in a democratic country, he lived as secluded a life as possible, telling his story to no one, moving from place to place in and around South Boston, keeping his family apart from neighbors, earning his living by shoemaking as a trade which could be pursued in comparative solitude.

His children—six sons and one daughter—Thomas Rimmer educated himself and apparently effectively; their heads were filled with history and poetry; they really understood music—he made a silver flute for each of them; they fenced; they painted; they studied natural history and did experiments in physics. At times the family life was rich and gay and interesting but there was always poverty at its base and the children were constantly aware of their father's frustration and despair. Thomas Rimmer, as he grew older, became more and more embittered. He thought all mankind unjust and hard. He had a dangerously violent temper. In the end he drank himself to death.

William, the eldest son, took over at an early age his father's attitude of the betrayed prince, and this became the basis of all his actions. He seems, though, to have been free from his father's violence. He was a fascinating conversationalist who charmed men well educated enough to understand him; most of his South Boston neighbors thought him queer and often dangerous. His artistic skill was evident early. He drew well under his father's teaching and during a period when the family lived near a quarry he began to cut statues from gypsum. A single one of these has survived. It is a small nude figure seated on a rock in an attitude of tension, the right hand clutching the right ankle, the left clapped over the mouth. The features are those of Thomas Rimmer. It is called *Despair* (*Pl. 15*). A curious piece of work for a boy to have made, it is full of power and promise.

At fifteen William tried to augment the family income by engaging in occupations more profitable than shoemaking. He painted portraits and signs, set type, and worked for a time with a lithographer. The admirable desire for all kinds of knowledge which his father had stirred in him led him to an interest in anatomy; he read all the books he could lay hands on, pored over plates and engravings, and studied the casts in the Boston Athenaeum. This knowledge was to be augmented and exploited later.

At twenty-four William Rimmer married Mary Peabody, a New Bedford Quaker, settled in Randolph, and began to raise a family; he had six children, three of whom died in their youth. To his shoemaking Rimmer added the painting of religious pictures for neighboring Catholic churches. The priests were his good patrons, especially Father John Roddan, a great builder of churches. Rimmer also played the organ and trained the choir in Father Roddan's church. Finally, in need of still more income, he decided to study medicine and fortunately found a friend and teacher in Dr. A. W. Kingman of nearby Brockton. Kingman, impressed by Rimmer's ability as so many men were, lent him books, tutored him, and got him access to the dissecting room of what was to become the Harvard University Medical School. Rimmer learned fast and well. He tried first, unsuccessfully, to establish a practice in Chelsea and then moved to East Milton, where he used his skill on the granite quarry workers in Quincy, not a very lucrative clientele. They respected him, though, for his patience and kindness as well as for his ability, and his theories and his cures so impressed the regular members of the medical profession that, after ten years of practice, he was granted a degree by the Suffolk County Medical Society and became Dr. Rimmer.

It was not until he was forty-five that Rimmer made any attempt at professional sculpture. He was practicing then as a doctor in East Milton and one of his few well-to-do patients there took, as Dr. Kingman had done, a great interest in him. This benefactor, whose name we do not know, insisted on introducing him, though Rimmer was shy of being patronized, to Stephen H. Perkins of Milton. Perkins was one of those patrons of art who was concerned not only to collect for himself but to discover and encourage American sculptors. He suggested that Rimmer make him a head in Quincy granite and the Doctor began at once upon a *St. Stephen.* He produced a powerful portrait of the martyr being stoned, the head thrown back, the throat muscles tense and distorted, the eyes full of suffering. The state of mind he depicted was evidently for Rimmer a kind of self-portrait. The *St. Stephen* bears no resemblance to any head hitherto made in the United States. The anatomy is remarkably accurate but it is not a study in anatomy but in pain. Rimmer cut the head as a modern sculptor would do straight out of the granite and became so moved with what he was creating that he worked with terrible impetuosity, straining his back and muscles and bruising his hands.

Perkins, much impressed by the work, put it on exhibition in Boston and was delighted at the attention it attracted among critics and connoisseurs. He was disappointed that it did not sell but one can scarcely blame the average Bostonian for not wanting that sort of emotion in his drawing room. Eventually Perkins himself purchased it for the Athenaeum. Perkins next offered to finance a project Rimmer had told him he had in mind, a *Falling Gladiator.* This life-sized figure, grasping a broken sword, is falling backward to his death. In part it is a demonstration of Rimmer's knowledge of anatomy—a falling figure is one of the most difficult of subjects —but, like all the Doctor's work, it is symbolic of his own state of mind and emotion.

The *Gladiator* was to be made in clay, a medium with which Rimmer had had no experience. He was too proud, or too impatient, to ask advice and simply went ahead as best he could, piling up the clay—he seems never to have heard of an armature—and cutting at it as though it were stone or gypsum. There were all sorts of difficulties: the clay froze, it fell apart, but he persisted in the hours he could snatch from his regular work and the remarkable *Gladiator* appeared.

Perkins had plaster casts made of both the head and the statue and exhibited them in London and in Paris, where they were admired by some experts but not widely enough to establish for Rimmer any reputation. This would have been, nevertheless, for most American sculptors, an inspiring start; it seems to have had small effect upon Rimmer. For all his instinctive knowledge and skill he was not devoted, as many of his less gifted contemporaries were, to the art of sculpture. When he began to make a statue he became absorbed in the task but he was impatient to be done and always worked too fast. It was drawing and painting that he most enjoyed and practiced for his own pleasure, with some very fine results, though he seems never to have acquired any skill in the use of color. His subjects were usually, like his statues, figures in violent motion, running or falling or fighting. He was reticent about this work and many of his admirers had no idea that he painted at all. His skill in drawing was well known because he employed it on the lecture platform.

Rimmer's career as a lecturer was one of the happy results of Perkins' exhibition of the *St. Stephen* and the *Gladiator*. Some distinguished Bostonians, eager to promote in their city a better understanding of art, insisted that he should come there to lecture on art anatomy. Rimmer hesitated long before accepting; he disliked always to leave his family and the idea of public appearance on a platform made him unhappy. He found, as he expected, that lecturing was a great nervous strain and he never came to enjoy it despite the success he made. His first course in Boston was attended by artists, art students, and art lovers who wanted to learn more about how to look at paintings and statues. Their enthusiasm was great. No one so learned in anatomy had ever lectured publicly in Boston before and Rimmer had all sorts of original theories about comparative anatomy and the animal characteristics of man, interesting and stimulating whether correct or not. Part of the excitement of his audiences was caused by his drawings. He worked rapidly on a blackboard with a sharp-pointed chalk, drawing first the structure of a bone, then of a muscle, then a limb in movement, then a whole figure. His listeners used to lament that this beautiful work should immediately be subject to the eraser.

Rimmer's lectures were a systemization of the process he himself had gone through in the dissecting room and in his study of the casts in the Athenaeum. The Greeks, he explained to his listeners, learned their anatomy not by dissection but by constant observation of the beautiful nude bodies of athletes. They recognized on the body certain "points of interest," joints or muscles which receded or protruded as the limbs moved. With these points the artist must be familiar. Rimmer demonstrated the structure of bone and muscle underlying each point, then showed what effect each produced on the surface of the body as it moved. Then he sketched whole figures or groups of figures illustrating the idea he was trying to convey. He paused after each drawing to give the art students time to copy it in their notebooks and, while they worked, he walked about the room giving comments and suggestions unless, as often happened, he was so exhausted by the strain on his nerves that he had to withdraw for a few moments and rest.

Among the many testimonials to the interest and value of these lectures one of the most significant comes from Daniel Chester French of the next generation of sculptors. French, then a very young man, attended Rimmer's lectures and counted them as the real beginning of his art education. In 1906, years after Rimmer's death, French had the *Falling Gladiator*, so much did he admire it, cast in bronze and thus it has been preserved for us.

The first series of lectures was so successful that petitions went to the Lowell Institute asking to have the course repeated there. When this was done the enrolment was so large that Rimmer had to give a special afternoon series for women.

During his sojourn in Boston Rimmer found himself for the first time in contact with a group of men interested in art and letters. Many of them were impressed by him and cultivated his society but he never really became a member of the community; he was moody and suspicious and they were aware that he came from an alien background. But the fault was his quite as much as Boston's.

One of Rimmer's Boston pupils suggested to a New York friend of hers, Mrs. Ann Lynch Botta, that she invite Rimmer to lecture at one of her weekly *conversazione.* There he was introduced to Peter Cooper, who asked him to take charge of the School of Design for Women at his Peter Cooper Union for the Advancement of Science and Art. To this Rimmer agreed and spent four years in New York which he often referred to as the happiest time in his life. He was doing something he liked, for, though the lecturing troubled him, he cared greatly for teaching and felt it important to help people to know; he was making enough so that he did not need to practice medicine; and he enjoyed his contacts with cultivated men and women among whom he felt less self-conscious than among the Bostonians.

The courses which Rimmer planned, and most of which he taught, for the School of Design were rich and learned but actually too fundamental and intellectual for women who were training for practical work in textile design. The trustees of the School finally decided to put its direction into more practical hands and asked Rimmer to stay on simply as a teacher. This he regarded as an insult and withdrew to Boston. William Morris Hunt suggested that they open an art school together but each of them had his own independent ideas on how it should be run and finally each began conducting classes of his own. Rimmer lectured not only in Boston but in Providence, in Worcester, at Harvard, at Yale, and at the National School of Design in New York. When the Museum of Fine Arts opened in Boston in 1877 he was asked to teach art anatomy there twice a week and to give instruction in modeling.

None of this work, influential as much of it was, brought in much money. Rimmer was always in debt, his wife was sickly, and he had three daughters to support. The three sons had died. Like so many of the literary sculptors he was inventive and ingenious and he tried to make capital of that. He invented an unbreakable trunk, a self-regulating counter for streetcar conductors, and a new type of gunlock, but nothing came of them. He became involved in plans for a model aquarium but had to abandon it before it opened, and he foolishly lent his name to a very dubious photo-sculpture concern.

His admirers tried in various ways to help him. One of them wanted to send him to Europe but Rimmer declined, partly because he did not wish to leave his family, partly because he had no interest in the usual sculptor's life in Rome or Florence. The effect on his work would probably have been small. To another patroness, Mrs. William Aspinwall Tappan of Boston, we are indebted for an interesting record of his teaching methods and theories. She arranged to have published, in 1877 under the supervision of Harvard College, a huge volume called *Art Anatomy* which contained eighty-one plates, beautifully drawn, of the kind of illustrations Rimmer was accustomed to put on the blackboard during his lectures. These are accompanied by comments such as he made in presenting his ideas to an audience. The book was so expensive that its circulation was not wide but it undoubtedly had some influence, as did the excellent textbook for children, *Elements of Design*, which he published himself in 1864.

Rimmer's most faithful patron, Stephen Perkins, pleased as he was with his protégé's success as a teacher, felt sure that he ought to be contributing also to American sculpture. While Rimmer was doing his first teaching in Boston Perkins arranged a commission for a public statue which he thought should be the next step in the sculptor's career. A group of wealthy Bostonians who were building mansions on the new Commonwealth Avenue had received permission from the city to ornament it with a statue of Alexander Hamilton which was to be the gift to Boston of one of their number, Thomas Lee. Perkins persuaded them to give the commission to Rimmer, who went at it with his usual impatience. He finished the clay model in eleven days and was pleased with it himself though he said later that he wished he had spent more time on the back. Neither the public nor the critics liked it at all. The general feeling was that Rimmer had had his chance and failed. This is one point at which contemporary taste was too far behind him, for the modern critic is impressed by the way the head, powerfully revelatory of Hamilton's character, rises from the enveloping cloak in a manner suggestive of a much later work, Rodin's *Balzac*. Mr. Lee expressed himself as satisfied but when he presented another statue to the city the commission went to J. Q. A. Ward.

Two other commissions did come to Rimmer, one from the Argentine politician Sarmiento, then consul in Boston. For him Rimmer made two fine heads, of Lincoln and of Horace Mann, but the transaction was marred by a bad spot in the marble which Sarmiento thought seriously spoiled the effect of the Mann bust while Rimmer insisted that it was a matter of no importance. In 1875 Hammat Billings, the architect of the Pilgrim Monument in Plymouth, asked Rimmer to make a figure of *Faith* to top it. He produced a charming nude figure, lightly draped, but this did not suit Billings' plans. He turned Rimmer's statue over to a plasterer who reconstructed it so that Rimmer's conception was completely lost.

During the sixties Rimmer made three life-size statues, a *Chaldean Shepherd*, an *Endymion*, and an *Osiris*. The first two were disliked but since they perished in the plaster we cannot tell with what justice. The *Osiris* Rimmer preferred to anything else he ever modeled. A figure in repose, it was intended as a contrast to the *Gladiator*; repose he thought a higher form of art than violent motion. *Osiris* was exhibited for a time in a gallery on Tremont Street, until complaints were made about its nudity, and later in New York at the Cooper Union. It was finally broken and only photographs remain to us, but they are impressive.

It was for his own pleasure, apparently, that Rimmer made two small groups both of which fortunately were cast in bronze, the *Fighting Lions* and the *Dying Centaur* (*Pl. 16*). His interest in animal anatomy was great and lions, of course, were part of his royal symbolism. He studied them wherever he could, at the zoo or whenever a traveling circus came into the neighborhood, but in making this group he worked, as usual, without a direct model.

The *Centaur* is a kind of epitome of Rimmer's life and thought. He dies in agony, lying on his side, one leg bent painfully under him, his body strains up from the ground, the right arm lifted toward heaven. Rimmer broke the arm off just below the elbow, partly to give the effect of an ancient statue, chiefly to intensify the passion of the dying appeal. In the *Centaur* we find Rimmer's interest in animal and human anatomy, his concern with man's struggle against the animal elements in his nature, his sense that he was going down in cruel defeat. His own death took place in 1879 when he was sixty-three.

There must be some significance, one feels, in this curious special instance among the literary sculptors but it is difficult to seize it. Rimmer's personality bulked larger than his genius. He seems to have been born, as Saint Gaudens was in the next generation, with a talent beyond that of any of his contemporaries but how much influence his work might have had if he had been able to fraternize with his fellow artists one can only guess. Certainly his teaching had effect and the statues, had he produced more of them, might have intensified the lessons. One does not feel that he was born out of his time, for his peculiar character would have spoiled life for him in any age. Enthusiastic recognition might have spurred him to more extensive effort but, as we have seen, he had many opportunities of which he was unable to make use. He belongs to the history of the period chiefly because his excellencies emphasize some of the weaknesses of his contemporaries.

6

The Nudo

The American sculptors who lived in Rome always spoke of it as "the *nudo*," which sounded somehow much more naked than nude and added to the diffidence the layman felt in approaching an undraped statue. That the unclothed human form may be contemplated with emotions which are aesthetic rather than erotic was one of the most difficult art lessons nineteenth-century Americans had to learn. Except for the widely traveled—a comparatively small group—the citizens of the United States were not accustomed, like their European contemporaries, to visiting galleries filled with Greek and Renaissance statues. Only in a few large cities—Boston, Philadelphia, New York—were casts from the antique to be seen and, where they were exhibited, inspection was attended with certain difficulties. Mrs. Trollope, for instance, describes, with her usual relish, her experience in 1830 in the Pennsylvania Academy of Fine Arts.

While she was reading the sign on the door of the Antique Statue Gallery, an old woman, who appeared to be the official guardian, bustled up to her and whispered,

> "Now, ma'am, now: this is just the time for you—nobody can see you—make haste."
> I stared at her with unfeigned surprise, and disengaging my arm, which she had taken apparently to hasten my movements, I very gravely asked her meaning.
> "Only, ma'am, that the ladies like to go into that room by themselves, when there be no gentlemen watching them." [1]

This state of mind seems to the mid-twentieth-century American almost incredible. He, like the ancient Greek, is accustomed to the daily sight of half-clothed bodies, on the beach, or even in the A&P.

He discounts, therefore, the force of the nineteenth-century instinct for covering things up, putting shawls on mantelpieces and scarves on pianos, crowding walls with pictures, encasing young ladies in layers of petticoats, and concealing raw emotions in elegant phrases. Even simple facts might require drapery. If, for instance, you were serving a young lady with chicken, you must inquire her preference for light or dark meat, since you could not in her presence utter such words as breast and leg.

The *nudo* was to be seen even less often in pictures than in sculpture. The paintings with which Americans were most familiar were the portraits, always thoroughly dressed, which hung in many homes, and the historical and religious pieces, which they saw frequently in engraved copies. There were also, in the drawing rooms of the well-to-do, copies of old masters brought from France and Italy, but these were usually religious subjects or perhaps landscapes by Claude or Salvator Rosa. Among native American paintings Rembrandt Peale's *Io* and Vanderlyn's luscious *Ariadne*, sleeping couched upon the grass, were exceptions, and dubious ones many thought. When *Io* was exhibited in Philadelphia in 1814, together with a *Danaë* by the Danish artist Wertmüller, society was divided. The majority considered highly indecorous exhibitions to which both sexes could not be admitted at the same time, but there were also "men and women of strict morals" who pronounced *Io* "elegant and decent, voluptuous but not lascivious." [2] *Ariadne* was much admired in the Paris Salon of 1812 but in Philadelphia she was a scandal. This seems, in part at least, to have been Vanderlyn's intention. His reasons for using the *nudo* were very different from the lofty purposes of most of the nineteenth-century artists, whether painters or sculptors. They felt the *nudo* essential to the expression of certain emotions and ideals; Vanderlyn saw it as a good way of making money. He exhibited his *Ariadne* in company with two copies (he was an expert copyist) of nudes, Titian's *Danaë* and Correggio's *Antiope. Antiope*, he wrote on 3 July 1809, "may not be chaste enough for the more chaste and modest Americans, at least to be displayed in the house of any private individual, to either the company of the parlor or drawing-room, but on that account it may attract a greater crowd if exhibited publicly." [3] We have no record of other serious nineteenth-century artists who thus exploited the nude.

Unless he had a mercenary motive like Vanderlyn's it was not really essential for an artist to paint the *nudo*, but the sculptors were obliged to model it often since their criteria were derived from the revered Greeks, whose marble masterpieces they studied daily in Rome or Florence. For the layman a marble nude was harder to accept than a painted one. The size of the sculptured figure and its three dimensional presence made it look alarmingly like a real person whom one ought not to encounter in undress. The early American "ideal" figures had before them a long and difficult educational mission.

The work of enlightenment was begun by that fine carver in wood, William Rush. He was known among his contemporaries chiefly for his figureheads, which were so famous that scores of people went down to admire whenever one of the ships they adorned put into a London dock. In 1809 Rush, a member of the Philadelphia Water Committee, was asked to carve a statue to commemorate the establishment of the waterworks which would supply the city with water from the river Schuylkill. He asked the daughter of one of his colleagues on the committee, Mr. James Vanuxem, a respected merchant, to pose for a nymph of the Schuylkill, and cut in wood a charming graceful figure, holding on her shoulder one of the great bitterns which in those days haunted the river sedges. Water spouted from the big bird's uptilted bill. The Nymph wore a willow withe on her head and willow leaves as a girdle about her light drapery, whose folds suggested the ripple of the river waves. This diaphanous costume seemed indelicate to the good citizens of Philadelphia and the fact that a young lady, a celebrated belle, had posed for the figure distressed them. Fortunately the Water Committee had the good sense to admire the statue and to set it up at the site of the new waterworks in Central Square. (The wooden figure has decayed but a bronze replica stands now in the Philadelphia Museum.)

Both Rush and his young nymph seem to have approached their artistic collaboration much as a modern sculptor and model would do. This one infers from the painting of Rush at work made many years later by Thomas Eakins, who had his own troubles with American prudery. In Eakins' carefully documented canvas, which shows Rush at work on the nymph, the young model is chaperoned by a placidly knitting elderly relative. (Painted in 1877; Eakins made two other versions in 1908.) This was not only historical painting on

Eakins' part but propaganda as well. He wanted his fellow-townsmen to realize that the *nudo* must be taken for granted as an element in art. To persuade Philadelphia and the rest of the United States to this point of view took many years.

Twenty years after Rush's carving of the *Nymph of the Schuylkill* the first of the "Italian" American sculptors, the Bostonian Horatio Greenough, found himself struggling with the problem of the *nudo* and public taste. His little group of *Chanting Cherubs,* made for James Fenimore Cooper, was inspired, as we have seen, by two young angelic figures in Raphael's *Madonna del Baldacchino.* Raphael was the most respectable of painters but the three-dimensional version of his cherubs presented them to home-keeping Americans as distressingly naked. In 1832 this was for many citizens of the United States the first piece of sculpture they had ever seen. How very little they knew about the art is indicated by what happened to the *Chanting Cherubs* in New York. Cooper's friend Dr. J. R. De Kay, who took charge for him of the exhibition of the little group, wrote him, 1 April 1832, about their reception.

> The Cherubs failed here, owing it is said to their name. Our literal folks actually supposed that they were to sing, and when the man turned them round in order to exhibit them in a different position, they exclaimed, "Ah he is going to wind them up: we shall hear them now." [4]

The exhibition a year later of Greenough's *Medora* put an even heavier strain on public taste. The heroine of Byron's *Corsair* lies on her bier, covered only by a light sheet drawn over the lower part of her body.

> In life itself she was so still and fair,
> That death with gentler aspect wither'd there.

What impression this lovely form made upon New England female delicacy we know from a letter written on 19 December 1833 by Miss Prudence Ward, who boarded for many years with the mother of Henry Thoreau.

> Last Friday I summoned courage . . . and went alone at twelve at noon [when gentlemen were supposed not to be present]. . . . On a platform covered with green a foot high in the center of the room was the bier on which lay the beautiful Medora. . . .

I was horrified at the size of what Moore calls woman's loveliness which actually took my eye so that I could not see the face. . . . The left side of the figure is entirely naked except a sheet drawn up under the arms. It is represented to be of so delicate a texture that the form is distinctly traced. For myself I can say it would have pleased me much better had it been drawn a few inches higher, for I felt for a while completely out of countenance. There was one gentleman present.[5]

Not only young ladies from the country but some of the traveled and sophisticated had their reservations about the *nudo*. George W. Hillard, for instance, whose highly interesting *Six Months in Italy* (1853) was the indispensable American guidebook of the day, asked himself as he stood before Titian's Venuses, in the Tribune, whether it would not have been better, on the whole, if they had never been painted. No subject, he decided, ought to be put on canvas "which a man would hesitate to look at in the presence of his children, or of the woman that he loves." [6] This instinctive recoil Hillard buttressed by a curious rationalization:

It is easy, comparatively, to make a naked nymph or Grace of a certain degree of excellence. All that is wanted are good models and mechanical skill: but to deal with drapery so that it shall reveal and not overlay the figure; to make it expressive, and yet not so elaborate as to attract attention to itself; to make it heroic, dignified, or graceful, according to the character of the form which it shrouds,—this requires skill, invention, and delicate creative power—qualities, in short, which distinguish the artist from the mechanic.[7]

Even the dashing N. P. Willis said in his *Pencillings by the Way* that "a little drapery would do no harm" to any of the nudes in the Sistine Chapel.[8] This comment should not, perhaps, be taken too seriously. Willis was a popular writer and he may have been trying simply to propitiate the anxious mamas, for he was quite aware that a good many young ladies of his day were far more knowing than they could let themselves appear. In his novel *Paul Fane*, published in 1857, there is a handsome Miss 'Phia Firkin from Cincinnati who, accompanied of course by her mother, comes to sit for her portrait in the Roman studio of an American painter, Wabash Blivins, who is very much in love with her. Blivins' friend Paul Fane asks permission to make a study at the same time and the young lady suggests that she be modeled as "anything you and Mr. Blivins think of most when you see me." "When I see Miss Sophia Firkin," announces Blivins handsomely, "I see the Goddess of American Liberty!" The idea of appearing in a helmet and a tunic does not give much pleasure to Miss 'Phia. She welcomes far more happily Fane's remark that she suggests to him Cleopatra applying the asp. " 'Oh, delightful, delightful!' " cried Miss Firkin, " 'Cleopatra in a reclining position, holding the serpent to—to—just below her heart isn't it?' " [9]

A little later 'Phia writes to her dearest Kitty that she is " 'breaking ground' as we say at the West, to *have my bust taken*, and so be done even more justice to, perhaps after all. Most anything is proper *in marble, you know*." [10]

This would suggest—and certainly Willis was an expert on the contemporary young lady—that the mind of the American female was not always quite so pure as her countrymen liked to think. Miss Firkin might almost have made that celebrated response of the Princess Pauline Borghese which both English and American journalists liked so much to quote. Canova modeled the Princess as Venus Victrix, reclining upon a couch, undraped except for a very light scarf about her waist. When an English friend asked her how she had managed to endure the exposure, the Princess answered sweetly that it was really not at all trying; the room was well warmed.

The non-professional model, of course, sometimes added complications to the delicate business of carving the *nudo*—except for the sculptresses. Harriet Hosmer, for instance, could persuade her friend and patron the beautiful Lady Adelaide Talbot to serve as model for her *Beatrice Cenci (Pl. 8)*, sleeping in prison the night before her execution. The graceful Beatrice, lying on her right side, is only partially draped and Fanny Kemble tells us that when Miss Hosmer's teacher, the great John Gibson, looked at the finished statue he exclaimed, "in his slow, measured, deliberate manner, 'And to think that the cursed prejudices of society prevent my seeing that beautiful back!' " [11] We are told, though, that Hiram Powers, because of his reputation for "purity and uprightness," was able to enlist, when he was modeling the *Greek Slave* in Florence, the cooperation of a very beautiful young girl, not a professional model. The *Literary World* (13 September 1847) which states the fact, does not, of course, mention her name.

The most effective work toward the education of the American public to a rational acceptance of the *nudo* was done by the tour made in 1847 by Hiram Powers' *Greek Slave*. Powers seems to have been quite unconscious of the dangers his lovely maiden might face when he sent her across the Atlantic. He was complacently aware that she had been admired by many visitors to his studio in Florence and that the enconiums of his fellow-artists were loud. He felt himself that she was technically good, and he knew that she "told a story," with political implications which would move American hearts. He did not realize, apparently, that most Americans were still unconvinced that it is possible to be at the same time nude and chaste.

Fortunately the painter friend who acted as his American agent foresaw some of the difficulties. Miner K. Kellogg of Cincinnati began by circulating admiring English estimates of the statue, for London had received the *Slave* with enthusiasm when she arrived there in 1845. She had been bought for $4,000 by Captain John Grant of the British Navy, introduced to Powers by Mrs. Trollope. Grant put the *Slave* on exhibition in London in the rooms of Messrs. Grove in Pall Mall and lines of carriages, half a mile long, so the report ran, blocked the adjacent streets for days. The statue was eventually sold to the Duke of Cleveland.

The marble from which the *Slave* was cut was much admired. It came from the quarries of Seravezza, finer even than those at Carrara, discovered to be so, it was said, by Powers' Yankee ingenuity. Powers had perfected, too, a process of finishing, with tools of his own devising, which gave the marble an extraordinary flesh-like quality; it seemed as porous as living skin. The English were pleased, also, with the *Slave*'s anti-Turkish propaganda and moved by her story, which could be imagined without great difficulty. Powers himself related it thus:

> The Slave has been taken from one of the Greek islands by the Turks, in the time of the Greek revolution; the history of which is familiar to all. Her father and mother, and perhaps all her kindred, have been destroyed by her foes, and she alone preserved as a treasure too valuable to be thrown away. She is now among barbarian strangers, under the pressure of a full recollection of the calamitous events which have brought her to her present state; and she stands exposed to the gaze of the people she abhors, and awaits her fate with intense anxiety, tempered indeed by the sup-

port of her reliance upon the goodness of God. Gather all the afflictions together, and add to them the fortitude and resignation of a Christian, and no room will be left for shame. Such are the circumstances under which the Greek slave is supposed to stand.[12]

It was this story, rather than her artistic qualities, which moved Elizabeth Barrett Browning to write a sonnet, much quoted in the United States: "Hiram Powers' 'Greek Slave.' "

> Appeal, fair stone.
> From God's pure heights of beauty against man's wrong!
> Catch up in thy divine face, not alone
> East griefs but west, and strike and shame the strong,
> By thunders of white silence, overthrown.

While she was on exhibition in England the *Slave* had been recommended to Americans by the United States Consul at Genoa, C. Edwards Lester. Writing in the *American Review* of August 1845 he said:

> I think my residence abroad has only made me prize more than ever the bright gem which adorns the American woman—that primitive virtue which recoils from the very shade of impurity. And so far from feeling any apprehension that the exhibition of these statues [*Eve*, sent later, and the *Greek Slave*] in America, would have any tendency to introduce among our women *foreign indelicacy*, characteristic of every country in the world, but our own and the British Islands at home, I am persuaded they would be warmly greeted by all the enlightened and all the pure of both sexes, and leave every spectator with more exalted conceptions of the beauty and the divinity of virtue. And I would even venture to say, that I should be compelled to fear of every one, who, after seeing them, should pronounce a different opinion, that the character of the *spectator* was not right.

This was the note which Mr. Kellogg emphasized in the pamphlet [13] he circularized to herald the exhibitions of the *Greek Slave*. It made effective use of a pronouncement (*Union Magazine*, October 1847) by the Reverend Orville Dewey, a Unitarian minister who had not only traveled in Europe but published a book about it, *The Old World and the New*. The Reverend Mr. Dewey eulogized Powers' statues as works of art and discussed, very delicately, the principles of the *nudo*. "There ought to be some reason for exposure *besides* beauty, like fidelity to history, as in the Eve, or helpless constraint, as in the Greek girl."

Plate 17

Erastus Dow Palmer, 1817–1904, in his Albany studio, painted by Tomkins H. Matteson, 1857. (*Courtesy of Albany Institute of History and Art*)

Plate 18

Horatio Greenough,
1805–1852, painted by
John Gadsby Chapman.
(*Courtesy of the Boston
Athenaeum*)

Thomas Crawford,
1813–1857, by an
unknown artist. (*In Villa
Crawford, Rome, owned
by Countess Eleonora
Marion-Crawford Rocca*)

Plate 19

Edmonia Lewis,
1845–? (*Photograph in* Negro
History Bulletin, *March,*
1939)

Hiram Powers,
1805–1857. (*Photograph in*
Charles E. Fairman, Art and
Artists of the Capitol,
Washington, 1927)

William Wetmore Story,
1819–1895. (*Photograph in*
Mary E. Phillips, Reminiscences of William Wetmore
Story, *Chicago and New York,*
1897)

Harriet Hosmer,
1803–1908, drawn by Emma
Stebbins, 1815–1862. (*In*
Eminent Women of America,
Hartford, 1868)

Plate 20

Harriet Hosmer at work on her *Benton* for St. Louis. (*Photograph in Cornelia Carr*, Harriet Hosmer, Letters and Memories, *New York, 1912*)

Plate 21

Vinnie Ream, 1847–1914, painted by George Caleb Bingham. (*Courtesy of State Historical Society of Missouri*)

Plate 22

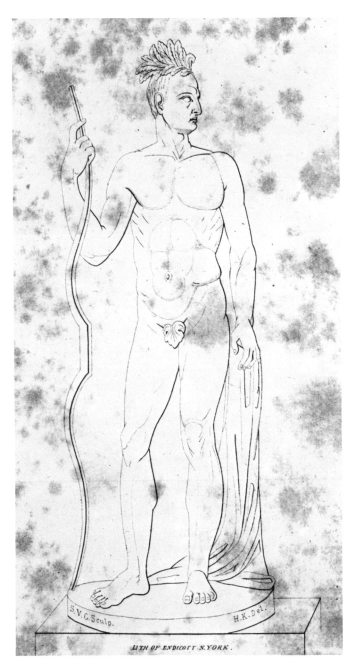

The first statue of an American Indian, made in Rome,
1843, by Shobal Clevenger; engraved for
the *United States Magazine and
Democratic Review,*
Feb., 1844.

Plate 23

Larkin Mead, *Recording Angel.* (*Courtesy
of Vermont Historical Society*)

Plate 24

Memorial Hall, at the Centennial Exhibition of 1876 in Philadelphia, contained one hundred and sixty-two pieces of American sculpture. (*Engraving in Potter's American Monthly, May 1876*)

The *Slave* he thought more beautiful than the *Venus de Medici* because "there is *no* sentiment in the Venus but modesty. . . . She has neither done anything nor is going to do anything, nor is she in a situation, to awaken any moral emotion." "I would fain," was his climax, "assemble all the licentiousness in the world around this statue, to be instructed, rebuked, disarmed, converted to purity by it."

It was Powers' second replica of the *Greek Slave* (there were eventually six, perhaps more) which was exhibited in the fall of 1847 at the National Academy of Design in New York. She stood on a revolving pedestal four feet high and was admired daily by hundreds, not only New Yorkers but "the finest spirits of Boston and Philadelphia," so said the *Literary World,* who made the journey to Broadway because they were unable to restrain their impatience to study this epoch-making figure in American art. The impression the statue made upon her viewers was carefully noted and described.

> It is most curious [wrote Mrs. Caroline Kirkland in her *Union Magazine,* October 1847] to observe the effect produced upon visitors. They enter gaily or with an air of curiosity; they look at the beauteous figure, and the whole manner undergoes a change. Men take off their hats; ladies seat themselves silently, and almost unconsciously; and usually it is minutes before a word is uttered. All conversation is in a hushed tone, and everybody looks serious on departing.

Sometimes the *Slave*'s power extended even beyond this. Miss E. Anna Lewis, writing on Powers for *Graham's Magazine* (November 1855), recalls her visit to the *Greek Slave* in 1847. Enchanted by the statue's beauty she dropped into one of the chairs placed before the pedestal and began to share in imagination all the emotions through which the maiden must have passed. When she awoke from her trance she found, so she states, that she had sat before the statue for five hours. Some spectators, she adds, objected to the *Slave*'s nudity because they did not realize that the human form is the only one in which the sculptor can embody those passions which are the soul of art. "Grace Greenwood," in the *Home Journal* improves on this: "One is scarce conscious of gazing upon a nude figure, clothed as the poor girl seems in the love and the sorrow of the angels." [14]

Many masculine admirers of the statue expressed their emotions in verse. These gentlemen were moved, not, like Mrs. Browning, by the *Slave*'s political propaganda but by her powerful combination of nudity and chastity.

> Naked, yet clothed with chastity, She stands;
> And as a shield throws back the sun's hot rays,
> Her modest mien repels each vulgar gaze.

That tribute appeared in the *Knickerbocker Magazine*, October 1847. Henry Tuckerman, one of our earliest art historians, was often moved to poetry by the paintings and statues he described. In speaking of the *Greek Slave* in his *Book of the Artists* he indited a six stanza tribute which indicates the state of mind the figure produced.

> Some pent glow, methinks, diffuses o'er those limbs a grace of soul,
> Warm with Nature, and yet chastened by a holy self-control.[15]

Or, as a sonneteer put it in the *Literary World* (18 September 1847):

> I had not looked upon thee had a line
> Breathed of the myrtle goddess of thy clime,
> But such a sinless, meek rebuke is thine,
> That thy mute purity abashes crime.

After its exhibition in New York the statue was seen in Washington, Baltimore, and Philadelphia. Another replica, the property of Lord Cootes, reached America in June 1848 and toured New England—Springfield, Boston, Salem, Providence, and Portland.

Next, the *Slave* went West, visiting of course Powers' own Cincinnati, where she had again to run a gauntlet of criticism. A committee of clergymen of various denominations were invited to scrutinize her carefully in a preview; they announced unanimously that she was pure. Most of the citizens felt then that they should visit her, but agreement was not complete. In the *Ladies Repository* (November 1848), published in Cincinnati by the Methodist Church, the Reverend A. Stevens expressed his feeling that, since even the voluptuous Florentine Venus shrinks and extends her hands in modest self-protection, we should expect in a Christian maiden "the most exquisite expressions of agonized sensibility"; but in the *Greek Slave* there is "no crouching, no shrinking," little emotion of grief, only resignation. Some have even said, he went on, though he thought this going too far, that, with the chains removed, the *Slave* might be taken for a nymph or a bather.

That the *Greek Slave* really did educate large sections of the United States to an acceptance of the *nudo* seems indubitable. Two years after her tour there were expressions of pleasure when the American Art-Union included among the works of art distributed by lot to members, twenty copies of a nude bronze statuette (twenty-two inches high) by H. K. Brown. *The Choosing of the Arrow* was Brown's title for his young Indian hunter, quite naked except for a quiver and a fig leaf. Male nudity is, to be sure, more respectable than female and Indian nudity is both historical (like Eve's) and to be expected of a savage, but the fact that the Art-Union felt no compulsion to mention the Indian's lack of dress suggests an attitude somewhat in advance of that which welcomed the *Slave*.

Even more impressive is the fact that in 1857, ten years after her original appearance, the *Slave* herself was presented for allotment by the Cosmopolitan Art-Union. This was no statuette but a life-size marble replica. It was won by a Mrs. Coleman of Cincinnati, who kept it on view at the Düsseldorf Gallery in New York. Eventually the Art-Union repurchased the statue for $6,000 and offered it again for allotment. The winner this time sold the statue to A. T. Stewart, the New York merchant. Comments on these events are strikingly different in tone from the solemn verses which greeted the *Slave*'s 1847 tour. "Belle Brittan" (Hiram Fuller), for instance, wrote about the *Slave* in one of her lively letters to the *Boston Transcript*. Cousin Lou, she said, is a subscriber to the Cosmopolitan Art-Union and is counting on winning for himself the lovely *Slave*, "whose charms will never wither, and who will be entirely satisfied with 'Nothing to Wear,' forever." [16]

The *Bulletin* of the American Art-Union at the same time remarked that the report that Mr. Stewart would display the *Greek Slave* in his famous New York emporium was incorrect; she would certainly spoil his trade in crinolines.

At a little later date the *Slave* began to appear in drawing rooms. Henry James remembered her in his youth "so undressed, yet so refined, even so pensive, in sugar-white alabaster, exposed under little domed glass covers in such American homes as could bring themselves to think such things right." [17] And Edith Wharton, expert like James in the significances of interior decoration, put a life-sized copy of the *Slave* into one of her fictional parlors. The heroine in "The Reckoning" recalls the apartment in which the evenings of her first marriage had been passed: "a wilderness of rosewood and upholstery, with a picture of a Roman peasant above the mantelpiece, and a Greek slave in 'statuary marble' between the folding-doors of the back drawing-room." [18] This is, of course, later than James's recollection. The *Slave*'s nudity does not disturb anyone, but taste has changed and she is no longer the height of artistic fashion. What the "art lover" now examines is her technical excellence, her plastic values, her beauty or her insipidity.

But this is not the whole story. For many years after the *Slave*'s 1847 tour, even after she had appeared again in England, at the Crystal Palace, and had scored another triumph, her propriety and that of all her kind continued to disturb earnest Americans. One can set no precise date for the artistic enlightenment of the United States. The convolutions of taste all through the nineteenth century are curiously devious. It moves forward and then spirals back.

In August 1850, for instance, Henry Ward Beecher was writing from Paris in one of his *Star Papers*:

> I am willing always to see the human form sculptured or painted when it seems to subserve a good purpose. If it be natural that it should under such and such circumstances be disrobed, I do not turn away from it, provided the sentiment is noble, and predominates to such a degree as to make the condition of the figure a secondary and scarcely perceived affair. [19]

One would expect at least as much liberality as Beecher's in that early art journal *The Crayon*, but in July 1859 we find the *Slave* and two other Powers nudes, *Eve* and *California*, denounced as "faulty in anatomy . . . low in character and vulgar in sentiment." A little later (December) appears a bitter diatribe on "Naked Art."

> Paganism loved to worship the naked body—to steep the senses in luscious physical forms, to become inebriate with the tantalization of fleshly outlines and protuberances, to forget the soul. . . . Christianity arose that it might effect the resurrection of the spirit through the proper subordination of the flesh. Art became its ancillary, . . . it delicately draped the body that the evolution of the spirit might not be impeded.

This introduces an attack on a statue then being exhibited in New York: "Will any man of unperverted intellect and moral sensibility . . . tell us, what new art revelation he finds in the White Captive [*Pl. 11*] of Palmer?" What some critics were finding, as they do today, in that charming youthful nude, was a characteristically American figure. The *White Captive* is, said the *Atlantic Monthly* (January 1860), not Greek but "one of us." Her nudity, they explained, is simply "a coarse chance of her overwhelming situation, for which she is no more concerned than for her galled wrists or her disheveled hair."

But opposition to the *nudo* was not confined to expression in print. It took the form at times of direct action. In 1859, for instance, public outcry forced the Boston Athenaeum to remove from exhibition on its walls William Page's *Venus Guiding Aeneas*. During the sixties the Pennsylvania Academy of Art decreed that when its students organized life-drawing groups—the Academy itself was interested only in teaching them to copy from the antique—they be strictly regulated: the supervisor of the School must always be in attendance; the female models were forbidden to speak to any of the students; and, while they posed, they must wear masks. When Eakins became director of the School he insisted that the basis of teaching must be the nude figure. He not only taught life classes but arranged to have anatomical lectures given by a leading physician and followed by dissections performed by the advanced students. All this troubled the conservative directors but Eakins was so good a teacher that they found it impossible to interfere until the increasing number of women students brought matters to a climax. In 1886 Eakins, demonstrating the pelvic muscles to a class of women students, asked the male model to remove his loin cloth. Some of the young ladies complained to the directors and they asked for Eakins' resignation. Most of the other students protested vigorously and a large group withdrew from the Academy to form a separate school with Eakins as their instructor.

Not all teachers of anatomy, though, shared Eakins' attitude. William Rimmer, for instance, though he taught women in his art anatomy classes, was horrified when some of them suggested that their knowledge might be improved by drawing from live models.

Closely related to the problem of the *nudo* was the question of sculptural dress. If your statue was to be shown fully clothed, must it be in the ungainly costume of the present day or was some artistic compromise possible? With a female figure, it certainly was. The lady could be supposed to be wearing some fanciful creation, light, elegant, and flowing, in the Greek manner. Actually contemporary females, unless they were queens, were seldom sculptured in full length, except perhaps on their tombs. Queen Victoria, standing on a pedestal, could be made impressive and not ungraceful in her royal robes, and when Harriet Hosmer modeled the Queen of Naples she dressed her in the riding habit and long cloak she wore when she walked, encouraging her soldiers, on the battlements at Gaeta. It was the great man, the hero, of this or a precedent generation, who presented the real problem.

Benjamin West had faced the dilemma in historical painting as early as 1771 when George III, Sir Joshua Reynolds, and Archbishop Drummond all tried to persuade him not to clothe the figures in *The Death of Wolfe* in "boots and breeches." In 1821 the citizens of North Carolina, proud as they were of the statue they had commissioned Canova to make for their capitol at Raleigh, were disturbed to find George Washington clad in Roman armor, sitting in a marble chair, writing an address with a stylus. The Raleigh *Register* explained to them that the Roman dress was "consonant to the purest taste, and that Canova, a Roman himself, has been so long accustomed to the classical costume that it would have been difficult for him to have done justice to the subject in any other garb."

By the middle of the nineteenth century, however, the Revolutionary costume was beginning to assume a certain picturesqueness, and Thomas Crawford even went so far as to say that the uniform of the Continental Army was the American classical costume. Most of the American sculptors who made statues of Washington dressed him as a Continental General, but Horatio Greenough, when he apotheosized the Father of his Country for the national Capitol, saw fit to clothe him as the Jupiter Olympus, whom he resembled in his seated pose and gesture. Washington's only garment is a sort of toga which covers the lower part of his body and is pulled over the shoulder of the right arm, which points to heaven. The outstretched left arm holds a sword symbolically reversed. The usual interpretation of these gestures by an unregenerate public was: "Here is my sword;

my clothes are in the Patent Office yonder." Only a few Americans
were ready to echo Emerson's "nobly draped below, and nobler nude
above," [20] though many of them tried hard to admire the statue, as
W. T. Thompson's comic character Major Jones did. The Major, in
one of his travel letters dated 19 May 1845, put it this way: "It made
me feel bad when I looked up and saw Washington's bare busum. The
veneration which Americans feel for the character of Washington is
shocked at the exposure of that noble breast whose every throb was
for his country. . . . I tried my best to overcum my prejudices
. . . because it was an American work, but it was no go." [21]

When one came to contemporary heroes the problem was even
more difficult. What could be done with tight trousers, frock coats,
and Wellington boots? Sometimes the sculptor just doggedly modeled them anyway, often delighting the public by the recognizable
accuracy of his details. Sometimes he resorted to subterfuge, as
Harriet Hosmer did when she wrapped Senator Benton in a cloak
draped like a Roman toga. Actually Benton had flung his nineteenth-
century cloak about him in much that way and his Missouri con-
stituents were pleased with the effect.

But this was not a real solution of the problem. In the middle of
the century it was quite seriously proposed that an international
alteration in dress, sponsored by courts and governments, should be
undertaken in the interests of Art. At the time of the Crystal Palace
Exhibition (1851) the Commissioners expressed a readiness to consider the display of articles of dress which showed beauty of design,
and a group of English artists seized the occasion to present their
views on the necessity for reform. The *Bulletin* (July 1851) of the
American Art-Union in New York reprinted their manifesto:

We are anxious to draw general attention to the subject of costume; that which is now prevalent in Europe being devoid of all
the requisites for dignified historical painting, utterly incongru-
ous with sculpture, and no less unfavorable to the living figure,
both as regards appearance and convenience. . . . No costume
of which there are any traces was ever so inconsistent with grace,
simplicity, and dignity of aspect, none so uselessly complicated,
as a European's of the present day. The unity of the figure is
frittered away. Stiff lines and angles disguise the body, and an uncouth hat crowns the disfiguration. Groups of men in the ordinary
garb gratify no taste but that of caricature; neither painting

nor sculpture can advantageously transmit to futurity a faithful representation of any event constituted of such a group. Nor does admixture of female fashions often obviate the difficulty. . . . Historical subjects must continue to be sought in remote periods. . . .

The cause of truth, the interests of our own times, and the satisfaction of posterity, alike require the removal of such an impediment to artistic faithfulness.

The *Bulletin* added a note of its own on the current dress controversy in America over the bloomer costume, but, it concluded sadly, the tunic and trousers are even uglier than the "stiffly extended skirt and rectilinear waist." The proposed reform, unfortunately, never got beyond the petition stage.

What was probably the ultimate word on the subject of costume was spoken by Harriet Hosmer to a committee who waited upon her to discuss the erection of a monument to a local dignitary recently deceased. He must be portrayed, said they, in his habit as he lived; they would send her his hat, his overcoat, and, most important of all, his boots; he was famous for having the largest feet in the county. Miss Hosmer lost the commission by suggesting that it would be more original and less expensive if they simply cast the boots in bronze and set them on a pedestal.

Some of the artists who were also writers tried in various ways to explain to the public their point of view about costume and, more important, about the *nudo*. Horatio Greenough, for instance, in his essay on "Aesthetics at Washington" (1851), wrote angrily on the taste of people who repudiated his naked little *Chanting Cherubs* and his semi-nude *Washington* but crowded eagerly to see French "harlot" dancers. (Greenough did not condemn all dancers. In 1846 he had written an appreciative essay on the Austrian Fanny Elssler, a sensation in many capitals: "Do Not be Afraid of Grace and Beauty!") Greenough's younger brother Henry, who was a painter, tried to instruct the public in fiction. He published in 1858 a novel called *Ernest Carroll or Artist-Life in Italy*. In one scene in Florence the hero spends the evening in a class in life drawing. While he studies the model, posed as a Bacchante at rest, the author takes occasion to tell us that

To an artist, nothing is more exciting, than the study of the *nudo*. The strong, artificial light, concentrated upon the figure, throws it into broad masses, infinitely varied by the most subtle details. The gradations from high light, through semi-tints, to shadows and reflexes, are to the painter's eye a most melodious gamut of light, shade, and color. He sees before him a picture, such as was never transferred by the hand of man to canvas. It seems impossible not to catch something of that grace and beauty which grows under his eye, as he endeavors to copy it. His knowledge and facility of handling, increasing almost from moment to moment, he works assiduously and *con amore*, to the very brink of exhaustion.[22]

W. W. Story, who was a man of letters as well as a sculptor, wrote late in life an "idyl," full of sentiment, called *Fiammetta* (1886). Its painter-hero discovers during a summer in the hills a beautiful *contadina* who seems to him to embody the naiad in a picture of which he has been dreaming. One day he finds her alone in the woods, sitting by a brook, "utterly unconscious of the presence of any human being." She had taken off her shoes and stockings; "her head was uncovered, her upper dress had been loosened, and exposed her shoulders and bosom."

There was no bashfulness, no sense of being surprised, no indication of offended modesty in her reception of him. Why should there be? She was perfectly innocent, and the mere fact that her arms, bosom, and legs were nude, did not carry with it to her mind any idea of impropriety. The legs and arms of half the girls that toiled over the hills were bare as hers were then. *That* meant nothing, and never had meant anything to her mind, or to the mind of any of the peasants with whom she lived. All such ideas are merely the result of habit and convention.

Nor for a moment did Marco attach any significance to this. He was an artist, and he knew how little nudity had to do with modesty.[23]

This was a point of view which the nineteenth-century lady found it difficult to grasp. Hiram Powers put it to her more effectively, perhaps, than Story, by translating it into the language of the ballroom. Powers was not a writer but his talk so impressed his acquaintances that more than one of them took the trouble to transcribe it. C. E. Lester, the Genoa consul who certified the *Greek Slave* to American modesty, set this down:

I've seen women in a ball-room who would be shocked at a sight of the Venus de Medici, or any nude statue, however delicate and chaste, who, from the pretext of fashion, or more probably a secret wish to allure, have so dressed themselves, that the effect upon the beholder was a thousand fold more contaminating to good morals than all the naked statues in the world.[24]

7

Wounded Indians, Armed Freedom, *the* Libyan Sibyl*–John Rogers, Erastus Dow Palmer*

The first statue of an American Indian was made in Florence in 1842 by Shobal Clevenger of Ohio. It attracted, so report runs, a good deal of attention as the earliest work of sculpture with a genuinely American theme, but it was never seen in the United States. Clevenger died before he could put it into marble and the clay figure has disappeared. Fortunately, though, we have an engraving (*Pl. 22*) made for the *United States Magazine and Democratic Review* (February 1843), where it accompanied an obituary eulogy of the sculptor and an announcement that subscriptions were being taken to purchase the Indian for the Mercantile Library of New York, a project which did not materialize. The *Indian Chief* of the engraving is a tall, stalwart, nude figure who holds in his right hand a bow, one end resting on the ground. Except for this and a tuft of feathers in his short straight hair there is little to suggest his race. We have no reason to think that Clevenger knew very much about Indians but the *Chief* is, nevertheless, a landmark, the first attempt to carve an Indian in marble. Americans had made Indians before but only in wood or iron, as figureheads or weathervanes.

The second modeler of Indians, Henry Kirke Brown, really knew something about them and did much to make them an accepted theme for sculpture in the United States. Brown first saw Indians in the Middle West when he was working as a railroad surveyor to earn his passage to Italy. He had been established in Cincinnati as a successful portrait painter—well trained in Boston under Chester Harding—when he discovered that his real bent was for sculpture. That art, he believed, required the Italian experience. Railroad surveying, which injured his health, did not provide the money necessary for the journey but the modeling of portrait busts in Albany did, with the addition of loans from some generous friends. Unlike most Americans, however, Brown did not find Italy at all to his taste. He seems to have been aesthetically at that point which many of the painters had already reached: he had a complete distaste for the neoclassical, combined with a strong desire to model what he actually saw in his own land. He spent four industrious years in Rome and dutifully turned out an *Adonis*, a *David*, a *Ruth*, a *Rebecca*; but he was glad to go home and soon after he reached New York, in 1846, he began to model Indians, working also, of course, at portrait busts and sepulchral monuments. He spent a good deal of time among the Indians of the Middle West, studying them, making drawings and wax models, and the statues and statuettes worked up from these sold well. *Choosing the Arrow* and the *Aboriginal Hunter* were distributed by the American Art-Union, to the pleasure of its subscribers, who liked the idea of patronizing distinctively American art. Brown's largest group was an *Indian and Panther*, the Indian killing the panther which has attacked his little son. As a further demonstration of his Americanism Brown devised a method of casting his statue in bronze. The fashion for Indians was definitely set and more and more American sculptors modeled them.

All these early Indians are, like Brown's, presented as heroic or romantic figures, sad occasionally, but never terrifying. The sculptors, few of whom had traveled the Oregon Trail or lived in the border settlements, seem to have accepted the conception of the noble savage. They made Indian hunters and Indian sages, Indian maidens (often called Pocahontas) and wounded Indians, but, in the first half of the century, only one really murderous savage. This is the Indian in Horatio Greenough's group *The Rescue* (*Pl. 2*), commissioned by Congress for one flank of the steps to the east door of the Capitol. A variety of accidents prevented *The Rescue* from being set in place before 1853 but as the commission was given to Greenough in 1840 his Indian may actually antedate Clevenger's.

Greenough's instructions were to make a group representing Settlement to balance Discovery on the other side of the steps, commissioned from the Italian sculptor, Luigi Persico. Though by training a thorough neoclassicist, Greenough had thought much about the theory of his art and was persuaded that the modern artist must not copy the Greeks but study them and "learn from them to be American." His group shows a frontiersman seizing from behind the arms of an Indian who is raising his tomahawk to strike the white man's wife and child; a dog, not greatly concerned, looks on. The "story" was approved but there was some criticism of the Indian as a slight and feeble creature. This seems to have been Greenough's intention; he wanted to show the superiority of the white race and his "Anglo-Saxon," as he called him, was much admired. The feeble Indian is at least far more realistic than the Italianate Indian maiden who accompanies Persico's Columbus in a pose suggesting a Polynesian hula.

Some of the other American sculptors shared Greenough's conception of the Indians as inferior creatures. They show them as a dying race though they feel some sorrow for their inevitable extinction. The group Crawford made for the Senate pediment of the Capitol included an Indian Chief (*Pl. 4*) which was often reproduced. The fine manly figure sits in deep despair, his elbow on his knee, his bent head resting on his hand; behind him are a squaw and a papoose; behind them, an open grave. Even the thoroughly classical Hiram Powers modeled, toward the end of his career, a fleeing Indian maiden which he called *The Last of Her Tribe*.

But Indians, after all, were not true representatives of the United States and the sculptors began to think about presenting real American citizens. The American by this time was thoroughly conscious of himself as a definite national type and he was proud of his individuality. His sense of freedom, the courage and energy essential to the kind of life he led had shaped some distinctive physical characteristics. The painters had been making recognizably American portraits even before the Revolution. Now the sculptors began to model busts and statues which were stamped with national character. Webster, Jackson, Clay could not be mistaken for Europeans. Greenough's Anglo-Saxon Rescuer was one of the earliest attempts at an "ideal" American figure and the idea pleased his countrymen. The Rescuer's features, said a writer in the *Home Journal*, "present, perhaps, the noblest type of native manliness that ever issued from

the imagination of the sculptor. They are thoroughly national
. . . . You would say at once, 'this person is unmistakably a native
American.' " The precise qualities of differentiation the critic did
not attempt to define but he felt the "inherent grandeur" of one
"whose destiny is to convert forests into cities; who conquers only to
liberate, enlighten and elevate." [1]

The London *Art Journal* recognized similar American qualities in
the figures in Crawford's pediment, where the dying Indians are
balanced by types of the enlightened conquerors. This critic, who
inspected the statues in Crawford's studio in Rome, wrote that the
Soldier drawing his sword was full of "untamed valor"; the two
Schoolboys had a *"go-ahead"* air about them; the Mechanic, who
leans upon a wheel, darted from his eyes "fiery energy" admirably
characteristic of "the fresh young life in the fecund West." [2] Crawford included also another important American type, the Merchant,
who sits upon a bale of goods and gazes at a globe.

A few single figures of which we have record present even more
typically American vocations. Henry Dexter, for instance, made a
Backwoodsman; Launt Thompson modeled a *Trapper;* and Rinehart used for supporters of the great clock in the Senate Chamber an
Indian and a white Hunter. Of other forms of labor there was some
celebration though not so much as one might expect in a country
which thought work so important. Louisa Lander was asked by a
wealthy patron to make for niches in his drawing room a Miner and
a Sailor, symbolic of the industries by which he had amassed his
fortune. The group which the state of South Carolina commissioned
from H. K. Brown for the State House at Columbia included workers in the rice and cotton fields. Just how these slave laborers were to
be related to the accompanying allegorical figures of Justice and
Hope we unfortunately do not know; the uncompleted group was
destroyed in the burning of the city in 1865.

The American types included also American angels. Both Erastus
Palmer and Franklin Simmons made Angels of the Resurrection
which have in their pose and expression nothing Greek or Gothic or
Renaissance. Nor do they resemble each other, except that both are
seated figures of vigorous young men. Palmer's Angel, who leans
forward intent upon what he is seeing, suggests qualities which were
recognized in the sculpture for the Capitol, "fresh young life,"

destined "to convert forests into cities." Simmons' Angel is more contemplative, a quiet hooded figure who, with his right hand, lifts the great cloak covering his head to look at wonder. Though the position of the arms is different, one is instantly reminded of Saint Gaudens' *Silence* and his Adams monument. Could he have taken from Simmons the suggestion of the solemn enveloping garment?

At female American types the sculptors tried their hands more slowly. Greenough's pioneer mother being rescued from the Indian is a special instance. Most of the American artists when they made female figures continued to work along the conventional Grecian lines, though they began gradually to give their ladies American names. Powers made a nude *California,* a divining rod in one hand, a thorn in the other, the thorn symbolizing the ill success of Powers' brother who had joined the Gold Rush. Haseltine made an *America Victorious;* Vinnie Ream, a *Young West;* Louisa Lander, a *Today,* crowned with morning glories and wrapped in the starry flag.

Most conspicuous of the sculptural figures was the colossal bronze *Armed Freedom* (*Pl. 5*) made by Crawford for the Capitol dome. The model of this statue seen close to is somewhat frightening but *Freedom* in her lofty dominance is impressive. Crawford calculated, or guessed, successfully the exaggerations and simplifications necessary for the angle from which she presides over Washington. In his original model he crowned *Freedom* with a Liberty cap, but Jefferson Davis,[3] then in charge of the work as Secretary of War, took exception to this because it is the badge of the freed slave and Americans had never been slaves. (There was certainly also some Southern apprehension here.) He presented his alternate suggestion, of a helmet, with much polite deference to the sculptor's desires and Crawford accepted it, fitting *Freedom* with a helm and crowning that with a tuft of feathers, like those worn by some Indians.

The practice of making allegorical American females began actually very early in the century. Some we know were made of wax, like the *Liberty* and *Justice* which flanked the figure of John Adams in the Columbian Museum in Boston. William Rush carved, in 1790, as the figurehead for the frigate *United States,* a *Goddess of America* who wore, on a chain about her neck, a medallion portrait of George Washington; in one hand she carried a spear; in the other, the Constitution. In the more serious medium of marble the

Italian sculptors of the Capitol produced a surprising number of symbolic ladies, *Agriculture, Art, Commerce,* and *Science* appeared in high relief over the entrance to the Hall of Representatives. *Justice* and *Fame* were in the Supreme Court Room. A spirited *Muse of History* rides in the winged chariot of Time to record the proceedings of the House of Representatives. One wheel of the chariot circles the dial of the clock. When, in 1825, an elaborate group was wanted for the east pediment, suggestions were invited from American artists and they sent in many, but President Adams was pleased with none of them. He opposed the idea of adorning a legislative building with emblems of heathen mythology or of military might. Finally Bulfinch, then the architect, contrived a group of three whose significance satisfied the President. In the center stands *America,* an eagle at her side; in one hand she holds the Constitution; with the other she points toward *Justice,* who, her eyes unbound, is gazing at her scales. On the left *Hope* leans upon her anchor. The moral, Bulfinch explained, is that "while we cultivate Justice we may hope for success," and he added that "an appropriate inscription would explain the meaning and moral to dull comprehensions."

This kind of manufactured mythology was carried almost as far as it will go by Randolph Rogers when he completed the Washington Memorial made by Crawford for the city of Richmond. For the six eagles Crawford had intended to set on the outposts of the monument Rogers substituted six small female figures. He called them: *Independence, Justice, Colonial Juries, Revolution, Bill of Rights,* and *Finance*—she holds a ledger. J. Q. A. Ward improved, perhaps, even upon this when he modeled a *Genius of Insurance.* Henry James, one sees, was scarcely exaggerating in *Roderick Hudson* when he had Mr. Leavenworth, the Ohio borax magnate, commission the young sculptor to make for his library "an allegorical representation of Culture."

The American landscape, which turned the eyes of so many painters toward their native habitat, had small effect, of course, upon the sculptors, though one does see its influence occasionally in details. Their attention was sometimes engaged by American flora and fauna. The most interesting sculptural use of indigenous plants is an early one, the corn and tobacco capitals designed by Benjamin Latrobe for the Capitol at Washington. In the vestibule of the

Senate wing he substituted for the usual fluted columns bundles of cornstalks bound with rope, with capitals of ears of corn, the husks partly open to show the kernels. These were skilfully carved by the Italian sculptors and the congressmen were more delighted by them than by "all the works of magnitude or difficulty that surround them." [4] So Latrobe wrote (28 August 1819) when he sent Thomas Jefferson the model for the "corncob capitals" to use as a dial stand in the garden at Monticello. Again, when he was supervising the rebuilding of the Capitol after the burning, Latrobe designed for the small rotunda in the Senate wing capitals in which the acanthus is replaced by the leaves and flowers of the tobacco plant. The model for these, too, went to Jefferson's garden.

American flowers and foliage are to be found also on mantels and moldings in some of the houses where American carvers worked during their apprenticeship, before they made bold to assume the title, sculptor. In most cases the artist's name is not recorded, but several fine houses in Baltimore boast that they have mantels by Rinehart. There are occasional American trees and flowers, too, on tombstones, another medium in which the young sculptor often learned his trade. John Frazee carved ivy leaves on his headstones and wild flowers from the New Jersey fields. Some of the ideal busts, Hope, Faith, Flora, Hesper, and so on, rise from wreaths of blossoms which any American should recognize. Larkin Mead crowned his reclining figure of *The Father of Waters* with tobacco leaves, pine cones, and water lilies and put in his right hand a stalk of Indian corn, from beneath which he peers at an alligator.

Birds for the nineteenth-century sculptor had none of the fascination they hold for the artist of the twentieth century. To the neoclassicist repose was an essential element in sculpture and birds are not at their best in repose. Eagles, though, it was essential to have in the national Capitol and Latrobe experienced difficulties here with his Italian sculptors. They had made plenty of eagles at home but those were stylized eagles bearing small resemblance to the great American bird. Finally the architect entreated help from Charles Willson Peale. One of his Italians, he wrote, in 1806, was modeling an eagle

but it is an Italian, or a Roman, or a Greek eagle, and I want an American Bald-eagle. May I therefore beg the favor of you to request one of your very obliging and skilful sons, to send me a drawing of the head and claws of the bald-eagle of his general proportions with the wings extended, and especially of the arrangement of the feathers below the wing when extended. The eagle will be fourteen feet from tip to tip of the wings, so that any glaring impropriety of character will be immediately detected by our Western members.[5]

With the Peale assistance the huge eagle in the center of the frieze of the House materialized without disturbing the Congressmen.

The next important American bird of which we have record is the great bittern which spouts water from the shoulder of William Rush's charming wooden *Nymph of the Schuylkill* (1809). The bittern was a true inhabitant at that time of the river's sedges. The doves and little birds which later accompany ideal maidens or portrait statues of children have seldom anything national about them.

In animals American sculptors seem to have had very little interest. The panther which Brown's Indian is killing is one of the few attempts to find an animal subject in the wilderness. There are some dogs and there are, of necessity, horses in the equestrian statues but not until the end of the century does anyone seem to have tried his hand at a bison. (Interestingly enough, there is an excellent bison in the "America" group on the Albert Memorial.)

The wood-carvers who made ship's figureheads seem to have been far more inventive. We have record of alligators and of American fishes made for the bows of the naval vessels named after them: a grampus, a dolphin, a shark.

Another source of native subjects the sculptors found in American poetry and novels. Edmonia Lewis combined poetry and Indians by modeling the *Courtship* and the *Wedding of Hiawatha*. Since she herself was Negro-Indian and had been brought up among the Chippewas, her details and accessories were accepted as interestingly authentic. Louisa Lander made an *Evangeline* sleeping on her journey and most spectators were moved, though *Harper's Magazine* (May 1860) thought that the figure had no character, was just any young woman asleep on the ground. Powers also made an *Evangeline*. Mozier modeled the heroine of Cooper's *Wept of Wish-ton Wish*, at the moment when she, brought up among the Indians, is trying to recall the Christian cradle hymn her mother used to sing.

The demand for American genre art which the painters were now supplying was harder for the sculptors to meet, but they managed. The New Englanders found good subjects in shipwrecks, though critics sometimes thought these groups too mournful. Brackett's *Shipwrecked Mother*, for instance, with her dead baby in her arm, was deplored for its sadness but also admired for its realism. It is supposed to present the precise moment when life has become extinct in the two bodies, and the Boston *Medical Journal* devoted a long article to its accuracy, advising its doctor-readers to study the statue for reasons quite other than aesthetic. Eventually the *Shipwrecked Mother* found an appropriate location on a grave in Mount Auburn Cemetery. More generally acceptable were Palmer's *Mariner's Wife*, seated on a rock gazing out to sea, and MacDonald's *Shipwrecked Boy*, clinging with one hand to the spar on which he sits and, with the other, waving his shirt as a rescue signal. Palmer also celebrated the frontier in his *Emigrant Children*, a small boy clinging to the arm of an older sister while they gaze at the skull of a stag.

A genre element was not infrequently introduced into portrait statues of children. The son and heir might appear as The Young Scholar, with a book, or The Young Musician, with a flute. Little girls were often shown with flowers or butterflies. Occasionally children played with dogs or kittens. Horatio Greenough even conceived the idea of showing two boys—life-size portraits—playing at shuttlecock. They stood on opposite sides of the drawing room and the freshness of the idea and the spirit of the composition were much admired.

Scenes from American history, which West and his followers had thought it right to add to their classical and biblical canvases, were almost outside the range of sculpture. Palmer proposed, to be sure, a Landing of the Pilgrims for a pediment of the Capitol but it was never commissioned. Congress rejected the idea, not, however, because they thought it unsuited to the medium but because it seemed too narrowly regional for a national edifice—America had other founders beside the Pilgrim Fathers.

American history was used extensively, however, by Crawford, Rinehart, and Randolph Rogers on the bronze doors in the Capitol. The intention was to emulate the small pictorial reliefs which make up Ghiberti's portals to the Baptistry at Florence. The American sculptors, however, thought it best to draw their subjects not from the Bible but from the history of the New World. Their little scenes have some of the qualities of John Rogers' Groups and visitors to Washington still study them with pleasure. Randolph Rogers' doors for the Rotunda showed scenes from the life of Columbus. Crawford, for the doors of the Senate, set War—Bunker Hill and other battle scenes—opposite Peace—Washington taking the oath of office, laying the cornerstone of the Capitol, and so on. Crawford also made designs for various scenes from American history for the doors of the House and these, after his death, were modeled by Rinehart.

Contemporary history was recorded in the memorials set up by cities all over the North after the Civil War. Many of these monuments followed a distinctively American pattern, set probably by Martin Milmore's monument on Boston Common. On a massive shaft rises an allegorical female figure, Victory or Liberty or the Republic. About the base, singly or in groups, stand Union soldiers and sailors, life-size or smaller. Sometimes there are bas-reliefs of allegorical figures or scenes of battle. The small town which could not afford one of these elaborate structures felt nevertheless that it must have a statue and set up one of those cast iron soldiers which have become an indigenous and touching element in the Northern landscape. Southern towns, as soon as they could afford it, set a Confederate soldier in the central square.

One of the most grandiose of American historical subjects was conceived, and executed, shortly before the Civil War by Henry Dexter, a blacksmith who became a highly successful maker of portrait busts. The power of Democracy, Dexter thought, might be gloriously illustrated by gathering in a great circle busts of the governors of all the states in the Union, dominated by a bust of the President of the United States. He had already modeled President Buchanan and he made a round of the state capitals, in each of which he was received with hospitality and enthusiasm. Only California and Oregon were too distant, he felt, to visit. All the governors Dexter saw consented to sit and he was able to present a panoramic portrait of American government in January 1860. The busts were exhibited in the rotunda of the State House in Boston and thirty thousand Americans came to study them.

More magnificently American still, though it took a long time to come to fruition, was the national Statuary Hall invented by Congress in 1864. When the House of Representatives moved in 1857 to its new chamber, the old semicircular room it abandoned was not designated for any particular purpose and became by degrees an untidy passageway and clutter hole. Sellers of apples and ginger-bread set up their stands there; idlers lounged and chatted; government bureaus with more files and equipment than they had place for found space for them against the curving walls. Eventually some energetic congressmen called it to public attention that the place was a disgrace and moved to restore the chamber to a condition worthy of its location. They conceived the idea of a Statuary Hall to which each State should be invited to send statues of two of its most illustrious sons, so that eventually there would be an impressive circle of American heroes—military, governmental, scholarly. The invitations were extended by the President and it was expected that inter-state rivalry would do the rest. But 1864 was not an auspicious moment for unnecessary expenditure. It was not until 1871 that the first statue arrived, from Rhode Island, *General Nathanael Greene,* modeled by H. K. Brown. Rhode Island's second worthy, *Roger Williams,* by Franklin Simmons, came in 1872. In that same year Connecticut sent its two representatives, *Jonathan Trumbull* and *Roger Sherman,* both modeled by a native son, Chauncey Ives. New York followed with *Governor Clinton* by Brown and *Robert Livingston* by Erastus Palmer, still the finest portrait statue in the collection. By 1880 a few more worthies had been added, from Massachusetts, Richard Greenough's *John Winthrop* and Anne Whitney's *Samuel Adams;* from Vermont, Larkin Mead's *Ethan Allen;* from Maine, *Governor William King* modeled by Franklin Simmons of Maine. But the ranks swelled slowly and it was not until the twentieth century that the growing number of states and their increasing readiness to expend funds on art began to overcrowd the semicircle.

None of these experiments and devices for the production of genuine American sculpture worked rapidly enough to satisfy the critics who were continually urging the sculptors on to be more national. There was a strong conviction that sculpture is a form of expression peculiarly adapted to the American temperament. Our youth, our energy, our delight in overcoming obstacles, the qualities which were subduing the wilderness, might well exercise themselves, it was thought, on granite and marble. Margaret Fuller considered it "perfectly natural to the American to mould in clay and carve in stone. The permanence of material and solid relief in the forms correspond to the positiveness of his nature better than the mere ephemeral and even tricky methods of the painter,—to his need of motion and action, better than the chambered scribbling of the poet." [6] Climate and race, James Jackson Jarves believed, worked to our advantage. "The fusion of bloods in our civilization, joined to the absolute freedom of the popular will to follow out its own convictions, is preparing a more favorable ground in America than exists elsewhere." [7] "Out of Yankee whittling," wrote *Harper's* Editor of the "Easy Chair" (February 1857), "comes American art. The department of art in which we are most famous is sculpture, and what is our sculpture but the flower of our whittling genius? Its great excellence is its mechanical perfection. It manipulates marble in a manner to have made Praxiteles fashion a statue of Joy. The great sculptors to-day are American sculptors." Charles Sumner, writing of Thomas Crawford as early as 1843 (*United States Magazine and Democratic Review*, May), prophesied that "The star of Art, perhaps, shall follow that of Empire in its western way. Already we see its mild effulgence."

As to just what form the American statues should take the writers were less clear. They were very sure that Greek myths and Greek gods held small interest for the Christian citizen of the United States but with what, beside Indians, should they be replaced? As the Reverend Samuel Osgood acknowledged (*Harper's*, August 1870), peace and democracy are not as easy to symbolize in marble as war and royalty. He had no suggestions about the creation of a new mythology but he felt sure that it would come.

The desire for a thoroughly American art produced one interesting phenomenon which has no parallel in Europe, the famous Rogers Groups. Whether these charming little plaster scenes are really "sculptural groups" as their maker called them is perhaps debatable today, but certainly within their self-imposed limitations they could hardly be better and the thousands of Americans who purchased them in the nineteenth century had no doubt at all that they were art. The critics praised them in the same terms they used for sculpture in marble. The National Academy of Design accepted them for its exhibitions and, in 1863, elected Rogers to membership. The English, too, took them seriously. It is said that Charles Reade, the novelist, purchased all eighty of them for his London mansion.

Even if this artistic judgment was not very sound the effect of the Rogers Groups upon the average American citizen was an excellent one. From them he learned not to be afraid of sculpture, to think of it as something natural and pleasant to have in the home. The men who could spend $4,000 for an ideal marble figure were few but thousands of Americans were quite able to lay out fifteen dollars, or even twenty-five, on a plaster group. And one did not need a mansion or a drawing-room to house a Rogers Group. Most of them were between twenty and twenty-four inches high; they rested comfortably on a marble-topped center table in the family sitting room or on a black walnut bracket fixed to the parlor wall. Rogers designed and sold these brackets, which he advised should, for the best effect, be set forty inches from the floor. A Rogers Group, a very correct wedding present, was often accompanied by a bracket to set it on.

Each of the groups tells a simple story, often mildly humorous. The old grocer, for instance, who is kindly *Weighing the Baby* (*Pl. 14*) on his counter scales, is amazed at what they register; he does not see that a mischievous older brother is tugging at the edge of the baby's blanket. A young lover who has made bold to clasp his lady's hand is alarmed by *A Tap at the Window*. A shy young couple are *Coming to the Parson*, whose cat is suspicious of the young man's dog. *We Boys* are riding a horse which has stopped to drink out of a brook. *The Photographer* and *The Pedlar* are characteristically engaged. There are scenes also from popular plays and books, *Courtship in Sleepy Hollow*, Joseph Jefferson as Rip Van Winkle, Edwin Booth as Iago or Shylock.

John Rogers (1829–1904) was by profession a draftsman and mechanic but his particular pleasure, in his spare time, was the modeling of little clay figures. In 1858 he decided to become a sculptor and went for study to Paris and Rome. The neoclassical lessons he learned there were so thoroughly distasteful that he abandoned his hopes of being an artist and returned to the United States. He took a drafting job in Chicago but a small group, *The Checker Players*, which he presented to a charity bazaar being held in the city attracted so much attention that he decided he could make a living by the kind of sculpture he wanted to do. He gave up his job, went to New York, and began to model and sell "sculptural groups" in wholesale quantities. In addition to the pleasure he took in the work he shared the contemporary desire to educate America in the arts. He was genuinely eager to put sculpture within reach of the average householder and he found a way to do it.

The figures were cast in plaster which was colored with an oil wash, usually slate grey or fawn. All the work had to be done by hand and Rogers carefully trained and supervised his workmen; before long he was employing sixty of them. Rogers patented each group so that his designs could not be pirated and distributed them through stores in New York and other cities. He also—a practice hitherto unheard of in the arts—ran a flourishing mail-order business. In all his work Rogers was insistent on quality. Again and again he declined to "publish"—his word for patenting and reproduction—a group which did not come up to his own standard of excellence, but between 1859 and 1892 he produced more than eighty groups and he sold eighty thousand copies.

Rogers was fascinated, as the genre painters were, by the details of everyday American life. He knew just what sort of chair would stand in a farmhouse kitchen, what kind of cheese would be on the counter of a country store, exactly how a young lady would dress for church. He solved easily the problems of costume which so often caused trouble for the sculptors in marble. The intricate details of waistcoat buttons and cravat, of ruffled basque and flowered bonnet, which in marble looked clumsy and absurd, acquired in plaster and in minia-ture a definite charm, and the unselfconsciousness and ease of his figures, who never seem to be posing on pedestals, lent a grace of composition and line. This came in part from Rogers' real knowledge of anatomy, in part from the fact that he worked from his friends and family more often than from professional models and did not so much pose them as watch them. He watched with the same keenness and discrimination the distinguished men of whom he sometimes made plaster portraits. His Lincoln, for example, in *Council of War* with Grant and Seward, sits in a natural and apparently character-istic position in his arm chair, one knee bent forward, his feet crossed, his eyes fixed intently on the map in his hands. We are not surprised to learn that Mr. Lincoln's family thought this a better likeness of the President than any of the formal monuments.

Rogers' skill with animals was built up in the same way, by the study of anatomy and by constant observation. He kept both horses and dogs on his New Canaan, Connecticut, farm and was genuinely fond of both. The horses in his life-size equestrian statues—he did some work in marble and bronze—are superior in vitality and grace to those of most of the contemporary makers of military monuments, who looked at horses only when they had to.

The Rogers Groups presented another type of subject not usual in sculpture—propaganda. Bronze and marble through the ages have celebrated causes after they have been won but are seldom directed toward their winning. We find arches commemorating battles, portrait statues of victorious generals, monuments to the heroic dead. These are intended to inspire pride and patriotism but not to incite to action. The idea that statues might help in political and moral reform was a thoroughly American one and Rogers was not the only artist who entertained it. Some of the sculptresses, as we have seen, made propaganda statues; so did a few Americans in Rome. The cause which precipitated Rogers' sculptural impulse was abolition.

The first group he offered for sale in New York, in 1859, was a little sculptural tract called *The Slave Auction (Pl. 14)*. It shows an auctioneer at a high desk on either side of which stand a Negro man and his wife with two small children. The stores in which Rogers had hoped to display *The Auction* declined to put it in their windows lest it offend their Southern customers; so, with his usual ingenuity, Rogers engaged a tall Negro to set it on his head and hawk it about the streets and at the doors of selected houses. This attracted the attention of some distinguished abolitionists and many copies were sold. Later Rogers made *Uncle Ned's School,* a Negro cobbler learning to spell out the Bible, and *The Fugitive's Story,* a slave woman, baby in arms, recounting her escape to Whittier, Beecher, and Garrison, excellent small portraits of all three. These groups were modeled after the war, so their interest was partly historical; but they were designed also to move the spectator to sympathy with the freedmen.

Often American sculptors were impelled by their neoclassical principles to put their propaganda into symbolic form. Anne Whitney's *Africa*, for instance, a neoclassical Ethiopia, is just rising from sleep; she shades her eyes against the breaking dawn. Story's *Libyan Sibyl* [8] was an imaginary portrait of Sojourner Truth, the extraordinary Negro woman who escaped from slavery and became a powerful abolitionist orator. When Harriet Beecher Stowe was in Rome in 1856 she breakfasted with the Storys and told them of her meeting with Sojourner Truth, imitating her wild prophetic utterances. This gave Story an idea for a statue which, he said to Mrs. Stowe, he would call the *Libyan Sibyl*. In 1860, when Mrs. Stowe was again in Rome, Story told her that the idea for his Sibyl was still working in his mind and asked her to tell him again of her meeting with Sojourner Truth. She told the story as dramatically as before and shortly afterwards he brought her his model of the *Libyan Sibyl*.

During the war Rogers made propaganda groups of a slightly different kind. He tried to encourage the soldiers' families to bravery and patriotism by giving them, to set in their homes, small battle pieces, *Sharp Shooters*, *The Picket Guard*, *Wounded to the Rear* (*Pl. 14*), and scenes from the daily routine of camp life in the Union army. The figures are always private soldiers and the groups have the same homely detail and simple humor that enliven *Weighing the Baby*. They show such scenes as *Camp Fire or Making Friends with the Cook*; *Card Players*, using a drum for a table; *Mail Day*, a youth struggling to compose a letter home.

We have brief record also of some propaganda on the Confederate side. Alexander Galt (1827–1865) of Norfolk made an ideal head of *Virginia* and another of *The Spirit of the South*, but they perished in the burning of Richmond. Albert Harnish made an equestrian *Lee* for Richmond; Robert Launitz, a Battle Monument for Frankfort, Kentucky; David Richards, a Confederate Soldier for Savannah.

The critics eager to welcome the development of an American art rejoiced loudly when, in the fall of 1856, the Palmer Marbles went on display in New York. Here at last was an exhibition of sculpture made entirely in America, not only modeled by an American who had never been to Italy but put into marble by American workmen trained in his studio in Albany. The exhibition was held in the hall of the Church of the Divine Unity on Broadway and sponsored by a committee of clergymen who were impressed not only by the beauty of Palmer's work but by its ennobling influence. Art critics had been saying for some time that it was ridiculous for Americans to make statues of Greek gods and goddesses since they did not believe in the Greek pantheon. However technically good their work might be it lacked the spirit of faith. Palmer's work had that spirit. It was colored by a deep religious feeling which seemed to his contemporaries to parallel the inspiration of the Greeks. Though not a member of any sect, Palmer was a devout believer in Christian principles so that his *Faith, Mercy, Supplication* expressed far more than the usual female head. And Palmer had another asset: before becoming a sculptor he had been an expert carpenter who worked by the craftsman's highest principles.

Except for his translation from local to world renown Erastus Dow Palmer's life was uneventful. He was born in Pompey, New York, in 1817. His father, a farmer, was not prosperous enough to allow him much schooling beyond his eleventh year when, being already a good carpenter, he began to add to the family income. At seventeen he left home to ply his trade in larger communities, settling finally in Utica, where his reputation as a craftsman rose steadily. He was in special demand for elaborate work like ornamental staircases.

When he was in his thirties Palmer saw for the first time a cameo portrait. It filled him with delight and he was eager to make one like it. The right kind of shell was not hard to procure but the tools and the method of cutting he had to improvise. Working slowly and carefully in his spare time he made a profile of his wife and when it was done it seemed to him good. He took it to a lawyer neighbor who was purported to be learned in matters of art. Tuckerman makes a dramatic incident of the little scene, using the words of the neighbor, although he does not give us his name.

"I took it from his hand, turned it to the light, and carefully examined the outline and finish. Little did I then realize the earnest feelings which agitated this new species of client; my surprise and delight were immediate. 'This,' said I, 'is beautiful; you have extraordinary talent.' Hearing no response, I looked from the exquisite medallion to the artist's face, and saw the tears of gratified sympathy in his eyes." [9]

Cameo cutting seemed to Palmer a much higher calling than carpentry and he pursued it with pleasure and success. When his reputation mounted he was asked to move to Albany, where he settled for the rest of his life. But after two years the delicate work began to tell seriously upon his eyes. Again he consulted the learned lawyer, who suggested that he transfer his skill to the larger medium of bas-relief. This he did with ease and after a time grew confident enough to try modeling in the round.

His first attempt at a statue, *The Dawn of Christianity*, was included in the New York exhibition of the Palmer Marbles and received enthusiastic praise. It shows an Indian maiden holding in her hand a little crucifix which she has found in the forest; her left hand clasps the feathers she has been gathering for her adornment; her blanket trails behind her on the ground. No one seems to have taken exception to her partial nudity.

The other pieces in Palmer's New York exhibition were bas-reliefs and medallions with such titles as *Spring, June, Infant Ceres, Infant Flora, Sappho, Hope, Mercy, Resignation.* The occasional classical name represented no classical influence. Of Grecian statues Palmer knew nothing. He worked directly from live American models, often his own daughters, one of whom was probably the model for his best known and most charming work, *The White Captive* (*Pl. 11*). This is a nude young figure bound by her wrist to a stake, waiting the pleasure of her Indian captors. By pose and title she invites inevitable comparison with the *Greek Slave* and illustrates strikingly the difference between the artist under neoclassical influence and the artist working from "nature." Modern taste prefers the American maiden and so did many of her nineteenth-century critics.

But Palmer, though he had no desire for European training in his art, was acutely aware of the defects of his education and worked hard to overcome them. He made and followed systematic plans of study and had his wife read aloud to him while he worked. He liked solid books full of facts or ideas, and also the novels of Dickens and Thackeray because they taught him so much about the human emotions he wanted to depict in marble.

The New York exhibition spread Palmer's reputation far beyond his native state. Particularly gratifying was a letter asking him to exhibit his work in Boston for it was signed by such distinguished names as Everett, Sparks, Agassiz, Longfellow, Prescott, Lowell. Commissions began to come in in pleasing numbers. Palmer, who was fond of Albany, did not want to move to a larger city; soon after the war he built himself a big house with a well-planned studio where his work could be efficiently put into marble. Tuckerman wrote a glowing account of the place, so like the best studios in Rome and Florence, and rejoiced that such a home of art could now be found in the United States.

When he was fifty-six Palmer did finally go to Europe and spent two years there. During part of the time he worked on the statue of *Chancellor Robert Livingston* which New York State had commissioned for Statuary Hall, and had it cast in bronze in Paris. It is a pity that he did not set down his impressions of the Grecian statues and of life in Rome, but he was not a writer. The only printed pronouncement we have of his is an essay in *The Crayon* (January 1856) on "The Philosophy of Art." In this he expresses, as he seems often to have done in conversation, his distrust of art schools. Their tendency, he thought, was to stereotype students, blurring their individuality. He saw no reason why other serious artists should not teach themselves as he had done.

Palmer performed yet another service for American art in the wide distribution of his work through pictures. Photography, which would eventually spoil the market for portrait busts, was in its early years a real asset to sculpture, presenting it in a form which could be inexpensively enjoyed at home. Photographs of Palmer's religious statues and medallions adorned, like Rogers Groups, many middle-class parlors. Most frequently reproduced was *Faith*, made first as a bas-relief and then as a life-size statue for St. Peter's Church in Albany. A beautiful young woman, clad in a long graceful robe, stands with clasped hands, her eyes turned upward toward a cross. For modern taste she is perhaps a little sentimental but Palmer's contemporaries found it inspiring to gaze at her in moments of trial. She was capable of teaching them not only religious trust but a good deal about beauty of line. So many of Palmer's marbles were photographed that a German art critic who had never seen the originals was able to write an enthusiastic article about them for the Berlin *National Zeitung* (20 November 1865). It is a bit of American luck that these two thoroughly American figures, Rogers and Palmer, were both skilful workmen so that the admiration for their statues excited by their unsculptural qualities actually advanced the education of Americans; while it taught them to appreciate artistic virtues, it satisfied their growing desire for statues with American themes.

8

Patrons, Public and Private

On the morning of New Year's Day 1857 the citizens of Brattleboro, Vermont, were astonished to see, standing at a road-fork opposite the school house, a great white angel, majestic and serene. In his
right hand he held a stylus; in his left, a tablet; he seemed to have
just finished recording Brattleboro's record of sin and virtue for the
year. So carefully was the eight-foot figure shaped and modeled that
it seemed to be carved in marble but, looking closely, one saw that it
was made of snow, new-fallen on New Year's Eve. It did not take
long to discover that the Angel was the work of young Larkin Mead,[1]
clerk in a Brattleboro hardware store and full of ambition to become
a sculptor.

For two weeks, in the good Vermont cold, the Recording Angel
stood at the road-fork. His great wings were crossed about his feet;
his eyes turned toward heaven; on his shoulder perched a dove. The
people of Brattleboro took pride and pleasure in his presence and
spread wide the news. The local paper published a full description
and some of the big city dailies sent reporters to Brattleboro. The
story in one of these came to the attention of a Cincinnati millionaire
who was interested in art and believed ardently that the young
United States ought to have more sculptors. Nicholas Longworth
thought that a young man who could model an eight-foot snow Angel
might be of real service to America. He wrote the Brattleboro postmaster and asked for information about the artist.

The postmaster's reply was encouraging. Larkin Mead was the
son of a respected lawyer. He had a satisfactory job in a hardware
store but wanted to make statues. Two years ago a visitor to the
Water Cure—Brattleboro had a famous one—had seen the young

man working at odd moments behind the counter, cutting a pig out of Vermont marble. He suggested that Mead ought to have training, and a place was found for him in the New York studio of H. K. Brown, who was working then on his *Washington* for Union Square. When Larkin Mead came back to Brattleboro after a year and a half he opened a drawing school in the Town Hall, but so far none of his fellow townsmen had ordered any statues. This may have been what the Angel was recording on his tablet. Longworth was pleased by the postmaster's story. He wrote Mead and gave him his first commission: a marble replica of the snow Angel.

Longworth's artistic gamble was a good one; it launched Mead on a successful career. In 1863 he went to Florence and lived there most of his life but he made statues for America: the colossal *Vermont* for the Capitol dome in Montpelier, *Ethan Allen* for Statuary Hall in Washington, a *Lincoln* monument for Springfield, Illinois, and many others, including a later version of the *Recording Angel* (*Pl. 23*) for All Souls' Church in Brattleboro.

Longworth's action was characteristic of the man himself and of the early American patron of sculpture; he not only assisted aspiring young artists, he encouraged them to aspire. His interest was aroused not so much by the quality of the work a man was doing as by the fact that he wanted to be a sculptor. The patron was proud to be able to co-operate in the advancement of American art.

Longworth was one of the most interesting and picturesque of these co-operative patrons. (His less interesting, though not undistinguished, grandson who carried on the name became Speaker of the House of Representatives.) The first Nicholas Longworth made his fortune in a typically nineteenth-century American fashion. Brought up in Newark, New Jersey, and trained in the law he had, when he was twenty-one, gone out to Cincinnati, then, 1805, a raw village of eight hundred inhabitants. He completed his legal education in the office of Judge Jacob Burnet. His first case was the successful defense of an alleged horse-thief who paid him with two copper stills. Longworth swapped the stills for thirty-three acres of land most people thought were worthless. But the city grew in that direction and before long the thirty-three acres were valued at two million dollars. A little later Longworth bought the Judge's cow pasture for $5,000, on instalment. Pretty soon it was worth a million and a half. The story goes on like that. Eventually Longworth was paying the highest realty taxes in the country next to W. B. Astor's. He was reputed to be a merciless creditor and given to sharp legal practices but he did enjoy giving away a good deal of the money he made and was, apparently, a likable person—Longfellow, for instance, was a friend—and he had a genuine desire to do service to the young nation.

This service took two forms, the patronage of art and horticulture. By the time Longworth was forty he was able to retire from the law and devote himself to the occupation he most enjoyed, the raising of grapes and strawberries. With the berries he made some valuable experiments but his great contribution was the successful making of Catawba wine. His concern here was partly moral; he believed that the heavy drinking in which too many Americans indulged could be modified by the substitution of wine for hard liquor. His sparkling Catawba and Isabella became popular and he has gone down in history as one of our leading horticulturists. His position on wine drinking was not, perhaps, thoroughly consistent, for much of his charity took the form of assistance to drunkards, thieves, and other members of the undeserving poor. "You must," he said to one of many scandalized neighbors, "find giving money only to those who are irreproachable citizens, a very economical method. . . . My charities are for the Devil's poor, because I am the only man in the city imprudent enough to help them." [2] Longworth distributed weekly, for instance, some five hundred loaves of bread to anyone who asked for them and had over his wine cellars barracks where poor laborers were allowed to sleep rent free. Very lawless and noisy they were.

The Longworth house was a huge one with plenty of space for paintings and statues but collecting was not Nicholas Longworth's chief method of advancing art in America. He preferred to encourage sculptors. Before his discovery of Larkin Mead he had become interested in a Cincinnatian, Shobal Clevenger, who was working in a marble yard and trying his hand at portrait busts in his spare time. Longworth made it possible for Clevenger to attend anatomy classes at the State Medical College and in 1840 lent him money for the journey to Italy, encouraging him to make visits first to Boston, New York, and Philadelphia, where he received numerous commissions for busts. Clevenger died of tuberculosis when he had been in Florence less than two years but he had already progressed well in his profession. He had real skill with the chisel and a serious desire to make each bust as "true" as possible. His *Everett, Clay, Van Buren,* and especially his *Webster,* were, Tuckerman tells us, "more widely circulated and popularly esteemed in the form of plaster casts, than any other works of the kind executed among us." [3]

Longworth's most spectacular protégé was an earlier discovery, another Cincinnati boy, Hiram Powers. He was, when Longworth became interested in him, making wax figures for Dorfeuille's Museum but he aspired to work in marble. Longworth offered to help him and their relationship grew into a real and lasting friendship, as Powers' correspondence indicates.

Before Powers was ready to go to Europe Longworth lent him assistance for a long stay in Washington. There Powers found, or rather was found by, two other patrons, the Prestons of South Carolina. Senator William Campbell Preston was much impressed by his busts of prominent statesmen and wrote of him in enthusiastic terms to his brother, who lived near Columbia. John S. Preston, a lawyer, had made a comfortable fortune from a Louisiana sugar plantation and was using a good deal of it to buy pictures and statues. He believed, like Longworth, in the cultivation of sculptors. Though he had never seen Powers or any of his work he accepted his brother's estimate and wrote the young man to draw on him for a thousand dollars to finance his journey to Italy, and to continue to draw anually for the same amount until he was well established in his profession. He invited the sculptor to come to Columbia before his departure to take busts of him and his wife.

Ten years after Powers went to Italy a discovery of sculptural talent was made in Baltimore by William Thompson Walters, merchant and railroad president. He was having some repairs done on a marble mantel in his house and was struck by the ability of the young workman sent for the job. He found that William Henry Rinehart [4] had ambitions to become a sculptor and immediately offered to help him. The details of the discovery, the patronage, and the life-long friendship vary in family memories but Walters certainly financed the second, if not the first, of Rinehart's journeys to Italy, gave him commissions for busts and monuments, took charge of his investments, and acted as executor of his will.

Rinehart's career, once launched, was a flourishing one. He became highly fashionable in Baltimore and across the country as a maker of portrait busts and he received several important commissions from the Federal Government so that he left, when he died, a substantial fortune. He had no family and arranged therefore, remembering what Walters' assistance had meant to him, that his money should be used to help young sculptors who wanted to study abroad.

Happy as Walters was to forward the career of Rinehart, his chief interest was not, like Longworth's, the discovery of sculptors. He was primarily a collector, but a collector with patriotic motives: he purchased statues and paintings not merely for his own pleasure but for the edification of his fellow citizens. He opened the galleries in his house from time to time to the public and after his death his son enlarged the collection and built the Walters Gallery for the city.

Some of the patriot collectors wanted only works by the great artists of the past; others desired to foster American talent and made a point of buying from American artists. One of these who was particularly interested in sculpture was W. W. Corcoran of Washington, whose gallery, opened in 1874, exhibited statues by Hart, Mills, Rinehart, and Powers. Corcoran usually bought the work of established artists but occasionally he lent a hand to a beginner. John Sartain, the engraver, tells us, in *Reminiscences of a Very Old Man*, that in Rome in 1863 he suggested to Corcoran that a small commission to a man just beginning to make his way might often work more good than a high price paid to a successful artist. Sartain was interested at the time in Larkin Mead, who had just arrived in Rome and he persuaded Corcoran to order from him a figure of *Echo*, which proved a good investment.[5]

Sometimes a patron became interested in sculpture because of his interest in an individual, rather than the other way about. Wayman Crow of St. Louis, for example, concerned himself with the career of Harriet Hosmer because she was a school friend of his daughter and impressed him by her serious determination to make statues. He helped her get instruction in anatomy, gave her her first commission, saw her through some financial difficulties, and managed her business affairs for her as long as he lived.

From whatever direction they began, the relationships between American sculptors and their patrons seem to have been singularly happy. The artists were able to combine gratitude and affection with independence and self-respect because, like the patrons, they felt that they were working for the good of the country. This is nowhere more apparent than in the correspondence of one of the earliest patrons of an American sculptor, James Fenimore Cooper. He made the acquaintance in Florence, in 1829, of Horatio Greenough, some twenty years younger than he, and became much interested in him both as an artist and as a friend. He gave Greenough his first commission for an ideal statue, made some important connections for him with distinguished clients, and stood behind him financially again and again. His letters are models for this sort of relationship.

> [Paris, 1 March 1833] I have no doubt that you will get the statue and the necessary price. . . . In the meantime, I am yet flush and can only say, if you want—"Lay on Macduff, and damn'd be he who first cries, Hold enough." [6]

> [Paris, 13 June 1833] I made a little memorandum on the subject of the 1600 francs, and it shall now be erased. As to any charges &c, that is quite out of the question. A trifling loan to a friend must not be dealt by like a broker's account— [7]

Even if he did not have much money a patron could sometimes be an effective friend to a sculptor. One of the most conspicuous examples is Charles Sumner,[8] the distinguished orator and abolitionist Senator. Sumner, while still a young man with only the promise of eminence, made the European journey in 1839 and in Rome was introduced by his friend W. W. Story to Thomas Crawford. Sumner was much impressed by the quality of Crawford's work and by his character and the two became fast friends. He did not have the means to give Crawford a commission but he lent him his energy and his persuasive tongue and pen. Sumner talked about Crawford to everyone he met; he insisted that travelers should visit Crawford's studio; he wrote about Crawford at length to his friends at home; and even, reluctantly, let Crawford make a bust of him because he was told that it would be helpful to the aspiring artist. When Sumner returned to Boston he personally solicited subscriptions to the amount of $25,000 to purchase for the Athenaeum one of Crawford's earliest ideal works, *Orpheus*. There were many delays in getting the statue into marble and across the Atlantic but when it at last arrived Sumner saw to it that it was well exhibited and that not only Boston but other sections of the country were made aware of its presence. Since the Athenaeum's rooms at that time were not properly lighted for sculpture he persuaded the society to build in their garden a little house where *Orpheus* could stand against a good background and under proper illumination. He talked constantly about the exhibition and wrote a laudatory article on it for the *United States Magazine and Democratic Review* (May 1843). His propaganda was effective. Crawford's reputation mounted rapidly and he received important commissions from the Federal Government. All through Crawford's life, cut short at forty-four, Sumner continued to help him by his friendship and his vigorous enthusiasm.

Though his intimacy with Horatio Greenough, whom he met on the same trip to Italy, was not so close as his friendship with Crawford, Sumner admired both the man and his work, his literary work as well as his sculpture, and did much to make him known to his countrymen.

For his closest artist friend, William Wetmore Story, Sumner campaigned with no less vigor but with much less success. Even after Story had made an impression in England it was long before he built an American reputation and few public commissions ever came to him. Sumner tried, unsuccessfully, to have Boston order from Story their statue of Horace Mann (made eventually by Emma Stebbins). He spoke eloquently in the Senate [9] on Story's behalf when, in 1866, a statue of Lincoln for the Capitol was under consideration, and was angry when the commission went to the pretty, engaging, totally inexperienced Vinnie Ream.

Less directly concerned for the cultural welfare of the country yet not totally unmindful of it were the wealthy men who commissioned works of art primarily for the adornment of their own homes. There were hundreds of these, chiefly at first on the eastern seaboard but eventually all across the country, even to California, where a group of railroad tycoons ordered statues from Rinehart. Many of these gentlemen, of course, bought some art works which were not quite so fine as they supposed. While criticism and connoisseurship were in their infancy it was not difficult to procure in Italy a "genuine" Titian or Murillo, even a Raphael, but Greek and Renaissance statues were not so easy to come by. The collector of sculpture was obliged to content himself with casts and copies or to patronize contemporary artists. He might think it more elegant, or more financially shrewd, to give his commissions to European sculptors, and fashion set now and then in that direction, but a good many rich Americans preferred to buy from American artists. They ordered portrait busts of themselves and their wives; they had life-size statues made of their little daughters; they wanted an ideal figure or two for their drawing rooms and for their libraries busts of some of the great men of the past and of contemporary clergymen or statesmen whom they admired. It is curious, but not incomprehensible, that they bought more when they were traveling than they did at home.

Some of these purchasers chose their art objects with knowledge and taste. Others were concerned only to follow the fashion and to make as good a display as possible. There are many satiric accounts of the uncouth, uneducated patron looking for a bargain. Every American sculptor in Rome seems to have entertained his friends with at least one story of a grotesque visitor to his studio. The uncouth patron is usually made to speak an extraordinary dialect, intended, apparently, to indicate that he is ill-educated and comes from the Middle West. He says "ain't" and "yourn," and "Gosh" and "Dew tell." He is in a great hurry because he has so few days to devote to Rome. He is boastful about his money and his previous art purchases and eager to make as good bargains in marble as he is accustomed to making in wheat and cotton. Sometimes he only looks and does not buy. Thomas Ball, for instance, in his autobiography, presents a specimen whose talk runs this way:

"We haven't much time to waste; we're just looking round a bit among the studios to see how prices range. What do you ask for that? . . . How much is that? Seems to me you're pretty stiff in your prices. They sell the real Carrary marble statues, over on the other side of the Arno, for about a quarter part as much as you charge, and they look pooty well, too, I tell you. Well, we must be off." [10]

Hiram Powers told a similar tale of a Tennessee visitor which a *Harper's* correspondent, Katharine C. Walker, set down in an article on "American Studios in Rome and Florence" (June 1866). The conversation ran like this:

> "Only just come to town!" said he; "had to wait in Paris to get my gallery packed. Bought a whole gallery of Old Masters— paid fifteen hundred dollars for 'em, too! How much is that statoo worth?"
> "Two thousand dollars."
> "My stars! Why I bought one t'other day for two hundred dollars, and it ain't plaster neither; for I drew my jack-knife right across her nose, and it never made a scratch."

Yet often the untutored visitor had a heart of gold, a delight in seeing a countryman prosper in a new field, and a disarming readiness to admit his lack of knowledge. Freeman, for instance, reports in his *Gatherings from an Artist's Portfolio* on a visitor of Crawford's who concluded a tour of the studio by clapping the sculptor on the shoulder and telling him that

> "I like that air image you are making in mud there; it's real cute and sweet, I tell you. I ain't no great shakes in judgin' of these air sort of things, but I guess that boy a-prayin' is *A, number one.* That's *my* opinion. When I git back hum, I shal tell our folks of the elegant effigies I have seen in your place; and I'll get somethin' put into the newspaper of our destrect tew." [11]

Henry James's borax merchant in *Roderick Hudson* is a slightly more sophisticated member of the same tribe.

Sometimes the wealthy citizens worked in concert for the advancement of sculpture. Early in the century, 1802, a group of rich New Yorkers established an institution which they thought would be of real value to art. They called it the American Academy of Arts and hoped that it might improve American knowledge and taste by exhibitions of casts from the antique. The idea had originated with Robert Livingston while he was Minister to France. He had some casts made from originals in the Louvre, which included at that time, thanks to Napoleon, many statues from Italy, the *Apollo Belvedere*, for instance, the *Venus of the Capitol*, the *Gladiator*, the *Laocoön*. A wave of curiosity when the casts were first shown brought many visitors, but interest soon waned and after a time the casts were placed in storage. In 1816 an attempt was made to revive the Academy, a good gallery was found and a number of pictures borrowed to add to the interest of the exhibit. Again there was a flash of public enthusiasm which quickly died. The art students, however, of whom there were now a considerable number in New York, were eager for the opportunity of drawing from the casts. Unfortunately the succeeding president, John Trumbull, was a gentleman-artist of the old school who had scant sympathy with the impecunious rising generation. In refusing to make arrangements easy for them he uttered one more of his famous infelicitous phrases: the students must remember that beggars cannot be choosers.

At the suggestion of S. F. B. Morse the artists then began to help themselves by organizing a Drawing Society, which grew before long into the National Academy of Design. Morse was familiar with the organization and practices of the European academies and saw to it that this society should provide the two things the artists most wanted: instruction in technique and opportunity to display their current work. The National Academy grew and flourished. Its first exhibition, held in 1826, though it was well attended, did not meet expenses; ten years later the annual exhibition brought in four thousand dollars. The Academy added to its good works the sponsorship of William Dunlap's *History of the Arts of Design in the United States* (1834), a record which is still invaluable for the period.

The success of the National Academy roused the jealousy of the American Academy, which made, in print, some bitter attacks on the new institution. Fortunately Morse was not only calm in combat but an excellent polemical writer so that the artists were usually in the ascendant during the many years of controversy. In 1841 the American Academy expired and the National Academy (which still goes on) bought its casts at auction.

The history of the Philadelphia group, inspired by New York's example, is less violent but not dissimilar. In 1805 some patriotic citizens organized the Pennsylvania Academy of Fine Arts, stating that its object was "to promote the cultivation of the Fine Arts in the United States of America, by introducing correct and elegant copies from the works of the First Masters in Sculpture and Painting." The Academy purchased land, erected a building, and in 1806 presented an exhibition of paintings by West and a few others with fifty casts from the antique selected for them by Nicholas Biddle, then Secretary of the Legation in Paris. This pleased the artists but did not satisfy them. They wanted the opportunity to exhibit their own work and they wanted schools to give instruction in anatomy and techniques. In 1810 they organized the Society of Artists of the United States. A union with the Academy did not seem feasible, but they were granted most of its privileges. In 1811 the combined forces for art held the first of the annual exhibitions which were later to offer many of the literary sculptors their first opportunity to secure recognition. Relations between the Academy and the Society were complex and stormy. The business and professional men, the patrons, who controlled the Academy felt certain that they knew better than the artists what the artists needed; the artists were not so sure. Eventually the Academy admitted enough artists to its board of directors to make the balance even, the Society disappeared, and the Academy vigorously survived. So important did it become that when, in 1845, its building was destroyed by fire a new and better collection was rapidly assembled by local generosity. Classes were organized and the annual exhibitions of contemporary work continued to excite interest and offer opportunity. The Academy's present building was dedicated at the time of the Centennial celebration of 1876.

From gifts of individual patrons and of the Academies and Art Associations municipal museums began to grow. Most of them burgeoned after the Civil War, though a few had made their start early in the century. By the time of the Centennial a number of cities in the North and Middle West were priding themselves on art collections of some kind. Casts from the antique and paintings imported from Europe were usually the foundation of these galleries but many citizens were genuinely interested in contemporary American art; they bought it for their collections and liked also to hold exhibitions of recent work. Of one of these collections of casts which grew into an important museum we have a detailed and interesting record, Mabel Munson Swan's *The Athenaeum Gallery, 1827–1873.*

At the time of the society's incorporation, 1807, Mrs. Swan tells us, the founders of the Boston Athenaeum expressed the intention of making it not only a library but also a repository for productions in the fine arts which might work toward "the correction and refinement of taste." The collection of books came first, however, and it was not until 1823, when this outgrew the original small quarters and was moved to the James Perkins house on Pearl Street, that an art gallery became practical. Then it was possible to display Stuart's portrait of Perkins and a collection of casts which had been presented to the Athenaeum by Augustus Thorndike. There were eleven casts in the collection, eight full size and three small, and about forty busts, two of them in marble. The casts included such recognized masterpieces as the *Apollo Belvedere*, the *Laocoön*, the *Venus di Medici*, the *Gladiator*, which Boston artists rejoiced to have the opportunity to draw. By 1839 the collection of both paintings and statues had been so much increased by gift and purchase that a special sculpture gallery was arranged and annual exhibitions of sculpture inaugurated. Eighty pieces, many of them lent from private collections, were displayed in the first of these. Soon work by American sculptors began to appear in the gallery and the Athenaeum records indicate that statues by almost every important American sculptor were exhibited there at some time; many were purchased for the permanent collection.

In 1851 the Athenaeum moved to a new building on Beacon Street where arrangements were made for a sculpture gallery opening from the entrance hall. By 1864 the library had grown so extensive and was so much used that it was decided to confine the Athenaeum's interest to books and to establish a separate Museum of Fine Arts. In 1876 the Museum was opened to the public on Copley Square. The Athenaeum had presented its casts and some of its larger statues, but many of the works by American sculptors still stand in the Beacon Street building.

The average citizen who could not afford to assist museums and academies or to purchase a statue for himself and yet wanted to advance the cause of art was able to play patron to the sculptors in a variety of small ways. He could, to begin with, do a little inexpensive purchasing, for often when a marble bust was made of some great man small plaster replicas were put on public sale; occasionally there were reproductions, in plaster or Parian, of some of the ideal statues, and Rogers Groups cost only twenty-five dollars.

The average man could also visit a statue when it was put on exhibition, and he did, with enthusiasm. He paid for the privilege, too, usually twenty-five cents, sometimes fifty. Occasionally an artist exhibited a number of his works together, the Palmer Marbles; sometimes only a single statue, the *Greek Slave*, but the art-lover thought exhibitions of either kind well worth a visit and often stayed for hours, admiring, analyzing, and discussing a new work.

Often purchasers of statues were ready to give the artist permission to exhibit a work for his own benefit before he made final delivery. The motives here were probably a mixture of pride and patriotism. The owner was pleased to have it known that he possessed so fine a work of art but he felt also that he was doing good to his fellow-citizens by giving them the opportunity to look at sculpture. Harriet Hosmer's *Zenobia*, for instance, purchased in 1865 by Almond Griswold, was shown by Mr. Griswold at a private reception in New York and then exhibited in public to some thousand visitors. The statue went on to Boston, Miss Hosmer's home ground, where curiosity about it was so great that the exhibition lasted for several weeks and was attended by more than seventeen thousand people. Some of these had cards of invitation but at least two-thirds, it was estimated, paid their way, to the sculptress's considerable profit. Several replicas of the statue were ordered, one by Mrs. Potter Palmer of Chicago, who exhibited it publicly there, another by Robert K. Emerson of Boston, who presented it to the St. Louis Museum of Fine Arts.[12] The famous tour of Powers' *Greek Slave* took place by permission of the purchaser of one of the replicas. Mr. James Robb of New Orleans granted Powers the right to exhibit the *Slave* for his own benefit but eventually quarreled bitterly with Powers' agent over which of the replicas then in America was to be assigned to him. He finally brought suit, obtained the version he wanted, and put it on exhibition in New Orleans for his own profit.

Another form of patronage the average citizen could exercise was to become a member of one of the Art-Unions.[13] These interesting, though short-lived, institutions flourished greenly during the forties and were credited with doing much to advance public interest in art. They marked, as Tuckerman put it, the era when art, "emancipated from the care of Kings and Popes, finds sustenance by alliance with commerce and the people." [14] The Union functioned as a sort of co-operative lottery. The idea originated in France and was adopted in both Germany and England before it was tried in America. The subscriber to a Union paid an annual fee, usually about five dollars, for which he received a statuette or an engraving and the privilege of sharing in the annual distribution by lot of works of art. To the great benefit of the artists the Unions purchased annually scores of paintings, engravings, and statues, putting them on public exhibition before the final distribution was made. Hundreds of visitors flocked to see them and members inspected them carefully, hoping that they might draw this piece or that. The night of the lot drawing was a festive social affair, full of talk and excitement. Not all the emotions aroused, perhaps, were aesthetic but at least art became genuinely interesting.

The Art-Union idea was introduced in New York by the Apollo Gallery, a co-operative association of artists. In a time of financial depression it had not been very successful in selling the work of its members. In 1839 it tried the lottery method and a few years later became the American Art-Union, which grew and flourished under directors who were well-to-do business men eager to promote American art. The American Art-Union *Bulletin*, started in 1848 and sent to all members, was the first American art journal; the free gallery, open from April to December, had in a year a quarter of a million visitors; annual subscriptions, which came from all over the nation, amounted at their peak to sixteen or eighteen thousand, so that the Union could purchase and distribute each year several hundred works of art. And the American Art-Union inspired the organization of Unions in other parts of the country—Boston, Philadelphia, Chicago, Trenton, New Jersey, and, in Cincinnati, a very successful Western Art-Union. Some proprietors of galleries also organized Unions for their own profit, interesting a still wider public though the American Art-Union directors regarded these commercial organizations with some skepticism.

The National Academy of Design, which wished to control artistic standards, fought the American Art-Union from time to time with varied success. Its members felt that the Union's businessmen directors were wrong in their policy of buying almost exclusively American works of art, that they were encouraging too many incompetent artists, and that they paid too little for everything they bought. Compromises were worked out but the Unions did not long survive. A somewhat extraneous issue destroyed them. The American Art-Union had granted an advertising favor to the *Times* which roused the jealousy of Bennett, who, in his *Herald*, accused the Art-Union directors of corruption. When they sued for libel he had the suit thrown out on the ground that the Union was an organization which promoted gambling. The lottery element in the Union's organization had been a frequent cause of discussion and criticism which this incident brought to a head. State laws against lotteries were invoked and the Unions, one after another, faded away. The artists and many others regretted them; they had done good work for the cause.

Probably the purest patriotism displayed by any art patrons actuated those groups of citizens who banded together to erect in their community a memorial to some great man. The intelligence, the efficiency, and the taste of these groups varied widely, but they coincided in the conviction that a statue of their hero would perpetuate not only his fame but his example, influencing for good the men and women who passed it every day. We still owe them gratitude for a number of admirable monuments in different sections of the country. Brown's Union Square *Washington* is a good example.

Some of the results of group patriotism, even though they did advance the cause of sculpture and give employment to an artist, were not altogether happy artistically. Consider, for instance, the statue of their hero projected by the Ladies Clay Association of Richmond. Who might make the monument they wanted the ladies did not know until they heard that one Joel Hart [15] was in their city taking busts. He was a Kentuckian with a high reputation at home because he had a knack for catching a likeness and because he had been permitted to model Andrew Jackson. That he was a stonecutter, just turned sculptor, who had never made a full-length figure did not trouble the Ladies Clay Association at all. They asked Hart to model a life-size statue of Henry Clay and offered him five thousand dollars. The Association was delighted by the care the sculptor took to get an exact likeness, even to the clothes, though somewhat disappointed in the length of time his easy-going disposition required for the completion of the statue, a matter of thirteen years. Nevertheless the unveiling was a great event and Hart promptly received orders for replicas, at ten thousand dollars each, from the cities of New Orleans and Louisville. The head of this statue has some quality but the body, in its accurately baggy trousers, looks to the modern eye rather ridiculous. On this one commission, the replicas, and busts of

Clay which he made whenever funds ran low, Hart lived happily in Florence all the rest of his life. He seems to have been a kindly and agreeable man though certainly not a vigorously working artist. His posthumous fame, and the cause of sculpture, were promoted by another organization of ladies, this time in Louisville. Hart's chief occupation while he enjoyed life in Florence had been a group called *Woman Triumphant*, in which a graceful girl holds an arrow just out of reach of a not very interesting Cupid. Hart never completed this work. "Why, my friend," he used to say, "it takes God Almighty eighteen or twenty years to make a perfect woman; then why should you expect me to finish one in less time?" He was quite ready, however, to show the group, so far as it had progressed, to studio visitors and critics, who were astonishingly enthusiastic. After Hart's death in 1877 a group of admiring ladies in Louisville raised enough money to have *Woman Triumphant* cut in marble and set up in their city. (It was later destroyed by fire.)

At a very different level of taste and knowledge were two organizations which gave commissions to Thomas Ball. He tells the stories in *My Three Score Years and Ten*.[16] Not long after the Civil War—he was living then in Florence—Ball received a letter from the Reverend W. G. Eliot of St. Louis saying that he remembered with great interest a small model Ball had shown him a few years ago of Lincoln and a freed slave. He thought it precisely the design the Freedmen's Memorial Society were seeking for the monument they wished to erect in Washington. Ball sent photographs and specifications, with which the Society were much pleased. They wrote that they would like to commission him to make the statue in bronze, nine feet high, if he could do the work for the sum they had at their disposal; it was much smaller than the price such a piece of sculpture should command but every penny of it had been contributed by freed slaves. Ball accepted the commission at once.

The other society of which Ball writes presented to the city of Boston his statue of *Washington*, usually agreed to be one of the best equestrian statues in the country. For several years there had been talk in the newspapers and on public occasions that Boston "owed it to herself," as the *Journal* put it, "to erect in some public square a memorial of Washington." In 1859 Ball showed to some of his friends a model of an equestrian Washington on which he had been working for his own pleasure. It seemed to them very fine. Some meetings were held and it was finally determined that the artists of Boston should undertake its erection. A great fair was decided on as the best means of raising money and the artists' lady friends—the nineteenth-century lady was expert in fair organization—rose to the occasion. The fair was held in November in the Music Hall and was a thorough success. Merchants contributed goods; artists contributed pictures; twelve thousand dollars were raised. This Ball accepted and began making the large model for the statue. The outbreak of war delayed its casting, for the foundry at Chicopee was making guns, and besides it was not considered patriotic to attempt to raise the necessary additional funds, but in 1868 the *Washington* was completed. The city made a grant toward its casting in bronze and the Everett Statue Committee contributed its surplus. On 3 July 1869 *Washington* was unveiled in the Public Gardens. The artists had become effective patrons of art.

Sculpture in this new era was patronized not only by private citizens but by many institutions as well as by the government. Associations like the Boston Athenaeum and the New-York Historical Society wanted for their collections busts of great Americans, Revolutionary and contemporary. Colleges ordered portrait busts of their presidents and distinguished members of the faculty. The students of Dartmouth College, for instance, commissioned from Thomas Ball a bust of President Lord. The students of Harvard asked Thomas Crawford to make them a bust of President Quincy.

Even business was beginning to think of itself as a patron of the arts. The *Bulletin* of the American Art-Union announced with pleasure in April 1851 that the Messrs. Appleton, publishers, who were building a new store on Broadway, had commissioned from H. K. Brown a bronze bas-relief to be set over the door. The five-foot relief, when it was completed, attracted much admiring attention. It showed a sage reading from an ancient volume to a group of fascinated young people.

To the credit of business also, perhaps, should be set the action of the New York wholesale drygoods merchants who employed Randolph Rogers as a clerk. That young man had ambitions to be a sculptor and did much modeling after business hours. He made busts of some of his employers' children which so delighted them that they told him he ought to leave their employ and go to Italy for study—and they lent him the money for the journey.

Public commissions for statues came more and more frequently as the century advanced. Cities and states awarded them as well as the Federal Government and they were much sought after for they were well paid and added greatly to an artist's reputation. Some of the fees—ten thousand, twenty thousand—seem large, but it must be remembered that the artist had to furnish the large block of marble, pay many workmen, and devote most of his time for several years to a statue. The earliest state commission was, as we have seen, North Carolina's, in 1816, for a statue of Washington. That did not go to an American sculptor, for there was none, but most of the later state commissions did, especially when they could be given to a native son. Missouri's *Thomas Benton*, for instance, was made by Harriet Hosmer, a native daughter by adoption; Vermont's *Ethan Allen*, by Larkin Mead of Brattleboro; Maryland's *Justice Taney*, by W. H. Rinehart of Baltimore. And cities were even more interested in monuments than were the states, especially after the Civil War. Morton Milmore, for instance, made soldiers' monuments for Claremont, Keen, and Peterborough, New Hampshire; Randolph Rogers was commissioned by both Providence and Detroit to make granite memorials fifty feet high. And the cities did not confine their admiration to military heroes. Brooklyn asked J. Q. A. Ward to make them a statue of *Henry Ward Beecher;* Portland, Maine, placed Franklin Simmons' seated figure of *Longfellow* in the center of an important public square.

Congress, too, was eager to give commissions to Americans as soon as there were Americans capable of executing them, but the choice of which American was always a difficult matter. Sometimes a friend of an artist, or the friend of a friend, introduced a bill granting a particular commission to him. This was the proceeding with Vinnie Ream and the *Lincoln* for the Capitol. Sometimes the selection of the artist was left to the architect or even to the engineer in charge of the construction of a building, as happened frequently with the Capitol; sometimes a committee was appointed to find the right man, with occasionally curious results.

One of the most fantastic of the commission committee stories concerns the choice of a sculptor for the equestrian statue of Andrew

Jackson which Congress decided should be placed in Lafayette Square.[17] The chairman of this committee was the Honorable Cave Johnson, Postmaster-General, who apparently had no idea how to go about the duty assigned to him. He was delighted, therefore, by a chance introduction to a young man on his way to study sculpture in Italy on funds provided by some wealthy gentleman of South Carolina who admired the bust of Calhoun he had made for the city of Charleston. Clark Mills was a Yankee who had drifted about the country doing a variety of jobs until he landed in Charleston as a stucco worker. There he tried his hand at portrait busts and found that he had a knack for molding clay and for catching a likeness which brought him plenty of orders. Finally he attempted to cut a marble bust of John C. Calhoun. He had no instruction of any kind but he succeeded so well that admirers of the statesman thought it the best likeness of him they had ever seen. The city council of Charleston purchased it from Mills and presented him with an honorary medal of praise. A group of wealthy gentlemen in the city decided that this young artist should study in Italy and agreed to finance his voyage. The Prestons, Hiram Powers' patrons, suggested to him that before sailing he should inspect the statues in the national capital. When Mills hesitated over the cost, John Preston offered to finance his trip and pay him beside for busts of his friends Crittenden and Webster which he might make while he was in Washington. Confident and happy, Mills went North, visiting on the way Richmond to inspect Houdon's *Washington*, the first statue he had ever seen. In the national capital he was enchanted by the statuary and more than ever determined to become a sculptor. He was particularly impressed by Franzoni's *Car of History*, which adorned the clock in the Chamber of the House of Representatives; he thought it sublime.

The Postmaster-General was pleased to meet this budding sculptor and almost immediately asked him if he would undertake to make a bronze equestrian statue of General Jackson. Mills, with becoming modesty, declined; he had never seen Jackson and he had never seen an equestrian statue. The Postmaster-General, however, quieted his scruples and Mills produced the first American equestrian statue (*Pl. 12*), which, if not a work of great value to American art, is certainly a monument to American mechanical ingenuity and resource. Mills thought it important that Jackson's horse be a spirited creature and devised a means of balancing him, rearing, by setting his hind hooves directly under the center of his body. This feat of equilibrium excited the admiration of Congress and of the majority of the inhabitants of Washington when the statue was unveiled in 1853. Mills's reputation soared. A few of the more sophisticated critics and journals cried out in horror at the ungainly trick which made the horse a good deal more conspicuous than the diminished General, but it was years before public opinion came to agree with them.

Actually far more remarkable than the balancing of the quadruped was the casting of the statue in bronze. Mills had to design and build his workshop, train his workers, try again and again with cranes that broke and furnaces that burst, until the statue emerged. An appreciative government added a grant of $20,000 to the $12,-000 they had agreed to pay. Then they awarded Mills another commission, $50,000 for an equestrian statue of *George Washington.* Mills was later entrusted with the casting of Crawford's colossal *Freedom* for the Capitol dome.

By the middle of the century the artists themselves were eagerly advocating competitions for congressional commissions, a practice usual abroad and employed not infrequently in the United States by municipal governments. There was agitation, too, for a Fine Arts Commission which should have jurisdiction over all art in the Capitol. A faint-hearted attempt to set up something of the kind was made in 1859 when Congress authorized a commission and President Buchanan appointed J. R. Lambdin, the portrait painter, J. F. Kensett, the landscapist, and H. K. Brown, the sculptor. The artists were pleased by the selection and hopes ran high that something useful for American art might be accomplished. The Commission went to work at once discussing the "art principles" which should govern the decoration of the Capitol, commenting on pictures and statues already in place, drawing up a list of what seemed to them appropriate and desirable additions. In about a year they presented to Congress recommendations for commissions which would total some hundred and fifty thousand dollars. The Senate, however, voted to limit the appropriation for the completion of the Capitol to "the work necessary to complete the building, exclusive of painting and sculpture." Since there would be, then, no employment for the Art Commission during the next year they recommended that it be suspended or abolished. "The causes of the repeal of the law providing for the Art Commission," said *The Crayon* (August 1860) bitterly, "are characterized with the coarseness, ignorance, and cunning, which are always brought into play in all matters, when government aid and protection are sought. They are due both to the craft of politicians, and to the impassive state of opinion in relation to the arts that prevails throughout the country."

Philadelphia, 1876

The Centennial Exhibition of 1876 taught Americans many things about their country of which they had not been aware. What the United States had produced and accomplished in the hundred years of its existence was spectacularly demonstrated in the buildings which sprang up all over Philadelphia's Fairmount Park and stood there from May till November.

Most conspicuous and impressive, of course, of the demonstrations was the industrial progress of the nation, the invention, production, and distribution of a wide range of goods and machines which were transforming the country's whole way of life. It was the possibility of understanding some of these, or at least becoming aware of them, which brought to Philadelphia thousands of people full of curiosity and excitement. But the visitors were impressed also by another demonstration which they had not anticipated, the extent of America's interest and accomplishment in the fine arts. That it was so great astonished many. Even the men who planned the exhibitions underestimated seriously the amount of space they would require for the display of pictures and statues.

This was the more impressive since the original plans were large. The works of art, national and international, were exhibited in Memorial Hall, one of the small number of buildings designed for permanent use by the city. Memorial Hall, it was proudly announced, was completely fireproof; it was built of granite, brick, glass, and iron; not a piece of wood in it. The architecture was "modern renaissance," a parallelogram relieved by square towers at each of the four corners and surmounted by a four-sided dome of glass and iron. The building was 365 feet long, 210 feet wide, and 59 feet high. It stood on a terrace and there was a good deal of external statuary so that the whole effect was striking.

The Director-General of the Exhibition, General A. T. Goshorn, had appointed, when he took office in 1873, an Advisory Committee on the Fine Arts but it was not until September 1875, eight months before the Exhibition opened, that he named as Chief of the Bureau John Sartain, the Philadelphia engraver, who proved to be energetic and fertile in ideas. Sartain discovered at once that the space allotted for painting and sculpture, large as it was, would be quite inadequate to house all the exhibits that were offered, so work was immediately begun on an Annex which practically doubled the available space. A third building was devoted to photography. In addition to putting up the Annex Sartain devised several ingenious methods of increasing wall and floor space. In Memorial Hall he had each gallery divided into three sections by removable partitions on both sides of which pictures could be hung. In the Annex he insisted that doors be placed, not as usual in the center of the wall, occupying one of the most effective spaces for the display of pictures or statues, but in the corners of the rooms. Sartain announced with pride in his report that the pictures exhibited made a band two and a half miles long and that the statuary occupied 10,962 square feet of floor space. Six hundred seventy-five pieces of sculpture were exhibited, of which 162 were American.[1]

There were other statues beside those exhibited in the galleries. Many of the ornate buildings were adorned with statues, usually made of cast iron. Memorial Hall itself was one of the richest in such decor. In front of it stood two enormous, and identical, bronze figures of Pegasus. The dome was surmounted by a colossal Columbia and surrounded by figures representing the four quarters of the globe. On the corners of each tower great eagles spread their wings and screamed. In the doors to the main gallery were set panels bearing coats of arms of the states and the pilasters between the doors were crowned by "emblematic designs illustrative of science and art."

In addition to such architectural ornaments a number of statues were set up to serve as rallying points for special groups. Organizations not large enough or rich enough to erect a building wanted a place where their members from different parts of the country might meet each other and wanted, too, some way of demonstrating to the nation their purposes and their accomplishments. A good means, they thought, was a statue. The Presbyterians, for instance, set up a figure of John Witherspoon, eminent scholar and divine, signer of the Declaration of Independence, and President of the College of New Jersey (Princeton). It was made by Joseph Bailly, who was born in Paris but had worked in the United States since the Revolution of '48. The Catholic Abstinence Association declared its purpose by a colossal fountain of marble and granite. Moses towered in the center surrounded by Catholic worthies: Charles Carroll of Carrollton, Archbishop Carroll, Commodore John Barry, and Father Matthew, the "Apostle of Temperance." The sculptor was Herman Kirn, a young Philadelphian trained in Germany. The Italian-Americans had a statue of Columbus, made in Italy, which they presented to the city of Philadelphia. The Order of B'nai B'rith erected an eight-foot monument to *Religious Liberty*. It was made in Rome by Moses Ezekiel of Virginia.

Inside Memorial Hall the sculpture was arranged by nations. Each foreign country was made responsible for the selection and placing of its own works of art. The Commission simply allotted the amount of space each nation asked for. The American entries were passed on by a Committee of Selection, which held sessions in New York and Boston as well as Philadelphia. Many of the states arranged to pay for the shipment to Philadelphia of the work of their artists. In Europe the Committee of Selection had deputies with whom the Federal Government co-operated by sending a ship to transport across the Atlantic paintings and marbles executed by American artists. This was a great benefit to the Americans with studios in Rome or Paris and a pleasant indication that the Government thought their work important to the nation.

Sartain was well content with the number and quality of the works sent from abroad, especially from England, and with the showing made by the American entries; visitors to the Exhibition flocked to Memorial Hall; but the judges appointed to evaluate the fine arts had many reservations to make in their report. The whole question of award or prize giving had been much debated during the planning of the Exhibition. None of the methods employed earlier in expositions in London, Paris, or Vienna seemed desirable to the Commissioners. The Crystal Palace system of prizes awarded by a jury had produced so many complaints and charges of undue influence that Prince Albert recommended that in future exhibitions the whole idea of awards be abandoned. Compromises tried in France and Austria had not proved very effective. Finally the Americans decided not to have juries but judges who should not make comparative estimates but simply cite such works—of art or of manufacture—as seemed to them to have especial excellence. Each citation was accompanied by a medal and a statement: "Commended for artistic excellence in sculpture of the bust"; "Commended for artistic excellence in the fine art of sculpture."

The judges' report, signed by their chairman, John F. Weir, Director of the Yale School of Fine Arts, was outspokenly critical of deficiencies and omissions in the exhibits.[2] The judges thanked Britain for her generous contribution of pictures and expressed their special pleasure that she had sent, in addition to contemporary work, some of her famous eighteenth century paintings, but they did not hesitate to register their regret that the British exhibit in sculpture was "slight," most of it by "deceased sculptors." "At the present time," they concluded in explanation, "England possesses no sculptors of more than average ability, nor is a susceptibility to pure form a national characteristic." They made no comment on the large British piece which Sartain had set up as the central object in the main gallery, directly under the dome, though this interested the public greatly. It was a terracotta replica of the *America* group, bison and all, from the Albert Memorial. Sartain surrounded it with some of the most important American statues in the exhibition.

The French exhibit, the judges said, reflected "some of the merits which are widely realized in French sculpture," particularly the attempt "to infuse into it the spirit and sentiment of modern life." The German exhibit they thought "not important." The Italian exhibit was very large but consisted chiefly of genre sculpture so the impression made on the judges was "not a favorable one." There was much display of intricate chiseling, they said, but little in the work that was vitally sculpturesque so that the collection, on the whole, was "frivolous and unimpressive." Other countries which exhibited paintings sent no sculpture.

With the United States exhibit the judges were frankly disappointed.

> In sculpture the American exhibit was not satisfactory. Many of our most prominent sculptors failed to participate, and the character of the display was that of being composed of odds and ends, with here and there an occasional work of decided merit. . . .

> The exhibit of sculpture, on the whole, lacked order and arrangement: the works were scattered, and were seldom to be seen to advantage. Nor was there any evidence of an attempt to illustrate the progress and present condition of this art in the United States, of which an interesting exhibit might well have been made.

Of the forty-three citations made for sculpture, only five went to the United States, though the American exhibit was larger than that of any other country except Italy. Two of the judges' choices have small significance: Isabella Gifford and Montague Handley are names which were seldom heard again, but the other three are interesting. Among the established sculptors whose work was well known about the country the judges chose to distinguish, indicating, it would seem, their concern for American subjects, John Rogers, who sent the complete set of his Groups, and Erastus Palmer, who showed his bronze *Robert Livingston* made for Statuary Hall. The other citation went to Howard Roberts of Philadelphia, who had studied in Paris at the École des Beaux-Arts. Roberts' *La Première Pose* attracted as much attention as anything in the Exhibition. The young model crouches on her throne, her legs drawn up and twisted tensely together, her arms trying vainly to shield her face and breast. She is a pretty creature and her extreme modesty is a comfort to the hesitant spectator; it makes him feel that he is not really looking at a nude. The workmanship is excellent.

Of the pioneers who produced the enthusiastic American interest in sculpture only a handful, as the judges complained, sent statues to Memorial Hall. Some of these artists were dead, some old, and some had achieved such solid reputations that it did not seem worth while to add to them. Those who did appear were welcomed by the public. Story's *Medea*, intending the murder of her children, excited continual interest. She stood in the circle about the Albert Memorial group. Story sent also his *Cleopatra, Semiramis,* and *Libyan Sibyl.*

Gould exhibited his *West Wind;* Ives, *Infant Bacchus;* Rinehart, *Latona and Her Children* *(Pl. 11)* ; Edmonia Lewis, her curious *Cleopatra,* shown at the moment of her death, a somewhat macabre piece which many viewers found distasteful. Margaret Foley's fountain was placed in Horticultural Hall but the group around the Albert Memorial contained her head of *Cleopatra.* Randolph Rogers sent *Atala, Ruth,* and his famous *Nydia (frontispiece).* Few of these were new works but there were many Americans who had never seen them.

Among the works of the rising generation the judges commented on the "very clever model in plaster" of D. C. French's *Minute Man,* but to another new name in the catalogue, highly interesting to modern eyes, they seem to have paid small attention. Augustus Saint Gaudens exhibited a statue and two busts: an excellent portrait of Senator William Evarts and a head of Admiral Farragut, made several years before the award of the commission for the memorial. The statue was *Hiawatha,* Saint Gaudens' first ideal work, made in Rome when the German advance in 1870 had forced him to leave Paris. The seated nude figure, in a pose of contemplation, has a quiver of arrows and a few other attributes by which his race may be distinguished. He is, Saint Gaudens tells us in his *Reminiscences,* " 'pondering, musing in the forest, on the welfare of his people,' and so on. This accorded with the profound state of my mind, pondering, musing on my own ponderous thoughts and ponderous efforts." [3] This, certainly, is as literary a subject as one can imagine though it is an American literary subject, not a neoclassical one, and there is nothing neoclassical about Saint Gaudens' Indian. The technique is the strong, competent work of a Beaux-Arts student. One saw here, as one saw in the work of Howard Roberts, that French training could have its effect on an American. After 1876 Italy ceased to be the land of the sculptor's dreams.

Whatever the quality of the work they looked at, whatever the reluctance of the judges, the curiosity of the visitors was admirable. They not only walked in a continuous stream through Memorial Hall and the Annex examining and discussing the works of art, they went back again and again to study certain paintings or statues which particularly interested them and they seemed to learn from experience. The lively reporter for *Potter's American Monthly* (October

1876) who thought the visitors the most interesting part of the Exhibition, estimated that at least 90 per cent of them had had no previous acquaintance at all with works of art. It took them some time to learn to distinguish plaster statues from marble but they did learn and they also became increasingly interested in the *nudo*.

> Nude paintings and statuary, at first slightly peeped at as it were over the shoulder are, on a second or third visit, looked over, studied, and their anatomical merits and demerits, the correctness and incorrectness of drawing, perspective, coloring and shading, all discussed by couples and groups of minors and adults with the utmost zest and evident enjoyment.

And when these enthusiastic visitors went home they purchased for their parlor tables elaborately illustrated volumes of Gems and Masterpieces of the Exhibition.

In the twenty years after the Centennial the increase in the number of sculptors and works of sculpture in America was very large. It was not so necessary now to have ideal figures in your drawing room and photographs were replacing portrait busts but cities were feeling more and more that memorials to their great men were essential indications of prestige and statues were springing up everywhere in streets, in squares, in parks. It came to be taken for granted that any public building, a court house, a city hall, a library, a museum, would have some external statuary, not only reliefs on the pediments but standing figures on the steps or portico. Business concerns, too, began to think that statues were an excellent way of indicating their importance. What the precise relationship should be between architecture and sculpture was not very thoroughly understood but at least it was accepted that a relationship was desirable. There was work enough for many mediocre sculptors as well as for the group, still small, of the really competent. Not all of this enthusiasm, of course, produced important art, but the work of the second generation of sculptors made some definite advances beyond that of the pioneers.

The most striking quality possessed by the second generation was their technical competence. They went to Paris, subjected themselves to the rigorous Beaux-Arts training, and emerged equipped to carry out whatever they could imagine. They had broken entirely free, too, of the neoclassical bonds. They could find their models in nature and in American nature. They seem, though, to have been quite as "literary" as their predecessors. One wonders why the opprobrious epithet is never attached to them. What is French's *Death and the Sculptor?* What are Saint Gaudens' floating females? What are Bartlett's *Columbus* and *Michael Angelo?* As a matter of fact the literary element continued in American sculpture well into the twentieth century. It did not really disappear until the abstractionists took over. And as for the element of Industrial Revolution allegory, it is worse in the second generation of sculptors than in the first because there is more of it. No work in the middle nineteenth century proliferated literary symbolism so violently as MacMonnies' Columbian Exhibition fountain, though Barnard's groups for the Harrisburg Capitol ran it a close second.

Critics of the post-Centennial day liked to compare with the Philadelphia Exhibition the decoration of the grounds and buildings in Chicago in 1893. There were statues everywhere in Chicago, more statues than any American had ever seen at once before and the total effect was a lively flamboyance which delighted the public and set the tone for the Exhibition.

Saint Gaudens, who made suggestions for the work and directed it, took pride in its co-operative nature and the fact that not since the days of Michelangelo had so many sculptors labored together on a single project. The artists seem to have been perfectly ready to work in "staff," a compound of plaster and jute fibre, which they knew could not endure for more than a few months. It gave them opportunity, though, to model ideal figures, elaborate allegorical groups, and picturesque structures for which they seldom found any demand in the less holiday world. Succeeding exhibitions blossomed with statuary in the same extravagant way.

That this second generation of sculptors was so vigorous and so flourishing they owed, far more than most of them realized, to their forerunners, the American pioneers. To only a few of the literary sculptors did the second generation pay any real attention. William Rinehart they admired; he was a classicist but he seemed to be working in the new day. J. Q. A. Ward they looked up to as an older colleague and leader. Augustus Saint Gaudens wrote of him: "His work and career, his virility and sincerity, have been a great incentive to me, from the day when he exhibited his 'Indian Hunter' at an art store on the east side of Broadway. It was a revelation, and I know of nothing that had so powerful an influence on those early years." [4]

This was admirable gratitude but it was narrow and it did not go back far enough; it took no account of the men who had made the work of Rinehart and Ward possible. The second generation of sculptors, conscious of their superiority, and exaggerating it, were inclined to look down much too complacently on the artists who had prepared the way for them. They did not begin to realize the importance and the extent of what the literary sculptors had accomplished in fifty years. Actually what the literary sculptors did for the country was comparable in many ways to the exploits of their brothers, the western pioneers. Each group tamed and civilized a wilderness.

The literary sculptors grew up in a country which knew nothing at all about statues, where most of the inhabitants had never seen one, not even a cast, yet, by the time of the Centennial Exhibition, there were statues up and down the land, monuments in squares and parks and cemeteries, marble figures in drawing rooms and gardens, busts in libraries and churches, works of sculpture in the museums which now stood in many of the cities of the North and even of the Middle West. States, cities, and private citizens had come to believe that money for statuary was well spent. They had learned that statues are difficult to make and must, in consequence, be well paid for. They had learned something, too, about their aesthetic qualities. They had some ideas about grace and proportion, many ideas about subject matter, and a growing impression that a nude statue is not necessarily obscene. Laymen not only flocked to museums and to exhibitions, they read about sculpture and talked about it. Weeklies and even daily papers were giving space to art notes and art criticism. Most of this writing, to be sure, was descriptive and laudatory rather than critical, but at least statues were being considered as though they were important. The literary sculptors had taken also the first steps toward genuinely American sculpture. They had experimented successfully with American themes and figures, adding them to the Greek and demonstrating to their countrymen that the New World had artistic subjects of its own.

The literary sculptors, too, had made the practice of their profession much easier for their successors. They themselves had been obliged to go to Italy for their training, for models, for workmen, for marble. Now there were many studios in the United States where techniques could be learned and expert criticism received. American marble was being discovered and quarried. A few Americans had learned how to cast in bronze. "Art life," too was beginning to flourish in a small way. The country had still much to learn about what the artist needs in his environment but the sculptor was no longer regarded as an eccentric or an impractical dreamer; the profession was recognized and any talented young man might be encouraged to enter it.

Gratitude to the literary sculptors should have been expanded, too, to include their patrons. Some of these men, of course, wanted sculpture only for their own aggrandizement. The statue in the garden, the bust in the library niche marked them, they thought, as men of wealth and culture, but the mere fact that they thought so added to the prestige of the art, as well as to the income of the artists. And there were many patrons who encouraged sculptors to model primarily because they believed it important for the United States to have statues.

It is for this especially that we owe gratitude to our pioneers. They were convinced that sculpture is an essential and a possible American art. They believed that, whatever the obstacles, it must develop and flourish, enriching American life. If the young United States needed statues, they would make them for her. These literary sculptors were thorough-going nineteenth-century Americans; it did not occur to them that there might be anything they could not do. They set to work as pioneers and cleared the trails. By 1876 the settlers could come in.

Notes

Chapter 1. Causes

1. Henry James, *A Small Boy and Others* (New York, 1913), p. 270.
2. Henry James, *William Wetmore Story* (Boston, 1903), II, 76.

Chapter 2. Rome

1. Margaret Fuller Ossoli, *At Home and Abroad* (Boston, 1856), pp. 375–377.
2. Henry James, *Foreign Parts* (Leipzig, 1888), pp. 167–168.
3. Nathaniel Hawthorne, *The Marble Faun* (Boston, 1889), I, 139.
4. *Harriet Hosmer, Letters and Memories,* ed. Cornelia Carr (New York, 1912), p. 211.
5. James E. Freeman, *Gatherings from an Artist's Portfolio* (Boston, 1883), II, 138.
6. C. E. Stowe, *Life of Harriet Beecher Stowe* (Boston, 1889), p. 300.
7. Carr, p. 32.
8. Rose Hawthorne Lathrop, *Memories of Hawthorne* (Boston, 1897), pp. 363–364.
9. Freeman, II, 216.
10. C. Edwards Lester, *Artists of America* (New York, 1846), p. 186.
11. Thomas Ball, *My Three Score Years and Ten* (Boston, 1891), p. 176.
12. H. W. Bellows, "Seven Sittings with Powers, the Sculptor," *Appleton's Journal,* II (1869), 470.
13. Carr, p. 27.
14. Henry James, *William Wetmore Story* (Boston, 1903), I, 102.
15. A. J. C. Hare, *The Story of My Life* (London, 1900), VI, 288.
16. Carr, p. 284.
17. William S. Rusk, *William Henry Rinehart, Sculptor* (Baltimore, 1939), p. 36.
18. *Ibid.,* p. 37.
19. James, *Story,* I, 108.
20. *Ibid.,* I, 134.
21. *Ibid.,* I, 137–138.
22. G. S. Hillard, "Thomas Crawford: A Eulogy," *Atlantic Monthly,* XXIV (1869), 51.
23. R. E. Launitz, "Reminiscences of Thomas Crawford," *Crayon,* VI (1859), 28.
24. Hillard, p. 53.
25. Thomas Hicks, *Eulogy of Thomas Crawford* (New York, 1865), p. 18.
26. George W. Greene, "Crawford," *Biographical Studies* (New York, 1860), pp. 138–139.
27. Quoted by Hicks, p. 24.
28. Robert L. Gale, "Thomas Crawford, Dear Lou, and the Horse," *Virginia Magazine of History and Biography,* LXVIII (1960), 175.
29. Hillard, p. 54.
30. James, *Story,* I, 266.
31. *Ibid.,* I, 299–300.
32. *Ibid.,* I, 298.

33. *Ibid.,* II, 71.

34. Nathaniel Hawthorne, *Passages from the French and Italian Note-Books* (Boston, 1883), pp. 442–443.

35. J. J. Jarves, *Art Thoughts* (New York, 1870), p. 311.

36. Mary E. Phillips, *Reminiscences of William Wetmore Story* (Chicago, 1897), pp. 203–204.

37. James, *Story,* II, 67–68.

Chapter 3. Florence

1. *Appleton's Journal,* I (1869), 342.

2. *Memoirs of Margaret Fuller Ossoli,* ed. R. W. Emerson and others (Boston, 1884), II, 216.

3. Henry James, *William Wetmore Story* (Boston, 1903), I, 245.

4. Henry James, *Charles W. Eliot* (Boston, 1930), I, 149.

5. T. A. Trollope, *What I Remember* (New York, 1888), p. 345.

6. *Memoirs of . . . Ossoli,* II, 311.

7. N. P. Willis, *Pencillings by the Way* (New York, 1852), p. 301.

8. *Letters of Horatio Greenough to His Brother Henry Greenough,* ed. Frances Boott Greenough (Boston, 1887), p. 117.

9. James, *Story,* I, 266.

10. *Journals of Ralph Waldo Emerson,* ed. E. W. Emerson and W. E. Forbes (Boston, 1912), VIII, 318.

11. William Dunlap, *History of the Rise and Progress of the Arts of Design in the United States,* new ed., ed. F. W. Bailey and C. E. Goodspeed (Boston, 1918), III, 225.

12. Horatio Greenough, *Travels, Observations, and Experiences of a Yankee Stonecutter,* by Horace Bender (pseud.), facsimile reproduction (Gainesville, Fla., 1958), p. 37.

13. H. T. Tuckerman, *Book of the Artists* (New York, 1867), p. 254.

14. Dunlap, III, 214–231.

15. *Ibid.,* III, 226.

16. *Correspondence of Carlyle and Emerson,* ed. C. E. Norton (Boston, 1883), II, 219.

17. Dunlap, III, 226.

18. *Ibid.,* III, 230.

19. H. T. Tuckerman, *Memorial of Horatio Greenough* (New York, 1853), p. 38.

20. *Letters and Journals of James Fenimore Cooper,* ed. James Franklin Beard (Cambridge, Mass., 1964), III, 220.

21. Tuckerman, *Book of the Artists,* p. 261.

22. Nathalia Wright, *Horatio Greenough* (Philadelphia, 1963), p. 229.

23. Tuckerman, *Book of the Artists,* p. 268.

24. Greenough, *Yankee Stonecutter,* p. 187.

25. Nathalia Wright, "Ralph Waldo Emerson and Horatio Greenough," *Harvard Library Bulletin,* XII (1958), 103.

26. Greenough, *Yankee Stonecutter,* pp. 116–117.

27. *Ibid.,* p. 126.

28. *Ibid.,* p. 131.

29. *Ibid.,* p. 134.

30. *Ibid.,* p. 133.

31. *Ibid.,* p. 145.

32. *Ibid.,* p. 38.

33. *Ibid.,* p. 180.

34. *Journals of . . . Emerson,* VIII, 390.

35. Trollope, p. 122.

36. Nathaniel Hawthorne, *Passages from the French and Italian Note-Books* (Boston, 1883), p. 306.

37. Percy Lubbock, *Elizabeth Barrett Browning in Her Letters* (London, 1906), p. 229.

38. Hawthorne, p. 335.
39. "Letters of Hiram Powers to Nicholas Longworth, Esq., 1856–1858," *Quarterly Publications of the Historical and Philosophical Society of Ohio,* I (1906), 51.
40. Hawthorne, p. 304.
41. *Letters of Horatio Greenough,* p. 99.

Chapter 4. *"Marmorean Flock"*

1. Percy Lubbock, *Elizabeth Barrett Browning in Her Letters* (London, 1906), p. 321.
2. Henry James, *William Wetmore Story* (Boston, 1903), I, 257.
3. *Harriet Hosmer, Letters and Memories,* ed. Cornelia Carr (New York, 1912), p. 9.
4. *Ibid.,* p. 22.
5. Mrs. E. F. Ellet, *Women Artists* (London, 1859), p. 340.
6. Carr, p. 35.
7. Mrs. Russell Barrington, *Life and Letters of Frederic Leighton* (London, 1906), I, 146.
8. Carr, pp. 93–94.
9. *Ibid.,* p. 126.
10. *Ibid.,* p. 50.
11. *Ibid.,* p. 154.
12. Nathaniel Hawthorne, *Passages from the French and Italian Note-Books* (Boston, 1883), pp. 150–151.
13. Carr, p. 122.
14. *Ibid.,* p. 236.
15. *Ibid.,* p. 193.
16. J. J. Jarves, *Art Idea* (New York, 1864), p. 276.
17. Hannah Sawyer Lee, *Familiar Sketches of Sculpture and Sculptors* (Boston, 1854), II, 217.
18. *Ibid.,* p. 218.
19. *Ibid.,* pp. 218–221.
20. Julian Hawthorne, *Nathaniel Hawthorne and His Wife* (Boston, 1883), II, 182.
21. James, *Story,* II, 176.
22. Elise B. Chatterton, "A Vermont Sculptor." Vermont Historical Society *News and Notes,* VII (1955), 11.
23. Georg Brandes, *Reminiscences of My Childhood and Youth* (New York, 1906), p. 316.
24. Ellet, p. 304.

Chapter 5. *The Exception*

The sources for this chapter are listed in the Bibliography under Rimmer.

Chapter 6. *The* Nudo

1. Frances Trollope, *Domestic Manners of the Americans* (New York, 1832), p. 216.
2. *Port Folio,* III (1814), 155.
3. *Collector,* XXXI (1918), 51.
4. *Correspondence of James Fenimore Cooper,* ed. J. F. Cooper (New Haven, 1922), I, 264.

5. H. S. Canby, *Thoreau* (Boston, 1939), p. 337.
6. George S. Hillard, *Six Months in Italy* (Boston, 1854), I, 122.
7. *Ibid.*, I, 246.
8. N. P. Willis, *Pencillings by the Way* (New York, 1852), p. 405.
9. N. P. Willis, *Paul Fane* (New York, 1857), p. 128.
10. *Ibid.*, p. 134.
11. Frances Anne Kemble, *Records of a Girlhood* (New York, 1863), p. 302.
12. C. Edwards Lester, *The Artist, the Merchant, and the Statesman* (New York, 1845), I, 88.
13. A. T. Gardner, *Yankee Stonecutters* (New York, 1945), p. 14.
14. Sarah J. C. Lippincott (Grace Greenwood, pseud.), *Greenwood Leaves* (Boston, 1850), p. 345.
15. Henry T. Tuckerman, *Book of the Artists* (New York, 1867), p. 286.
16. Hiram Fuller (Belle Brittan, pseud.), *Belle Brittan on a Tour* (New York, 1858), p. 221.
17. Henry James, *William Wetmore Story* (Boston, 1903), I, 114.
18. Edith Wharton, "The Reckoning," *Descent of Man* (New York, 1904), p. 168.
19. Henry Ward Beecher, *Star Papers* (New York, 1855), p. 85.
20. *Letters of Ralph Waldo Emerson,* ed. Ralph L. Rusk (New York, 1939), III, 122.
21. William T. Thompson, *Major Jones's Sketches of Travel* (Philadelphia, 1848), p. 48.
22. Henry Greenough, *Ernest Carroll* (Boston, 1858), p. 127.
23. William Wetmore Story, *Fiammetta* (Boston, 1886), pp. 112–114.
24. Lester, I, 85–86.

Chapter 7. Wounded Indians

1. *Home Journal,* quoted by *Bulletin of the American Art-Union,* Series for 1851, p. 97.
2. "Crawford and His Last Work," *London Art Journal,* reprinted by *The Crayon,* I (1855), 168.
3. Charles E. Fairman, *Art and Artists of the Capitol* (Washington, 1927), pp. 169–170.
4. *Ibid.,* p. 19.
5. *Ibid.,* pp. 9–10.
6. Margaret Fuller Ossoli, *At Home and Abroad* (Boston, 1856), p. 370.
7. J. J. Jarves, *Art Thoughts* (New York, 1870), p. 293.
8. Harriet Beecher Stowe, "Sojourner Truth, the Libyan Sibyl," *Atlantic Monthly,* XI (1863), 480–481.
9. Henry T. Tuckerman, *Book of the Artists* (New York, 1867), p. 363.

Chapter 8. Patrons

1. Charles E. Crane, "Larkin G. Mead," in *Vermonters,* ed. Walter H. Crockett (Brattleboro, Vt., 1931).
2. Clara Longworth de Chambrun, *The Making of Nicholas Longworth* (New York, 1933), p. 33.
3. Henry T. Tuckerman, *Book of the Artists* (New York, 1867), p. 605.
4. William Sener Rusk, *William Henry Rinehart, Sculptor* (Baltimore, 1939), *passim.*
5. John Sartain, *Reminiscences of a Very Old Man* (New York, 1899), p. 238.
6. *Letters and Journals of James Fenimore Cooper,* ed. James Franklin Beard (Cambridge, Mass., 1960), II, 370.
7. *Ibid.,* II, 383.

8. *Memoirs and Letters of Charles Sumner,* ed. Edmund L. Pierce (Boston, 1877), II, 98, 104–106, 117, 175–176, 230–232.

9. *Works of Charles Sumner* (Boston, 1874), X, 540–556.

10. Thomas Ball, *My Three Score Years and Ten* (Boston, 1892), p. 309.

11. James E. Freeman, *Gatherings from an Artist's Portfolio* (Boston, 1883), II, 273.

12. *Harriet Hosmer, Letters and Memories,* ed. Cornelia Carr (New York, 1912), pp. 199, 201, 202.

13. Mary Bartlett Cowdrey, *American Academy of Fine Arts and American Art-Union* (New York, 1953); James Thomas Flexner, *That Wilder Image* (Boston, 1962), chap. vi.

14. Tuckerman, p. 17.

15. Samuel Woodson Price, *Old Masters of the Blue Grass* (Louisville, Ky., 1902), pp. 149–181; Lorado Taft, *History of American Sculpture* (New York, 1903), pp. 98–104.

16. Ball, pp. 281–282, 366–379.

17. *Round Table,* I (1864), 340.

Chapter 9. 1876

1. United States Centennial Commission, *International Exhibition, 1876* (Washington, 1880), I, 131–160.

2. *Ibid.,* VII, Group XXVII.

3. *Reminiscences of Augustus Saint Gaudens,* ed. Homer Saint Gaudens (New York, 1913), I, 109.

4. Saint Gaudens, II, 52.

Appendix

Listed below are literary sculptors of whose work we have some knowledge. The brief biographical sketches attempt, so far as possible, to indicate where these men and women were born, why they decided to become sculptors, what sort of training they had, and what sort of success. Mention is made of some of their more important works.

AKERS, (BENJAMIN) PAUL, 1825–1861. Akers, christened Benjamin, was called St. Paul by his schoolmates because he was so serious and religious, and it was as Paul Akers that he was professionally known. In his father's saw-mill on the Saco River in Maine the boy developed a mechanical skill and a romantic love of nature. He tried writing and painting and was finally turned toward sculpture by the sight of a bust by the Maine sculptor Edward Brackett. He got some training in Boston and later in his studio in Portland successfully made portrait busts. In 1852 he went to Florence for a year of study, probably under Hiram Powers, and a little later opened a studio in Rome, where he built a reputation as a maker of ideal statues as well as portrait busts. He did a good deal of writing on art for magazines and newspapers. His head of *Milton* (Amherst College) and dead *Pearl Diver* (Sweat Museum, Portland) are described as Kenyon's in Hawthorne's *The Marble Faun*.

AMES, SARAH FISHER CLAMPITT, 1817–1901. Sarah Ames, wife of the painter Joseph Ames, studied in Boston and in Rome. She made busts of many distinguished men. Her bust of Lincoln is in the national Capitol.

BALL, THOMAS, 1819–1911. The death of his father, a sign-painter in Charlestown, Massachusetts, made it necessary for Thomas Ball to go to work at an early age. When he was an errand boy for the New England Museum in Boston he tried to copy the portraits and found he could do it so well that he set up as a painter and then tried modeling. He supported himself in part by church singing. In 1854 he went to Italy for three years and then lived in Boston. In 1864 he returned to Florence, where he remained for most of his life, living near his good friend Hiram Powers. Boston gave him many commissions. His autobiography, *My Three Score Years and Ten,* gives an interesting account of his successful professional life. His equestrian *Washington* and *Sumner* are in Boston; *Lincoln the Emancipator,* in Washington and Boston.

BARBEE, WILLIAM R., 1818–1868. Born in Virginia, Barbee practiced law for ten years to earn enough to study art in Italy. He settled in Florence, where he was much influenced by Powers and Hart. His son Herbert became a sculptor.

BARTHOLOMEW, EDWARD SHEFFIELD, 1822–1858. Bartholomew, born in Connecticut, was inspired to become an artist by reading the autobiography of Cellini. He studied painting but, discovering that he was color-blind, turned to sculpture. In 1851 he managed to go to Rome, where he studied and modeled vigorously though his health had been seriously weakened by smallpox. After he had established a foreign reputation Connecticut began to be proud of him. In 1857 Hartford honored Bartholomew and F. E. Church, the painter, with a public dinner. Many of Bartholomew's works are in the Wadsworth Athenaeum in Hartford. His *Eve Repentant* was particularly admired.

BARTLETT, TRUMAN H., 1835–1923. Bartlett, born in Vermont, worked in New York under Launitz and then studied in Paris and Rome. He spent his later professional life in Hartford, New Haven, New York, and Boston.

BRACKETT, EDWARD AUGUSTUS, 1818–1908. Brackett, born in Maine, became a sculptor in Cincinnati, where he grew up. He made busts there and in Washington and in 1841 opened a studio in Boston. He eventually gave up sculpture to become Chairman of the Commission on Land Fisheries. His *Shipwrecked Mother* is in Mount Auburn Cemetery, Cambridge, Massachusetts.

BROWN, HENRY KIRKE, 1814–1886. Brown, born in Massachusetts, was apprenticed to the Boston portrait painter Chester Harding. He worked in Cincinnati and then decided to become a sculptor. He spent four years in Italy but did not consider foreign study important. In 1846 he opened a studio in New York City, experimenting with American themes, chiefly Indians, and with casting in bronze. He had great influence on several younger sculptors who were his pupils. He was a friend of Walt Whitman, of whom he made a bust. He received many commissions for monuments. His equestrian *Washington* in Union Square, New York, is considered one of the finest works of the period.

CALVERLY, CHARLES, 1833–1914. Calverly assisted Palmer in his

Albany studio for about four years. Shortly after the Civil War he opened a studio of his own in New York City. He was especially adept at medallions.

CAREW, Joseph, ?–1870, and Thomas, active 1843–1859. The Carew brothers, working often together, devoted themselves particularly to mortuary sculpture. Much of it is in Mount Auburn Cemetery, Cambridge, Massachusetts.

CLEVENGER, Shobal Vail, 1812–1843. Clevenger, born in Ohio, was trained as a stonecutter. In Cincinnati his work attracted the attention of Nicholas Longworth, who helped him to study anatomy and then to go to Florence. A year later he died of tuberculosis. His *Indian Chief*, though never put into marble, was the first statue of an American Indian.

COGDELL, John S., 1776–1847. Cogdell practiced sculpture only as an amateur but his work seems to have been respected by his professional contemporaries. He was made an honorary member of the National Academy of Design and exhibited there, in the Pennsylvania Academy, and in the Boston Athenaeum. Born in Charleston, South Carolina, he was trained in the law and practiced it successfully, held various public offices, and was President of the Bank of South Carolina. Traveling for his health in 1800 he visited Italy and was inspired to try his hand at painting which he did well. Washington Allston, whom he met on a visit to Boston, encouraged him to model in clay. He studied anatomy and produced many successful busts. Examples of his work are owned by the Charleston Library Society.

CRAWFORD, Thomas, 1814–1857. Born in New York City, Crawford worked in the stoneyard of Frazee and Launitz and studied at the National Academy of Design. He went to Rome in 1835, married the heiress Louisa Ward, and spent most of his life in Italy. By industry and skill, though he was deficient in education, he made himself a high reputation on both sides of the Atlantic. He received several important government commissions, notably *Armed Freedom* for the Capitol dome. His untimely death was caused by an eye tumor.

DEXTER, Henry, 1806–1876. Brought up on a New York State farm, Dexter was apprenticed to a blacksmith but determined to become a portrait painter. He managed to get some instruction, and opened a studio in Boston. The chance acquisition of a mass of modeling clay showed him that his real vocation was sculpture and he became a very successful maker of portrait busts. In 1857 he exhibited in the State House busts of thirty-one state governors. His *Binney Child* was long the most admired monument in Mount Auburn Cemetery, Cambridge, Massachusetts.

DIXEY, George, ?-*ca*. 1853. Son of an Irish sculptor who emigrated to America, Dixey was trained by his father and worked with him in New York in the carving and gilding business.

DUBOIS, Mary Ann Delafield (Mrs. Cornelius), 1813–1888. Mrs. Dubois discovered her talent when called on to criticize a bust being modeled of her father. She was particularly skilful at cameo portraits. She worked so hard that her physician finally ordered her to stop modeling but she continued to instruct young ladies and to help aspiring artists, among them Edward Brackett.

DUNLAP, James Boliver, 1825–1864. Born in Indianapolis, Dunlap went to California for his health and opened a studio in San Francisco, where he made portrait busts. He later returned to Indianapolis.

EZEKIEL, Moses, 1844–1917. Ezekiel, born in Richmond, went to Berlin to study sculpture. He won a prize which took him to Rome for study and remained there most of his life, making occasional visits to America. He made the B'nai B'rith monument, *Religious Liberty*, for the Centennial Exhibition.

FOLEY, Margaret, ?-1877. Born in Vermont, Miss Foley practiced cameo cutting in Boston for seven years to earn enough for the voyage to Rome. There she worked happily and made many friends, among them the Mitfords.

GALT, Alexander, 1827–1863. Born in Virginia, Galt went to Florence for study in 1848, later returning to Richmond. During the war he served on the Governor's staff. Many of his works were destroyed in the burning of Richmond. His *Jefferson* stands on the grounds of the University of Virginia.

GARLICK, Theodatus, 1805–1884. Garlick, born in Vermont, learned stonecutting and then studied medicine, which he practiced in Ohio. He used his sculptural skill for pioneer experiments in plastic surgery. Later he became interested in photography.

GOULD, Thomas Ridgeway, 1818–1881. Born in Boston, Gould was successful in business there until the war came. He had amused himself with sculpture in his spare time, making busts of his friends, who included many prominent men, and he now became a professional artist. In 1868 he opened a studio in Florence. His *West Wind* was much admired. He made a statue of *King Kamehameha I* for Honolulu.

GREENOUGH, Horatio, 1805–1852. Greenough was born in Boston. His interest in sculpture was inspired by a statue in his father's garden. After graduating from Harvard he went to Italy, the first American professional sculptor to do so. He settled finally in Florence. His friend Washington Allston helped him to a government commission for a statue of *Washington*. Later he made *The Rescue* for the Capitol. In 1851 he returned to live in the United States. His critical writing was even more interesting than his sculpture, expounding the theory of significant form. *Travels of a Yankee Stonecutter* was published in 1852.

GREENOUGH, RICHARD SALTONSTALL, 1819–1904. Admiration for his elder brother Horatio turned Richard Greenough toward sculpture. He studied under Horatio in Florence and later settled in Rome. He was one of the first Americans to study and work in Paris. His *Franklin* stands near City Hall in Boston.

HARNISH, ALBERT E., 1843–?. Harnish, probably the son of a German lithographer, was born in Philadelphia soon after his father came to this country. He studied with Bailly, exhibited for many years at the Pennsylvania Academy, and about 1859 went to Rome. His *Boy in the Eagle's Nest* was much admired.

HART, JOEL TANNER, 1810–1877. Born in Kentucky, Hart was apprenticed to a stonecutter. Meeting Clevenger, who was modeling a bust of Clay, he tried his hand at sculpture. In 1846 the Ladies Clay Association commissioned him to do a life-size statue. It took him thirteen years, most of them spent in Florence, but the Ladies were delighted with the result. Hart remained in Italy for the rest of his life, working on a group called *Woman Triumphant*. He invented a complex pointing machine which made it possible to get very precise likenesses in portrait busts.

HARTLEY, JONATHAN, 1845–1912. Hartley, born in Albany, was a marble worker for Palmer. He studied in England, Germany, Paris, and Rome, then opened a studio in New York. He served as Professor of Anatomy at the Art Students League.

HASELTINE, JAMES HENRY, 1833–1907. Haseltine was born in Philadelphia, the son of an amateur painter. He studied under Bailly, exhibiting at the Pennsylvania Academy for the first time in 1855. He then studied for a few years in Italy and France, returning home to serve in the war. Most of his later life was spent in Rome.

HEMENWAY, CHARLES, ?–1887. Hemenway was trained in carving in a stoneyard in Providence, R. I. He made portrait busts and mortuary monuments. His monument to the Sprague children in Swan Point Cemetery was much admired. He lived a carefree, improvident life, becoming at the end an object of charity.

HOSMER, HARRIET, 1830–1908. First and most successful of the women sculptors, Harriet Hosmer showed the way to all the rest. She was born in Watertown, Massachusetts, studied modeling in Boston and anatomy in St. Louis. In 1852 she went to Rome, became a pupil of Gibson, worked with energy and intelligence, and soon established an international reputation. Her patrons and friends included European royalty and English aristocracy. In the United States she received some public commissions.

HOXIE, Vinnie Ream, 1847–1914. Vinnie Ream was brought up on the Missouri frontier and came to Washington when she was twenty. During a chance visit to the studio of Clark Mills it was discovered that she had a gift for modeling which her friends hailed as genius. Mills gave her instruction and some members of Congress persuaded Lincoln to let her make a bust of him. When, after the assassination, Congress voted $10,000 for a statue the commission went to Vinnie Ream. She lived in Rome for two years while she put her statue into marble and there had great artistic and social success. In 1878 she married Lt. Richard L. Hoxie, abandoned art, and became a popular Washington hostess. Her *Lincoln* stands in the Capitol, her *Admiral Farragut* in Farragut Square.

IVES, Chauncey Bradley, 1810–1894. Ives was born in New Haven. He was apprenticed to a woodcarver but decided to become a sculptor and went to Boston to study. In 1844 he went to Italy, where he was successful in making portrait busts and small marble groups for parlor ornaments. His *Roger Sherman* is in Statuary Hall.

JACKSON, John Adams, 1825–1879. Jackson, born in Maine, learned drawing in Boston and then went abroad, studying in Paris and in Italy, where he spent the greater part of his life. He modeled busts of many prominent men and ideal figures which were very popular. He made the Soldiers Monument in Lynn, Massachusetts.

JONES, Thomas D., 1811–1881. While working as a mason and stonecutter Jones taught himself to carve portrait busts and made them with success in Cincinnati, Detroit, Nashville, New York, and Boston.

KEYSER, Ephraim, 1850–?. Keyser, born in Baltimore, studied sculpture in Munich, Berlin, and Rome.

KING, John Crookshank, 1806–1882. King, born in Scotland, came to the United States in 1829 and found work as a machinist. In Cincinnati he met Hiram Powers, who suggested that he try modeling busts, at which he became highly successful. He traveled along the Ohio and Mississippi rivers modeling portraits and then, in 1840, opened a studio in Boston where he made busts of Emerson, Agassiz, Webster, and other eminent men.

LANDER, Louisa, 1826–1923. Louisa Lander showed in her childhood a knack for modeling which her family took for genius. She worked away in her native Salem and at thirty went to Rome to study with Thomas Crawford. She was quietly successful both with ideal figures and with busts. One of these was of Hawthorne, who studied her independent way of life when he was writing of Hilda's in *The Marble Faun.* Later Miss Lander had a studio in Washington.

LAUNITZ, Robert E. S. von der, 1806–1870. Born in Riga, Launitz was well educated in the classics and military science but decided to become a sculptor. He went to Rome to study. In 1830 he emigrated to the United States, worked in John Frazee's marble yard, and then became his partner. He published a book of tombstone designs which was widely used. Crawford received his early training under Frazee and Launitz. Launitz made the statue of *Pulaski* in Savannah and the *Battle Monument* in Frankfort, Kentucky.

LEWIS, Edmonia, 1845–?. Edmonia Lewis, half Negro and half Indian, was brought up among the Chippewas. She was educated at Oberlin, from which she was sent to Boston with letters to abolitionist sympathizers. The sight of Richard Greenough's *Franklin* roused her desire to become a sculptor. Brackett helped her, so did many others, and she finally made her way to Rome. There she lived with Charlotte Cushman and achieved a good deal of professional success.

MACDONALD, James W. A., 1824–1908. MacDonald, born in Ohio, had as a boy artistic ambitions and when he saw a bust of Washington decided that he must become a sculptor. He ran away from home and found work in St. Louis, studying art at night. After 1854 he managed to support himself by modeling. After the war he settled in New York City. He made several Civil War monuments and many busts and medallions.

MEAD, Larkin G., 1835–1910. Mead, brought up in Brattleboro, Vermont, wanted to be a sculptor and managed to get some training in H. K. Brown's New York studio. Returning to Brattleboro, he worked as a clerk in a hardware store until one night in 1857 he modeled in snow a colossal *Recording Angel* which attracted wide attention. Nicholas Longworth of Cincinnati heard of it and became Mead's patron. He helped him to go to Florence, where he spent most of the rest of his life. The state of Vermont gave Mead several commissions.

MILLS, Clark, 1810–1883. Mills, born in New York State, drifted about the country as a common laborer, finally making, with some success, an attempt at clay modeling. In 1846 the city of Charleston, South Carolina, purchased his bust of Calhoun and J. S. Preston helped him to commissions. While he was visiting Washington, Mills, by an odd chance, received a government commission for an equestrian statue of Andrew Jackson for Lafayette Square. He boldly attempted the work, which attracted national attention because it was the first equestrian statue by an American and because, by ingenious mechanical calculation, Mills balanced the horse rearing on his hind legs. He also devised a method of casting his statue in bronze and later cast Crawford's *Armed Freedom* for the Capitol dome.

MILMORE, Martin, 1845–1883. Milmore was trained in Ball's Boston studio and later studied in Rome. His Soldiers Monument in Roxbury was a model for many others all over the country.

MORSE, Sidney Henry, 1833–?. Morse, known chiefly as a Unitarian writer and editor of *The Radical*, also devoted much time to sculpture. He had a studio in Rome for some years. At home he went often to the New York studio of H. K. Brown, where he met and became the friend of Whitman, of whom he made a bust. He made a bust of *Channing* for the Arlington Street Church, Boston, and one of *Emerson* for the Second Church.

MOZIER, Joseph, 1812–1890. Mozier, born in Vermont, became a successful New York businessman. By 1845 he had made enough to retire, live in Italy, and devote his whole time to sculpture. He studied in Florence and then opened a studio in Rome. His ideal figures, especially *The Wept of Wish-ton Wish*, were very popular. He was hospitable and generous to other American artists.

NEVIN, Blanche, 1841–1925. Miss Nevin studied at the Pennsylvania Academy of Fine Arts and in Venice and achieved some small fame. She modeled chiefly for her own pleasure but made Pennsylvania's *Muhlenberg* for Statuary Hall.

PALMER, Erastus Dow, 1817–1904. Palmer was the first American to do extensive work in marble without study in Italy. Born in New York State, he became a skilled carpenter, then learned cameo cutting and, when it proved too great a strain on his eyes, tried marble. He had real talent and was immediately successful. The Palmer Marbles, exhibited in New York in 1856, attracted wide attention. He trained workmen in marble cutting and his studio in Albany resembled a sculptor's establishment in Rome. His *White Captive* and *Indian Girl* are in the Metropolitan Museum; many of his works are in the Albany Institute of History and Art.

PERRY, John D., 1845–?. Perry, born in Virginia, spent his professional life in Boston and in Rome. Harriet Beecher Stowe owned his plaster bas-relief *Two Buds*.

POWERS, HIRAM, 1805–1873. Born in Woodstock, Vermont, Powers grew up in Cincinnati. After his father's death he got a job in Dorfeuille's Museum because he was able to model figures in wax and to fit them with amazing mechanisms. He began soon to make portrait busts and in 1837 went to Italy, helped on the journey by Nicholas Longworth of Cincinnati and the Prestons of South Carolina. He settled in Florence and lived there for the rest of his days. The *Greek Slave* (now in the Corcoran Gallery), exhibited in London in 1845 and taken on a tour of America in 1847, established Powers' reputation on both sides of the Atlantic. He became the best known and most financially successful of all the American literary sculptors.

POWERS, LONGWORTH, ?–1904. Trained by his father Hiram Powers, Longworth Powers worked as a sculptor in Florence.

POWERS, PRESTON, 1843–?. Trained in Florence by his father Hiram Powers, Preston Powers practiced sculpture in America, living in Boston, Washington, and Portland, Maine.

REAM, VINNIE. *See* HOXIE.

RICHARDS, DAVID, 1828–1897. Richards, born in Wales, came to the United States as a young man and worked as a stonecutter in Utica. He studied modeling in New York and worked there and in Chicago, later spending two years in Rome. He made *The Confederate Soldier* for the city of Savannah.

RIMMER, WILLIAM, 1816–1870. Rimmer, the most talented sculptor of the period, never studied abroad and was quite uninfluenced by his American contemporaries. His father had been brought up to believe that he was the heir to the French throne and had been educated accordingly. When his hope of succession was dashed he emigrated to the United States and lived near Boston, making shoes for a living, and educating his children in art, music, and the languages. William, the eldest son, took over his father's haughtiness and bitter disappointment. This colored his whole life and made all his relationships difficult. He taught music, painted pictures for churches, practiced medicine, and taught, with striking success, art anatomy to classes in Boston. He illustrated his lectures with extraordinary free-hand drawings, many of which were collected in his *Art Anatomy*, published in 1877. He made a few remarkable works of sculpture, which were not appreciated until after his death. They are now in the Metropolitan and the Boston Museum.

RINEHART, WILLIAM HENRY, 1825–1874. Rinehart's father, a prosperous Maryland farmer, was disgusted by the boy's talent for drawing and modeling. Finally he apprenticed him to a stonecutter from whose quarry he went to a marble yard in Baltimore. His work attracted the attention of W. T. Walters, who helped him to go to Rome. As a maker of busts and of ideal statues Rinehart was highly successful, and he was one of the few artists of the period admired by the next generation of sculptors. He amassed a considerable fortune through his work and this, since he never married, he left to help young American sculptors to study in Italy. Much of his ideal work, *Clytie, Latona*, etc., is in the Peabody Institute in Baltimore. His *Justice Taney* is in Statuary Hall and in Annapolis.

ROGERS, JOHN, 1829–1904. Rogers, a draftsman and mechanic, wanted to be a sculptor but, after study in France and Italy, found the neoclassical fashion so distasteful that he abandoned the idea. In 1859, however, he found that he could sell the kind of work he wanted to do, little genre scenes about two feet high. He went to New York, perfected a process of reproduction in plaster, and launched a successful art business. He made more than eighty Rogers Groups and sold some eighty thousand copies. The Groups included abolitionist propaganda, scenes from soldier life, and scenes from country life. A large collection of Rogers Groups is owned by the New-York Historical Society.

ROGERS, RANDOLPH, 1825–1892. While working for a drygoods firm in New York Rogers modeled portrait busts of his employers and their familes which pleased them so much that they helped him to go to Italy. He settled in Rome, where he received many commissions both public and private. He made bronze doors for the Capitol, a *Seward* for Madison Square, New York, a *Lincoln* for Philadelphia. His *Nydia* was repeated one hundred times for American patrons. Rogers left all his casts to the Art Gallery of the University of Michigan.

SIMMONS, FRANKLIN, 1839–1913. Simmons studied sculpture in Boston and became an itinerant artist in his native Maine. In 1867 he went to Rome, where he remained for the rest of his life. He received many public commissions, among them a *Washington* for Valley Forge and a *Roger Williams* for Statuary Hall. His *Longfellow* and Civil War Monument stand in Portland, and replicas of many of his works are in that city's Sweat Museum.

STEBBINS, EMMA, 1815–1882. Born in New York, Emma Stebbins was encouraged by her well-to-do family in her efforts at drawing and painting. At forty, influenced by a visit to Italy, she decided to become a sculptor. She went to Rome, studied with Akers, and became a close friend of Charlotte Cushman, whose biography she wrote. Her *Angel of the Waters* stands in Central Park, her *Horace Mann* by the Boston State House.

STEPHENSON, PETER, 1823–ca.1860. Stephenson, born in England, was brought up on farms in New York State and Michigan. He painted as a child, then cut cameo portraits and at twenty decided to become a sculptor. He went to Boston, where by making portrait busts he earned enough to take him to Rome for two years. On his return he lived in Boston. He specialized in cameos but also made busts and ideal figures.

STONE, HORATIO, 1808–1875. The son of a New York State farmer who considered carving sinful, Stone ran away from home. He studied and practiced medicine, but, in 1848, he abandoned it for sculpture. He settled in Washington making portrait busts of many prominent men. During the Civil War he served as a surgeon. He was President of the Washington Art Association and a prime mover in the establishment of the National Gallery of Art.

STORY, WILLIAM WETMORE, 1819–1895. Story's father was an eminent jurist. He himself was trained at Harvard to the law and practiced it in Boston with distinction. He also did important legal writing but in middle life he decided to devote himself entirely to sculpture, which had long been his avocation. He had ample inherited means so he took his family to Italy and established them in a handsome villa in Rome where he and his wife entertained agreeably and well. He worked hard at his modeling and built an international reputation. His *Cleopatra* (in the Metropolitan) is described by Hawthorne as Kenyon's in *The Marble Faun.*

THOMPSON, LAUNT, 1833–1894. Thompson, born in Ireland, came to America as a boy. He studied medicine in Albany but abandoned it for sculpture and became a pupil of Palmer. In 1858 he moved to New York, in 1875 to Florence.

VOLK, LEONARD WELLS, 1828–1895. Volk learned stonecutting from his father and practiced as an itinerant workman. In 1848 he settled in St. Louis and began the study of sculpture. In 1855 he borrowed enough from a relative, Stephen Douglas, to spend two years in Rome. On his return he settled in Chicago, where he founded and was for many years President of the Chicago Academy of Design.

WALCUT, WILLIAM, 1819–1895. Born in Ohio and educated there as an engineer, Walcut, when he saw his first statue, decided to become a sculptor. He studied modeling for four years in various American cities, then in London and Paris. In 1855 he opened a studio in New York. He made the Perry monument for Cleveland.

WARD, JOHN QUINCY ADAMS, 1830–1910. Ward was one of the few among the early sculptors admired by the next generation. Brought up on a farm in Ohio, he discovered his vocation at eighteen when he visited the New York studio of H. K. Brown. For six years he was Brown's pupil and assistant; later he opened his own studio in New York. He received many commissions from the city. He was interested in modeling Indians and spent some time in the West studying them but was too busy with public commissions to work often on the subjects he would have chosen. The major part of his work was done after the Centennial Exhibition.

WHITNEY, Anne, 1821–1915. By the time Anne Whitney was forty she had established a New England reputation as a poet. She had also done a good deal of painting when she decided to become a sculptor. She studied in Rome, Munich, and Paris as well as in the United States. From her Boston studio she successfully filled both public and private commissions. An ardent abolitionist and suffragist she made busts of many of the reformers. Her *Leif Ericson* is on Commonwealth Avenue, Boston; her *Samuel Adams* in Statuary Hall.

WILSON, Mrs. ?, active 1840–1851. Mrs. Wilson's interest in modeling was excited by a visit to a sculptor's studio, possibly Hiram Powers'. She worked at her portrait busts with such energy that she often fainted away and her doctor husband was obliged to restrict her efforts.

Selected Bibliography

Rome and Florence

Listed here are books which give particularly interesting or informative accounts of the Rome and Florence the literary sculptors knew.

ABBOTT, JACOB. *Rollo in Rome*. Boston, 1858.

ABOUT, EDMOND. *Rome contemporaine*. Paris, 1861.

BUTLER, FANNY KEMBLE. *A Year of Consolation*. New York, 1847.

FREEMAN, JAMES E. *Gatherings from an Artist's Portfolio*. Vol. I, New York, 1877; Vol. II, Boston, 1883.

GILLISPIE, WILLIAM MITCHELL. *Rome as Seen by a New Yorker in 1843–44*. New York, 1845.

HAWTHORNE, NATHANIEL. *Passages from the French and Italian Note-Books*. Boston, 1883.

HILLARD, GEORGE S. *Six Months in Italy*. 2 vols. Boston, 1854.

PREZZOLINI, GIUSEPPE. *Come gli americani scoprirono l'Italia, 1750–1850*. Milano, 1933.

TROLLOPE, FRANCES. *Visit to Italy*. London, 1842.

TROLLOPE, T. A. *What I Remember*. New York, 1888.

WILLIS, N. P. *Pencillings by the Way*. New York, 1852.

Biography, History and Criticism

Listed first are dictionaries and works of general biography, history and criticism, then, under the names of individual sculptors, particularly useful books or articles on each.

GENERAL

BENJAMIN, S. G. W. *Art in America*. New York, 1880.

CLARK, EDNA M. *Ohio Art and Artists*. Richmond, Va., 1932.

CLEMENT, CLARA E. AND LAURENCE HUTTON. *Artists of the Nineteenth Century*. 2 vols. Boston, 1879.

DUNLAP, WILLIAM. *History of the Rise and Progress of the Arts of*

Design in the United States. New York, 1834; new ed., corrected and enlarged, ed. Frank W. Bailey and Charles E. Goodspeed, 3 vols., Boston, 1918.

ELLET, MRS. E. F. *Women Artists in All Ages and Countries.* London, 1858.

FAIRMAN, CHARLES E. *Art and Artists of the Capitol.* Washington, 1927.

FIELDING, MANTLE. *Dictionary of American Painters, Sculptors, and Engravers.* Philadelphia, 1926.

FRENCH, H. W. *Art and Artists of Connecticut.* Boston, 1879.

GARDNER, A. T. *Yankee Stonecutters.* New York, 1945.

GROCE, GEORGE C. AND DAVID H. WALLACE, eds. *New-York Historical Society's Dictionary of Artists in America 1564–1860.* New Haven, 1957.

HANAFORD, PHEBE. *Daughters of America.* Augusta, Me., 1882.

JARVES, J. J. *Art-Hints.* New York, 1855. *Art Idea.* New York, 1864. *Art Thoughts.* New York, 1870.

LARKIN, OLIVER. *Art and Life in America.* New York, 1949.

LEE, HANNAH SAWYER. *Familiar Sketches of Sculpture and Sculptors.* 2 vols. Boston, 1854.

MATHER, FRANK JEWETT, JR. *American Spirit in Art.* New Haven, 1927.

New-York Historical Society's Dictionary. See Groce.

POST, CHANDLER R. *A History of European and American Sculpture.* 2 vols. Cambridge, Mass., 1921.

TAFT, LORADO. *History of American Sculpture.* New York, 1903.

TUCKERMAN, HENRY T. *Book of the Artists.* New York, 1867.

INDIVIDUAL

AKERS
USHER, LEILA W. "Benjamin Paul Akers," *New England Magazine,* N.S. XI (1894), 460–468.

BALL
BALL, THOMAS. *My Three Score Years and Ten.* Boston, 1892.

BARTHOLOMEW
CRANE, SUSAN U. "Edward Sheffield Bartholomew," *Connecticut Quarterly,* II (1896), 204–214.

CLEVENGER
"Clevenger," *United States Magazine and Democratic Review,* XIV (1844), 202–206.

CRAWFORD
GALE, ROBERT L. *Thomas Crawford, American Sculptor.* Pittsburgh, 1964.

———. "Thomas Crawford, Dear Lou, and the Horse." *Virginia*

Magazine of History and Biography, LXVIII (1960), 171–192.

GREENE, GEORGE W. "Crawford," *Biographical Studies*. New York, 1860.

HICKS, THOMAS. *Eulogy of Thomas Crawford*. New York, 1865.

HILLARD, GEORGE S. "Thomas Crawford: a Eulogy," *Atlantic Monthly*, XXIV (1869), 40–54.

FOLEY

CHATTERTON, ELSIE B. "A Vermont Sculptor." Vermont Historical Society *News and Notes*, VII (1955), 10–14.

FREEMAN, JAMES E. *Gatherings from an Artist's Portfolio*. Boston, 1883, II, 133–136.

ROBINSON, HARRIET H. *Loom and Spindle*. Boston, 1898. Pp. 150–154.

GREENOUGH

GREENOUGH, FRANCES BOOTT, ed. *Letters of Horatio Greenough*. Boston, 1887.

GREENOUGH, HORATIO. *Travels, Observations, and Experience of a Yankee Stonecutter*, by Horace Bender (pseud). New York, 1852; facsimile reproduction with an Introduction by Nathalia Wright, Gainesville, Fla., 1958.

TUCKERMAN, HENRY T. *A Memorial of Horatio Greenough*. New York, 1853.

WRIGHT, NATHALIA. *Horatio Greenough: The First American Sculptor*. Philadelphia, 1963.

HART

PRICE, SAMUEL WOODSON. *Old Masters of the Blue Grass*. Louisville, Ky., 1902. Pp. 149–181.

HOSMER

CARR, CORNELIA, ed. *Harriet Hosmer, Letters and Memories*. New York, 1912.

LANDER

SHARF, FREDERIC A. " 'A More Bracing Atmosphere,' Artistic Life in Salem, 1850–1859," *Essex Institute Historical Collections*, XCV (1959), 160–162.

LEWIS

BROWN, WILLIAM WELLS. *The Rising Sun*. Boston, 1874. Pp. 465–468.

HANAFORD, PHEBE. *Daughters of America*. Augusta, Me., 1882. Pp. 316–318.

MEAD

CRANE, CHARLES E. "Larkin G. Mead," in *Vermonters*, ed. Walter H. Crockett. Brattleboro, Vt., 1931.

MORSE

    COOKE, GEORGE WILLIS. *Poets of Transcendentalism.* Boston, 1903. Pp. 319–320.

    KELLER, ELIZABETH L. *Walt Whitman in Mickle Street.* New York, 1921. Pp. 73–86.

PALMER

    INGRAM, CHARLES. "Erastus Dow Palmer, a Great American Sculptor," *Americana,* XXIV (1930), 7–21.

POWERS

    BELLOWS, H. W. "Seven Sittings with Powers the Sculptor," *Appleton's Journal,* I (1869), 342–343, 359–361, 402–404, 470–471, 595–597; II (1869), 54–55, 106–108.

    HAWTHORNE, NATHANIEL. *Passages from the French and Italian Note-Books.* Boston, 1883. *Passim.*

    KELLOGG, MINER K. *Justice to Hiram Powers.* Cincinnati, 1848.

    ———. *Mr. Miner Kellogg to his Friends.* Paris, 1858.

    LESTER, C. E. *The Artist, the Merchant, and the Statesman.* New York, 1845. I, 1–155.

RIMMER

    BARTLETT, TRUMAN H. *Art-Life of William Rimmer.* Boston, 1882.

    KIRSTEIN, LINCOLN. "William Rimmer," *Massachusetts Quarterly,* II (1961), 685–716, reprinted from the Catalogue of the Rimmer Exhibition of 1946–47, arranged by the Whitney Museum of American Art and the Boston Museum of Fine Arts.

    RIMMER, WILLIAM. *Art Anatomy.* Boston, 1877.

RINEHART

    RUSK, WILLIAM SENER. *William Henry Rinehart, Sculptor.* Baltimore, 1939.

ROGERS, JOHN

    SMITH, MR. AND MRS. CHETWOOD. *Rogers Groups.* Boston, 1934.

    WALLACE, DAVID H. Biography (in progress).

SIMMONS

    WHITING, LILIAN. "A Veteran Sculptor," *Outlook,* XCVIII (1911), 213–215.

STEBBINS

    HANAFORD, PHEBE. *Daughters of America.* Augusta, Me., 1882. Pp. 308–309.

STORY

    JAMES, HENRY. *William Wetmore Story.* Boston, 1903.

    PHILLIPS, MARY E. *Reminiscences of William Wetmore Story.* Chicago, 1897.

WARD

> Sheldon, G. W. "An American Sculptor," *Harper's Magazine,*
> LVII (1878), 62–68.

WHITNEY

> Livermore, Mary A. "Anne Witney," *Our Famous Women.*
> Hartford, 1888.
>
> Payne, Elizabeth Rogers. Life and letters (in progress).
>
> ———. "Anne Whitney, Sculptor," *Art Quarterly,* Autumn,
> 1962, pp. 244–261.
>
> Spofford, Harriet Prescott. *Little Book of Friends.* Boston,
> 1916. Pp. 43–66.

Index

(Numbers in italics refer to plates. Numbers in bold face indicate the most extended reference to a given topic or individual.)